PLAYING THE RACQUETS

Other Delta Books of Interest

The Family Tennis Book
by John Newcombe and Angie Newcombe
with Clarence Mabry

Inside Tennis: A Season on the Pro Tour by Peter Bodo
and June Harrison

PLAYING THE RACQUETS

The Complete Guide to the Basics of Tennis,
Squash, Racquetball, Paddle Tennis, Platform Tennis,
and One- and Four-Wall Paddleball

Carol Morgenstern

with photos by June Harrison

A Delta Book

A DELTA BOOK

Published by
Dell Publishing Co., Inc.
1 Dag Hammarskjold Plaza
New York, New York 10017

Delta ® TM 755118
Dell Publishing Co., Inc.

Printed in the United States of America

First printing—March 1980

Library of Congress Cataloging in Publication Data

Morgenstern, Carol.
    Playing the racquets.

    (A Delta book)
    1. Racquet games.   I. Title.
GV990.M67   796.34   79–25047
ISBN:0-440-57121-9

ACKNOWLEDGMENTS

Grateful acknowledgment is made for permission to reprint from the
    following:

USTA Yearbook (Rules of Tennis and Cases and Decisions):
    reprinted by permission of the United States Tennis Association, Inc.

The Rules of Squash: Official Playing Rules: reprinted by permission
    of the United States Squash Racquets Association, Inc.

Official Racquetball Rules: reprinted by permission of the United
    States Racquetball Association.

Official Rules and Regulations of Racquetball: reprinted by permission
    of International Racquetball Association. Published 1979 by Towery
    Press, 1535 E. Brooks Rd., Memphis, TN 38116.

Official Rules of Play—American Paddle Tennis League: reprinted by
    permission of American Paddle Tennis League, Inc., Beverly Hills, CA.

Paddle Tennis: Official Rules, Questions/Answers by Murray Geller:
    used by permission of Murray Geller, Official Rules Interpreter,
    United States Paddle Tennis Association.

APTA Official Rules: used by permission of the American Platform
    Tennis Association, Inc.

Official Rules and Regulations for One-Wall Paddleball: approved by
    the American Paddleball Association.

Official Rules—One-Wall Paddleball: written and copyright © 1976
    by Howard Solomon and Joel Skolnick. Used by permission of the
    authors and the Paddleball Players Association.

Official Paddleball Rules: used by permission of Rodney J.
    Grambeau, Ed.D., Physical Education Department, The University
    of Michigan, Ann Arbor, MI.

To Ronne Mandelker

Many people helped me with this book. For so generously sharing their time and expertise I particularly wish to thank Dewey Blanton, Bjorn Borg, Charlie Brumfield, John Bruschi, Gloria Dillenbeck, Trish Faulkner, Bill Ford, Murray Geller, Stu Goldstein, Rodney Grambeau, Howard Hammer, Lee Jackson, Judy Jolly, Tom Jones, Sharif Kahn, Harvey Kane, Darwin Kingsley III, Andy Krosnick, Duffy Lautz, Ken Levine, George McFadden, Edy McGoldrick, Mark Melamed, Dick Pitcher, William Plummer, Marvin Rosenberg, Harry Saint, Joel Skolnick, Rod Waywell, Sharon Wilkes, and the governing bodies of all the sports covered in this book.

My heartfelt gratitude to the following player/models for their enthusiasm and excellent form: Dan Agro, Bill Andruss, Dick Booker, Wendy Chase, Carole Dicker, Art Diemar, Steve Geller, Larry Hilbert, André Hopkins, Carolyn Lane, Greg Lawrence, Brian Lee, Marcy Lynch, Jim McCready, Kirk Moritz, Liz Munson, Pam Perrotty, Kitty Preston, Doug Russell, Ray Sanchez, Bobby Schwarz, Butch Seewagen, Scott Shannon, Barry Sheiber, Susan Wilson.

I also wish to thank my parents, Frank and Deborah Morgenstern, for their encouragement and support.

I am also grateful to my editors, Martha Kinney, Chris Kuppig, and especially Laura Wolff, whose diligence and wit I so much appreciated as I came down the homestretch; and to June Harrison, whose wonderful photographs are testimony to the extraordinary creative energy she brought to the project.

Special thanks are due to George Kondogianis, who let there be light, and to Ed Snider, Joseph Livoti, and Gerry Montesano of Images Unlimited, for a superb printing job.

Racquet sports clothing furnished by Jockey, Lacoste, Loomtogs Tennis Whites, Fred Perry Sportswear, Topseed, and Ultrasport. Gymnastic leotard by Danskin.

Equipment furnished by Ektelon, General Sportcraft, Marcraft, Mason's Tennis Mart, and Prince Racquets.

Locations courtesy of Beach Channel High School; Center Court Racquetball Club in Rockville Center, N.Y.; Courttime Racquetball Club in Lyndhurst, N.J.; East River Tennis Club in Long Island City, N.Y.; Stuyvesant Town; and Uptown Racquet Club in New York City.

CONTENTS

PLAYING THE RACQUETS

INTRODUCTION

Approximately seventy-five million Americans—one in three—regularly don shorts and sneakers to spend an hour or more at a time smashing various rubber balls over nets or against walls with an odd-looking assortment of flat-faced implements. In the unprecedented fitness boom that still shows not the slightest sign of waning, practically all participatory activities, from spelunking to skydiving, are enjoying a tremendous upsurge of popularity, but the racquet and paddle sports have been among the biggest gainers.

It's easy to see why. All of them offer an enjoyable, healthful, convenient, and sociable way to spend leisure time. All are relatively simple to learn and play, yet challenging enough to keep the interest keen. Most are suitable for men, women, and children of all ages. And finally, equipping yourself and renting court time for any of these sports is not an expensive proposition, unless you wish to play indoor tennis in a high-rent neighborhood.

Though it may sometimes appear otherwise, twentieth-century Americans were hardly the first people to recognize the many and varied appeals of racquet and paddle sports. The ancient Greek historian Herodotus informs us that his countrymen played a similar game in their *sphairisteria,* or places for ball play. It is speculated that the Greeks may have gotten the idea from the Egyptians or the Persians, for whom the ball was a fertility symbol. Anthropologists tell us that many ancient civilizations, the Incan and the Mayan among them, had a game that involved striking a ball with some sort of implement.

In more recent history, the first racquet sport to gain wide acceptance was court tennis. Now an extremely esoteric sport, with a total of twenty-nine courts and approximately two thousand players worldwide, court tennis was probably first played in the twelfth century by French monks, who used the courtyards of their monasteries as playing fields. The balls for *jeu de paume* (game of the palm), as it was known, were fashioned out of leather and stuffed with all manner of things—wool, feathers, bran, even human hair. The object of the game was to hit this ball with the hand back and forth over a crude wooden obstacle, or sometimes simply a dirt mound.

By the fourteenth century, *jeu de paume* had become a sport favored by kings. Soon the nobility was imitating the sovereigns, and before long people at all levels of French society were not only playing *paume* but also thronging to the courts to gamble on it, in such numbers and for such high stakes that in 1369 Charles V, himself an avid player—he built the first court at the Louvre in about 1368—issued an edict prohibiting the working class of Paris from playing the game. Despite this and later similar edicts, *paume* grew more and more popular, reaching its heyday in the sixteenth century. In 1600 the Venetian ambassador to France wrote that there were nearly eighteen hundred courts in Paris alone; an Englishman visiting France around the same time reported that there were as many tennis players in that country as there were ale drinkers in England. The game also attracted followers in other Western European countries and across the Channel.

Implements resembling the strung racquets used today in tennis, squash, and racquetball evolved slowly. First an ordinary glove was introduced. Then someone thought of binding cords between the fingers and across the palm of the glove. Next, simple wooden boards came into use, followed by short-handled *battoirs,* made at first of solid wood; later, one end was hollowed out and parchment was stretched tight across it. Around 1500, the handle was extended and the hollowed end was strung with sheep gut.

In the late fourteenth century the game moved indoors—an important development that would be echoed six hundred years later by *jeu de paume's* modern offspring, lawn tennis. The outdoor version, *longue paume,* continued to be played in streets and parks until the nineteenth century, but it was the indoor version—*courte paume*—that developed into the complicated and fascinating pastime that survives today.

The rules and procedures of court tennis are no less complicated than its elaborate court, with odd openings, abutments, and roofed sheds set into the walls. It has been said that months of study are necessary in order to understand the game completely. Court tennis would look bizarre even to a player of a related sport, with its lopsided racquet, handmade ball, and opponents changing ends in the middle of the point—a unique practice known as the chase.

By the late seventeenth century this intriguing pastime was on the decline in both France and England, largely because of gambling scandals. In France the sport's aristocratic connections brought about its downfall during the Revolution, but not until the tennis court at Versailles had become the scene of the Tennis Court Oath, when the third estate, locked out of its regular chambers by order of Louis XVI, met on the court on June 20, 1789, and vowed not to disband until they had given France a constitution. Today the court is a museum dedicated to the French Revolution.

By the end of the eighteenth century only fifty courts remained in all of France, and in England the game was being played only by the extremely wealthy; the *Times* of London reported in 1797 that "the once-fashionable game of tennis is very much upon the decline." Interest revived among the English upper class at the end of the nineteenth century but did not spread to less wealthy Victorians.

In the United States—where the game never caught on except with a handful of millionaires early in the twentieth century—only eighteen courts were ever built (the last completed in 1923) and only seven are in use today. There is little likelihood that any more will be built, since the cost for one would be well in excess of a quarter of a million dollars.

Just as court tennis is the ancestor of the net sports, hard racquets—or simply racquets—is the grandfather of the walled sports. Its lineage, however, is considerably more humble: it was invented early in the nineteenth century by restless inmates of London's Fleet Street Debtors' Gaol, to help while away the long, idle hours of incarceration. The prisoners used sawed-down old court tennis racquets and the hard-as-rock ball from the game of fives, or handball. Their court was the cobblestone prison courtyard and its surrounding high, stout walls. Hard racquets was a fast, simple game.

Once they had settled their debts, these inventive prisoners, many of them well-bred gentlemen who merely owed someone money, took their game beyond the prison walls, chiefly to the backyards of pubs and inns all over England.

From its lowly origins, racquets made its way upward in society, soon becoming a fashionable pastime among the solvent and even the rich. Its popularity and prestige received a tremendous boost in the early 1820s, when it was taken up by students at Harrow, the exclusive boys' boarding school. From Harrow, racquets spread to other English "public" schools, including Eton and Rugby, as well as to Oxford, Cambridge, and several swank gentlemen's clubs. It never really developed into a mass sport because it was a difficult game to play and the court became increasingly elaborate and expensive to build. Though similar to squash in court, racquet, and method of play, the game itself is much, much faster; Allison Danzig, a leading racquets authority, believes it is probably as fast a game as any known to man.

During its mid-Victorian heyday the sport was played all over England and introduced by the Royal Army and Navy to such remote outposts as Gibraltar, Malta, India, and Canada. From Canada it found its way to the United States. As with court tennis, however, the enormous cost of building racquets courts prevented it from ever becoming popular in the United States. There are only a dozen or so courts and probably no more than five hundred serious players in the entire country, and under three thousand worldwide. The game's staunchest adherents are found in the British public schools.

Court tennis and hard racquets may both be practically museum pieces, inaccessible to all but a few, but in their stead we have their modern offspring—half a dozen racquet and paddle sports that are far more available, easier and less expensive to play, and which offer every bit as much stimulation, exercise, and enjoyment.

One particularly gratifying aspect of the widespread new popularity of these sports is that many of the new racquet and paddle wielders are newcomers to sports altogether, people whose previous contact with athletics was limited to spectating. Women make up a significant part of this group. Long excluded from pickup basketball at the local playground and touch football in the park, women are welcomed to racquet and paddle sports and are physically well suited to them. Approximately 40 percent of all racquetball players and 40–50 percent of new squash players are women; most of the other sports discussed in this book can claim slightly less dramatic but still significant percentages of female players. Tennis, of course, has long been a "liberated" sport.

The next few pages will provide a brief overview of each of the sports covered in the text. It should soon become clear that wherever you live, whether you are interested in a strenuous workout or more mild exercise, whether you want an easily learned sport or a challenging one, whatever your age, athletic ability, and budget requirements, there is at least one racquet or paddle sport—and more likely several—to suit you.

Nearly everyone is familiar with tennis, which can be described as a game in which players use long-handled, strung racquets to hit a felt-covered rubber ball back and forth over a net that is hung across the center of a court. From its origins as a garden party diversion for the privileged few, tennis has come to be one of the best-known and most widely played sports in the world. There are currently about 150,000 tennis courts in the United States—in parks, schools, tennis and country clubs, resorts, apartment complexes, and tennis camps; on rooftops, and under bubbles. Some are private, many are public or commercial. Partly as a cause and partly as a result of the spectacular tennis boom that began in the late 1960s, there are now some fifteen hundred indoor tennis clubs in the United States, making tennis a year-round sport even in the northern states.

Though tennis has become widely available, it still retains some of its exclusive image and, in certain cases, exclusive prices: an hour of prime time indoors in Manhattan can run upwards of $30. The cost is considerably less in most other places, and many outdoor courts are public and available at no charge or for a nominal fee. Racquets cost anywhere from $10 to over $200, and they need to be restrung periodically. (These and all other prices given are, of course, subject to change.)

Besides being potentially the most expensive of all the racquet and paddle sports, tennis is also the most difficult to learn. A typical beginner can anticipate struggling through three to six months of utter frustration before he or she has mastered the basics sufficiently to hit the ball three times in a row. For those who get "hooked" on the game, the continual challenges it presents to one's stamina, reflexes, natural ability, and strategic sense are what make it so appealing; it is truly a sport that can be enjoyed from childhood (there is a well-organized junior development program) into old age.

Doubles is a less vigorous form of the game, which can be played by people of all ages. In 1977, the United States Tennis Association instituted a championship for men age eighty and over, in both singles and doubles.

For some people, the difficulty of learning to play tennis is a major drawback. Together with the rising expense of renting court time, it explains some of the defections from tennis to one of the other racquet or paddle sports. Several of them are adaptations and variations of tennis; all are easier and less costly to play.

Squash is played on a walled court with long-handled, small-headed racquets and a small, hard rubber ball. The court's four walls are all in play; the front wall is the target wall. On every shot, the ball must hit it above the 17-inch-high metal telltale before touching the floor.

Squash, which has been around almost as long as tennis, offers a slightly different configuration of appeals. First of all, it is easier to learn than tennis, especially since the introduction of the livelier 70-+ ball. Second, keeping the ball in play in the relatively small, four-wall court is simpler than on a tennis court, and retrieving miss-hit balls is less time-consuming. Though easier at the beginning, squash is just as difficult to master as tennis, requiring if anything greater stamina, quicker reflexes, more finesse, and a better sense of strategy and tactics. Thus it continues to challenge its participants, of whom there are currently about a million, at all levels of expertise.

Squash is a concentrated, convenient form of exercise that fits in well with today's fast-paced life. Despite its smaller court (one-tenth the floor area of a tennis court), it is a more strenuous game than tennis. The ball goes out of play much more quickly than a tennis ball, so you must run harder to reach it in time. Even for well-conditioned players, a half-hour of squash can provide a vigorous workout; of course, the game can be slowed down by the judicious use of lobs. There is also a doubles game, but because it is not widely played (there are only about two hundred facilities for it nationwide), it will not be discussed here.

Because squash courts are so much smaller than tennis courts, they are more efficient to build and operate; consequently, squash court time is typically about half as expensive as tennis time. Commercial clubs generally charge a small membership fee, $25 to $50, and $5 to $10 per half-hour of court time. Racquets range from about $10 to $40.

If you play squash, you will never be forced to cancel your game because of inclement weather. Furthermore, you can practice and work out alone. It is one of the more intellectual racquet sports; the importance of thinking two or three shots ahead have led some to compare it to chess. All in all, squash is a physically and mentally challenging way for both men and women to pack a lot of exercise into a short period of time.

Now for the drawback: there are currently only about thirty-seven hundred squash courts in the United States. Until recently, there were virtually no commercial squash facilities anywhere in the country; to play squash, a person pretty much had to be enrolled in a boarding school, college, or university or belong to a private athletic club. This situation has begun to change in the last few years: New York City now has more pay-for-play squash courts than indoor tennis courts. Outside of New York and Philadelphia, however, U.S. cities have no more than a handful of commercial courts.

Racquetball is essentially four-wall handball played with truncated tennis racquets and a lively rubber ball, which must hit the front wall before touching the floor, as in squash. Unlike squash, the ball may hit the ceiling as well as the four vertical surfaces, and it may hit the front wall at any height; there is no telltale to be aimed above. One- and three-wall versions of racquetball have been devised to accommodate existing handball courts.

The racquetball boom that has been followed with interest by business and the press for the past few years is fast bringing this newest racquet sport to every section of the United States, where there are more than seventeen thousand racquetball courts located in schools, YMCAs, community centers, and in about a thousand commercial racquetball clubs, hundreds of which are built each year. The sport is little known outside the United States, and is least represented in the Northeast, where it has more competition from longer-established sports such as squash, but it is reported that some people are now playing racquetball on squash courts. With an estimated eight to ten million racquetball players—up from a mere fifty thousand in 1970—the sport's association has its sights set on matching or even overtaking tennis in the next few years. Many women have been attracted to racquetball, and they now account for about 40 percent of its adherents. It has proven popular with youngsters too, as demonstrated by its flourishing junior development program.

Racquetball's meteoric success has been due to its many real appeals as well as to its expansion-minded governing body. First of all, it is probably the easiest of all the racquet sports to learn. Neither the strokes nor the strategies are at all complicated. Someone who already plays a related sport could probably pick it up very quickly, but it is also an excellent choice for a person with no prior racquet sport experience.

Like squash, racquetball is fast-paced and strenuous, offering concentrated exercise and requiring stamina, good reflexes, speed, and strength. Far less ability and experience, however, are needed to play well enough to get a good workout. There is also a doubles game, which is less strenuous.

Another advantage racquetball shares with squash is its low cost. Since racquetball courts are similarly smaller and less expensive to build and maintain than tennis courts, it is another indoor sport that is within reach of people whose budgets make tennis prohibitive. YMCAs and similar facilities charge only $3 or $4 an hour; most racquetball clubs charge between $8 and $10 an hour. Players generally find that they get a lot for their money: many racquetball clubs offer saunas, steam rooms, sophisticated exercise equipment, swimming pools, and facilities for a related sport. As with squash, weather and climate are no obstacles to play, and it is possible to practice alone. Racquets cost between $20 and $100.

Racquetball opponents are usually in close proximity on the court, and the game can be a bit rough at times, with players elbowing each other out of the way like shoppers at a sale. Occasionally they crash into the walls, floor, and each other in hot pursuit of the fast-moving ball. There are racquet sports sophisticates who feel that racquetball doesn't offer as much complexity and challenge as some of the others—which is an advantage or a drawback, depending on your point of view—but nearly everyone who tries it agrees that it's a terrific way to release tension and have a great deal of fun.

Paddle tennis is played on a court about half the size of a tennis court with wooden paddles and a tennis ball that has been punctured to deaden its bounce. Originally designed for children, it is a kind of miniature tennis. The grips, strokes, and strategies of the sport are almost identical with their counterparts in tennis, but the small court, short-handled paddles, and low net make it far easier to learn and play. There is a singles and a doubles game, and neither is as physically taxing as tennis. Thus it is a good children's sport and perfectly suited to older, slowed-down players. The institution of several changes in the late 1950s and early 1960s has made it possible for paddle tennis to be also a fast, strenuous, and challenging contest. Though it doesn't require the power or speed needed for tennis, it does call for aggressive tactics and quick reflexes for the rapid-fire exchanges that take place at the net.

Along with the ease of learning and playing, one of the chief appeals of paddle tennis is its low cost. Equipment is inexpensive—$15 to $20 for a paddle (paddles in general are cheaper than strung racquets, and of course never need restringing); court time is either free or inexpensive.

Though it has received less exposure, promotion, and attention than some of its sister sports, paddle tennis is an ideal family sport that can be played for a lifetime. Women make up 30 to 40 percent of the estimated seventy-five thousand people who play the sport regularly. Unfortunately, most of the approximately eight thousand courts are limited to the New York City area, southern California, and a few other isolated spots. The courts in New York are found mainly in public parks and playgrounds; in California, where the game is most popular, there are private paddle tennis clubs as well. Paddle tennis can be played year-round even in New York because the deadened ball is less affected by cold temperatures and blustery winds than an unpunctured tennis ball.

Platform tennis is frequently confused with paddle tennis, from which it developed, especially as both sports were once called by the same name and the newer sport still often goes by the nickname "paddle." The scaled-down court used in platform tennis, the same width but six feet shorter than a paddle tennis court, is usually installed on a raised platform. It is always surrounded by 12-foot-high taut wire screens that form part of the playing surface: you can let your opponent's shots rebound off them if you choose. Like paddle tennis, platform tennis is played with wooden paddles, but instead of a punctured tennis ball a soft, sponge rubber ball is used.

The rules and strokes for platform tennis are almost the same as those for tennis and paddle tennis. It, too, is easier to learn than tennis because of the smaller court and short-handled paddles. In addition, though they are often perplexing to beginners, the "wires" actually make the game easier by giving players a second chance to return hard-hit balls.

Platform tennis is not a particularly strenuous sport. Primarily a doubles game, it features long rallies but relatively little running, and power is less important than in most of the related sports. Thus it is a good mixed-doubles and family sport, although at the top levels platform tennis players are skilled, well-conditioned athletes.

Where commercial courts are available, platform tennis is not expensive. Paddles run about $16 to $50, and court time costs between $10 and $15 an hour. However, facilities are not widely available. There are about four thousand courts located in private country clubs or backyards in the northeastern United States, and the small number of commercial platform tennis clubs that have been built are also in the Northeast. The only other area where the sport is played in significant numbers is southern California; there it is called screen tennis, because the platform has been eliminated.

Platform tennis originated as a winter alternative to tennis, and in the Northeast it is still largely a cold-weather outdoor sport (there are no indoor courts). In really inclement weather, of course, you'd have to find an alternative, but hardy "paddlers" do play in light rain or snow. The surface of the court is roughened to prevent slipping, and most courts are built with hinged flaps, called snowboards, to facilitate snow removal. In iconoclastic California it is played year-round.

There are actually three versions of paddleball: four-wall, one-wall, and a rarely played three-wall variety. All three forms of paddleball, like racquetball, are spin-offs of handball, utilizing the same courts and similar rules but, of course, wooden paddles.

Once widely played, four-wall paddleball has been largely eclipsed by its better-promoted offspring, racquetball, despite the fact that it offers many of the same appeals. It is relatively easy to learn, inexpensive to play, and excellent exercise; singles, of course, is more strenuous than doubles. It is a slower-paced game than racquetball, but because the ball is softer and the paddle much heavier than their racquetball counterparts, four-wall paddleball requires considerably more strength.

While four-wall paddleball is currently most popular in the region of its birth, the Midwest, one-wall paddleball is almost entirely a New York City phenomenon, with thousands of concrete-walled courts located in schoolyards, public parks, and playgrounds throughout the five boroughs. Courts are abundant and free; the game is easily learned; equipment is inexpensive; no special attire is needed; and it is wonderful exercise. These factors make it the second most popular sport in town (basketball is first). Once played almost exclusively by men, it is now attracting increasing numbers of women.

One-wall paddleball is a fast, strenuous, physically demanding sport, even in the more common doubles form. Its relatively lenient rules regarding obstruction of and by one's opponent make it a comparatively rough sport that stresses power and aggressiveness.

Until recently, one-wall was entirely an outdoor and thus primarily a seasonal sport, but now, to the delight of the estimated two hundred thousand players, indoor one-wall paddleball establishments are beginning to appear. They charge about $6 to $8 for an hour of court time.

People who have had the good fortune to grow up with access to basements and backyards are probably familiar with table tennis and badminton. Although related to the games discussed here, they are omitted from this book because at present they are regarded, in the United States at any rate, more as recreation than as athletic sports; there are few public courts or clubs and little organized play for either of them. This is not the case, of course, in many other parts of the world, especially the Orient and parts of Europe, where both are major competitive sports. At the top levels, they are both tough, extremely demanding sports that call for as high a level of ability and skill as any of the other racquet and paddle sports.

"I'd really love to try squash [racquetball, paddleball, paddle tennis, etc.], but I'm afraid it would ruin my tennis [racquetball, paddleball, paddle tennis, etc.] game," is a sentiment often voiced by people who play one of these sports when the subject of another comes up. In truth, the notion that playing a new racquet or paddle sport will "hurt your game" in the one you already play is more myth than reality. These sports are more alike than they are different, and you have far more to gain than lose by playing several of them. All share the same basic goal: to win points by striking a ball with a racquet or paddle in such a way that your opponent cannot retrieve or return it. They share many of the fundamentals: the basic footwork and strokes, the importance of getting your weight into your shots, and hand-eye coordination. Because all these elements are important to all the sports, the skills you learn for one are transferable to any of the others. With each sport stressing different skills, your proficiency in one can be sharpened by playing another. To take tennis and squash as examples: If you play squash during the winter, then for five or six months you are challenging your speed, endurance, reflexes, and sense of strategy to the utmost; this can't help but make you a faster, smarter, and better-conditioned tennis player come spring. It is true that squash shots are made with wristier, more curtailed strokes than their counterparts in tennis, and some players do find themselves hitting with squashlike strokes at the beginning of the tennis season and vice versa, but such habits can be easily corrected by spending a little time practicing the appropriate strokes—you don't need a court for this—before the particular season gets under way. The more often the switch is made, the easier it will become for both mind and muscles.

More and more players are adding a second racquet or paddle sport to their repertoire, seeking variety as well as the flexibility to play one sport in cold or inclement weather, say, and another outside on warm days. A recent survey revealed that 20 percent of *Tennis* magazine readers also play the popular newcomer, racquetball. An interesting sidelight is that these sports are no longer strictly typed by socioeconomic status; the lines between them have become increasingly blurred as they have become more available and as players of one take up a second.

This book is designed both for the newcomer to racquet and paddle sports and for the player of one interested in learning another. There is information and advice about the equipment for each one, which will enable you to make informed choices when purchasing a racquet, paddle, balls, or attire. There are descriptions and diagrams of the courts, and an appendix with the official rules for each game. There are clear, detailed instructions and explanations of the fundamentals—the skills and strokes required for each sport as well as the basic strategies for both singles and doubles. The drawings and photographs accompanying the text will help you to visualize and practice what you are reading. I must apologize to left-handers and to women. For the sake of simplicity, this book is written as if all players were right-handed and male. Left-handers, kindly reverse the instructions as necessary.

Before you turn to the sport that interests you most, take a few minutes to read the first chapter, which deals with sports and health. It contains some important—and perhaps some surprising—information that could not only spare you an injury on the court but also help you to play better.

Beyond what you learn in this book, you may want to take some lessons from the pro at your club or park in order to get another perspective. An expert can tailor his instructions to your playing ability and help you correct the particular errors you are making. Most players who do take lessons agree that it is time and money well spent. The more proficient you become, the more enjoyment—and the more exercise—you will get.

Study this book, take a few lessons, practice your strokes, but above all, play; enjoy the exercise and the healthy competition. The more you play, the more you'll improve, which will make playing more fun.

BEFORE
YOU START

Whether your game is squash or paddleball, racquetball or one of the three versions of tennis, and whether you are a beginner or a ranked tournament player, one thing is certain: you do more running, reaching, arching, bending, and extending on the court than in any of your ordinary, everyday activities. Indeed, probably one of your main reasons for playing an active sport in the first place is to get a workout—to get into or stay in shape.

Whichever racquet or paddle sport you play, you can count on getting a good deal of exercise and being rewarded with greater fitness and a trimmer body. If like most people, however, you play your sport only once or twice a week and spend the rest of your waking hours sitting behind a desk or a steering wheel, you're not going to have enough flexibility, stamina, or strength to play your best, avoid injuries on the court—which are more likely to occur when muscles are tight, tired, or weak—or enjoy yourself fully from the first point all the way to the last. In an all-too-common syndrome, at some point in the game the twin evils of soreness and fatigue will take over, interfering with skill and desire. Instead of staying on your toes, going for every ball, and hitting your best shots, you're likely to be standing flatfooted and out of position, worried about whether or not you'll be able to last an hour on the court.

Many ingredients go into performing a sport well, including talent, sound techniques, which can be learned and practiced, and physical capacity—flexibility, endurance, and strength—which can all be increased by exercising. Not everyone can be a top athlete, but almost everyone can be in top physical shape.

FLEXIBILITY   In noncontact sports, tight muscles are the most common cause of injuries, and flexibility is the most important protection against injury. With vigorous exercise, muscles get stronger, but also shorter—"tighter"; you feel this as stiffness a day or so after engaging in unaccustomed strenuous activity. Muscles that are short and tight stand a much greater chance of being strained, sprained, pulled, or ruptured than muscles that are flexible. In addition, all the racquet and paddle sports call for sudden and extreme movements—reaching, lunging, twisting—movements that place extraordinary demands on your muscles. Therefore, no matter how often or how ardently you play your sport, you should do stretching exercises—*before* playing to prevent injuries and to allow you to reach for the ball at the fullest possible extension, and again *after* playing to rid your muscles of the tightness that has been built up by playing.

STRETCHING GUIDELINES   First, it is important to emphasize that flexibility exercises should be done regardless of the temperature on the court. Stretching your muscles is just as necessary in warm weather as in cold.

When doing any of the following flexibility exercises, stretch slowly and smoothly to the point where you feel tightness and a slight burning sensation. Never stretch to the point of pain and never bounce into a position, which could cause greater tightness and even damage to tissues. Unless other instructions are given with the exercise, hold each stretch for a period of ten seconds and repeat two or three times. Relax for a few seconds between repetitions, and try to reach slightly further each time. The entire series should take you ten to fifteen minutes. When you don't have enough time to do them all, at least do the six stretches that are asterisked; they involve the muscles most likely to be injured on the court.

Before you start stretching, it is a good idea to jog or run in place for a few minutes, just to break a sweat.

1. *Neck stretch.* Standing or sitting with your shoulders and arms relaxed, turn your head right and then left; tilt your right ear toward your right shoulder, then your left ear toward your left shoulder; bend your head forward, then back. For this stretch, hold each position for five seconds, and do entire stretch twice.

*2. *Shoulder stretch.* (a) Raise both arms overhead and clasp your hands. Without arching your back, pull your hands back until you feel the stretch in your shoulders. (Fig. 1-1) (b) Extend your arms out to the sides at shoulder height. Keeping them at this height, draw your hands behind your back and hold. (Fig. 1-2)

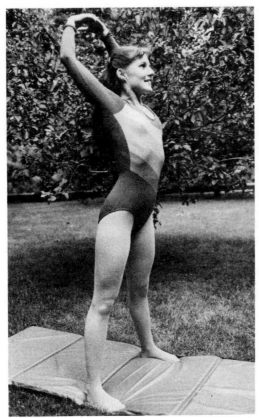

Fig. 1-1

Fig. 1-2 Shoulder Stretches

3. *Trunk rotations.* Stand relaxed, feet about shoulder width apart. Swing slowly and smoothly from side to side, keeping your feet stationary. Let your head turn and your arms swing with your body. Do five to ten swings in each direction.

*4. *Shoulder and hamstring stretch.* Stand with your feet a few inches apart and clasp your hands behind your back. Bend forward, press your head to your knees, and pull your hands up over your back. (Fig. 1-3)

*5. *Calf stretch.* Face a solid wall, standing at least four feet away from it. Place your palms on the wall and lean forward, bending your elbows and keeping your back straight. Keep your heels on the floor. (Fig. 1-4)

*6. *Inner thigh and waist stretch.* Kneeling on one knee, extend your other leg out to the side and bend sideways over it. (Fig. 1-5) Then reverse legs.

7. *All-over (cat) stretch.* From a squatting position, place your palms on the floor directly under your shoulders and extend both legs straight out behind you; you should be supporting yourself on your palms and toes.

Fig. 1-3 Shoulder-and-Hamstring Stretch

Fig. 1-4 Calf Stretch

Fig. 1-5 Inner Thigh-and-Waist Stretch

Lift your rear end up to form a V with your body; press your heels to the floor and bend your head to look at them. Hold. Then slowly lower your rear end, keeping your arms straight, until your back is arched; bend your head back.

8. *Groin stretch.* Sit on the floor, soles of your feet together. Push your knees toward the floor and bend forward.

9. *Plough* (for lower back and hamstrings). Lie on your back. Bend your knees to your chest, then raise them over your head and straighten them. Try to touch the floor with your toes.

*10. *Hurdler's stretch* (for hamstrings). Sit on the floor with one leg extended straight out in front of you and the other bent behind you. Bend forward from the waist over your straight leg, trying to touch your chest to your knee. (Fig. 1-6). Then reverse legs.

*11. *Sprinter's stretch* (for quadriceps). From a squatting position, place your palms on the floor directly under your shoulders and extend one leg straight out behind you, resting on your toes; your other knee is bent to your chest. Shift your weight forward. Hold. (Fig. 1-7) Then reverse legs.

12. *Quadriceps stretch.* Hold on to a support. Bend your knee and grasp your foot behind you with your hand. Lean forward and press your foot into your rear end. Then reverse legs.

Fig. 1-6 Hurdler's Stretch

Fig. 1-7 Sprinter's Stretch

The final step in a good pregame warm-up session is exactly where most players are accustomed to starting. After you've stretched out all your playing muscles, rally for about ten minutes. Start with slow, easy movements and increase the pace gradually; this will make the transition to more strenuous exercise safer and easier. Go through all the strokes and movements you'll be using in the sport, but don't tire yourself out; you've got a lot of running and hitting ahead of you.

CONDITIONING   You cannot get into top shape for a sport simply by playing the sport. If you want to feel and play your best until the last point is over, you need stamina and strength to spare. Even professional athletes, who play nearly every day of the year, do supplementary conditioning exercises to enable them to give 100 percent when they are competing. They know that in a long, tough match, it is often the better-conditioned player who has the edge. Before the match is over, an out-of-shape player is likely to be too tired to get explosive starts, set up properly, or hit his best shots; instead, he is preoccupied with the soreness in his legs, his aching back, the sheer effort required to move. The fact is, lazy footwork, bad habits, and loss of concentration are frequently the result of fatigue.

Besides improving your game (and your waistline) conditioning exercises will help protect you from injuries. Well-conditioned muscles, like flexible ones, are less injury-prone than sore, exhausted muscles. And if you do happen to injure yourself, good muscle tone will help you heal faster.

Conditioning helps prevent pulls and sprains in your arms, legs, back, and shoulders; an even more important effect is the protection it provides for your most vital muscle—your heart. Numerous studies have demonstrated that physical fitness plays a definite role in decreasing the risk of suffering a heart attack or dying from heart disease. This alone should be reason enought to start working out.

CONDITIONING GUIDELINES

Check with your doctor before undertaking any exercise program if you have any heart or other medical problems or if you are over thirty-five and out of shape. He or she may want to give you an exercise stress test to determine what level of activity your cardiovascular system can tolerate.

If you're just beginning to exercise, or if you're starting again after a layoff of even a week, go slowly. If you skip as many as three weeks, begin at the beginning. Unfortunately, getting out of shape is a much more rapid process than getting into shape.

How often should you work out? That depends on your seriousness. The more often (within reason), the more strength and stamina you'll build. Many tournament players work out daily. If you're an average club player, you should make time for conditioning exercises three times a week. That will give you enough strength and energy not only for your sport but for all your other activities as well.

How much should you do each time you work out? That depends entirely on your current strength and stamina. You want to exercise enough to get conditioning benefits, but not so much that it leaves you with persistent soreness and fatigue, signs that you are *overtraining*—going beyond your body's capacity. A distinction must be made between overtraining and *overloading*—doing a little more than your accustomed level of exertion—which is the correct way to build up. Use common sense to determine the right amount of exercise for you; learn to recognize the difference between enough and too much. As a general guideline, go to your limit, and then try to do one more—one more lap, one more sit-up, one more leg raise.

ENDURANCE   Two kinds of endurance are called for in all of these sports: long-term *(aerobic)* conditioning, so that you can last three long sets of tennis or three fast games of squash without running out of steam, and short-term *(anaerobic)* conditioning, for the quick bursts of speed often necessary to get to the ball. The most efficient way to build up both types of endurance is by running, but in two distinctly different ways.

To do any kind of running, it is important to wear specially designed running shoes, which have more cushioning and heel elevation than tennis shoes. If possible, avoid running on pavement, which is harder on your feet, legs, and spine than grass or a dirt or cinder track. Before and after running, do the shoulder and hamstring stretch, the calf stretch, the inner thigh and waist stretch, and the plough.

1. *Jogging* (for aerobic conditioning). A rough definition of jogging is running at a slow enough pace so that you can talk normally. Correct, safe form involves keeping your back straight (not leaning forward) and your shoulders relaxed. Take short strides, landing softly on your heels; don't pound. Start with a short distance and work up to one or two miles.
2. *Sprint/jog combinations* (for anaerobic conditioning). Alternate twenty yards of each. Sprints should be done at top speed. Work up from a few minutes of these to fifteen minutes. They will improve your stamina, leg strength, and quickness all at the same time.

STRENGTH   The other half of conditioning is strength. To run your fastest and play your best, all your running and hitting muscles have to be strong. The areas to concentrate on are your legs, abdomen, back, arms, and shoulders.

If you have any back problems, consult your physician before doing the push-ups and sit-ups.
1. *Push-ups* (for shoulders and arms). Women should support themselves on their knees, not their toes.
2. *Sit-ups* (for abdomen, back, and thighs). Everyone should do these with bent knees. Hook your feet under a chair or other heavy object if you can't raise your upper body smoothly without bracing yourself. Start each sit-up with a pelvic tilt; that is, push your lower back to the floor. Do these smoothly, not too fast, keeping your back round as you come up and go down.

3. *Chest and leg arches* (for arms, back, and legs). Lie on your stomach, arms extended in front of you. Raise your chest and both legs simultaneously, pulling your hands behind your back.

4. *Toe and heel raises* (for feet, ankles, and calves). Rise up on your toes, then roll back on your heels with your toes flexed.

5. *Side leg raises* (for legs and abdomen). Lie on your side, lower knee bent for support, upper leg straight; rest your head on your lower arm and use your other arm for balance. Raise your upper leg as high as possible. Lower and repeat. Then turn over and reverse legs.

6. *Knee bends* (for thighs). Do these slowly and don't squat too low—just until your thigh is not quite parallel to the floor; knee bends are hard on the knees.

7. *Wrist curls* (for wrists and forearms). Sit on a chair. Holding a dumbbell, book, or other weight in each hand, rest your forearms on your thighs. With palms facing up, curl wrists up. Then turn palms downward and curl wrists back. Forearms remain stationary.

8. *Ball squeeze* (for hands and forearms). Holding a racquet or paddle sport ball in each hand, squeeze tightly and vigorously.

Fig. 2-1

TENNIS

ABOUT TENNIS   Walter Clopton Wingfield, a retired British Army major and avid sportsman, is credited with the invention of modern lawn tennis in 1873, although his creation, with its hourglass-shaped court, five-foot-high net, and diamond-shaped serving box, underwent significant alterations before it much resembled what we call tennis. Wingfield's game, which he dubbed *sphairistiké* (Greek for ball playing), was a smashing success in fashionable society. Because it was played on a court laid out on the grass, people were soon calling it lawn tennis.

The first Lawn Tennis Championships were held on the newly laid courts of the All-England Croquet Club in the borough of Wimbledon in 1877. Wimbledon, as this oldest tennis tournament is known, is still acknowledged as the most prestigious event in the game.

Tennis soon spread to many parts of the British Empire. It reached the United States in 1874, after Mary Outerbridge of Staten Island saw it played in Bermuda by the British garrison stationed there. She brought balls, racquets, and a net home with her, and she and her brother laid out a court at the Staten Island Cricket and Baseball Club.

In short order tennis was all the rage on the East Coast among a coterie of moneyed players who could afford private courts or membership in one of the exclusive cricket clubs that set aside a portion of their turf for the new game. Leather shoes and street clothing were worn to play tennis. For the women, this meant long, full skirts with starched petticoats and large hats to protect them from the sun. Needless to say, the style of play in those days was rather more sedate than today's strenuous, athletic game.

In 1881, representatives of the leading tennis clubs formed the United States National Lawn Tennis Association, one of the first amateur sports-governing bodies in the country, in order to standardize the rules and equipment and to govern tournaments. The first national championships, for men only, were held in August of that year at the elegant Newport Casino in Rhode Island. A women's championship was inaugurated six years later. By 1895, tennis clubs were being organized all across the country and the USNLTA already had 106 member clubs.

The year 1900 marked the inauguration of the Davis Cup, a team competition for men of all nations. International competition for women began in 1923 with the Wightman Cup, an annual championship between British and American women's teams.

In 1960, there were only about five-and-a-half million tennis players in the United States; currently there are nearly thirty million. The phenomenal tennis boom that began in the late 1960s and lasted until the mid-1970s was due in large part to the advent, in 1968, of open tennis tournaments, in which professionals and amateurs were finally allowed to compete against each other. This led to high-stakes tournaments sponsored by huge corporations and exposed the game to millions of spectators on weekend television.

GOVERNING BODY United States Tennis Association
51 East 42nd Street
New York, NY 10017
Official newsletter: *Tennis USA*

COURT The tennis court is a rectangle 78 feet long and 27 feet wide for singles, and the same length but 36 feet wide for doubles, extended by 4½-foot-wide alleys on either side. The court is divided across the middle by a net that is 3 feet high at the center and 3 feet 6 inches high at the posts. The lines bounding the ends and sides of the court are called baselines and sidelines respectively. At the center of each baseline is a 4-inch line called the center mark. On each side of the net, 21 feet from it and parallel to it, are the service lines. The area in between the net and the service lines is divided into two equal service courts by the center service line.

There should be at least 21 feet of back space behind each baseline and

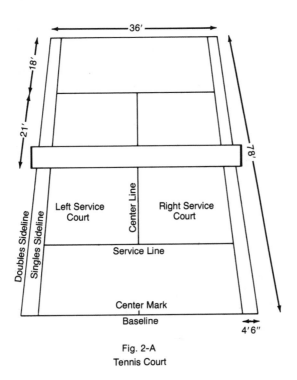

Fig. 2-A
Tennis Court

12 feet of side space outside each sideline, making the total area needed for a regulation tennis court 120 feet by 60 feet.

Tennis courts come in a variety of surfaces, each with its own particular playing characteristics. Generally thought to be the most important is the court's speed—how much time players have in which to reach the ball before it has bounced twice and is out of play. Variations in speed from one court surface to another can be striking; a shot that might be an outright winner on a fast court, such as grass, could very well be just another shot on a slow one—clay, for example.

On fast surfaces—cement, wood, and grass—rallies tend to be a good deal shorter than they are on slow courts, and the more aggressive, harder-hitting player—the serve-and-volleyer who hits forcing shots and follows them to the net—is favored over the player who remains in the back court. On both wood—the fastest of all—and cement, the surface is smooth, so that the ball takes a true and therefore predictable bounce, which is not the case on either grass or clay. Both wood and cement provide excellent traction, but cement is hard on feet, legs, shoes, and balls. Neither surface requires any regular upkeep besides hosing or sweeping.

Grass courts are soft and springy, a delight to run on. However, both the ball and the players skid on grass, and if the turf isn't in top shape, the ball will bounce unpredictably, which means that getting to the net, where you can hit the ball on the fly, is particulary important. Grass courts are expensive to maintain; if they are to thrive, they require experts to tend them and periods of rest as well as the right soil and climate. Consequently, this luxurious surface has become, alas, something of an endangered species, although the pre-eminent tournament, Wimbledon, is still played on grass.

On slow courts—clay and brand-name fast-dry surfaces such as Har-Tru—the ball takes a high, slow, and sometimes erratic bounce. Because it is possible to get to practically any shot, points are generally longer on these slow surfaces, favoring the steady, baseline player who has the speed to run down his opponent's shots along with the patience to wait for openings. The surface texture of these soft courts makes sliding into the ball both possible and useful for saving time and energy.

Today there are new methods of constructing hard courts that are either asphalt-, concrete-, or cement-based and acrylic-coated. These are the so-called "all weather" courts, playable soon after a rain because the drainage is off the court surface rather than through to the base of construction. All share the attractive characteristic of low maintenance, but they vary widely in other respects—speed, resilience, footing, porosity, and durability. There are also dozens of rubber, felt, plastic, and textile surfaces marketed under almost a hundred trade names that are used for indoor courts.

RACQUETS During the last ten years, there has been a veritable racquet revolution. The great increase in the number of tennis players, many of them affluent and ready to spend money on equipment for their favorite sport, has been an enormous incentive to the tennis racquet industry to make use of highly advanced technology in order to develop more and better products. Nowadays, racquets are evaluated for such qualities as torque resistance, longitudinal flexibility, and vibration damping, and there is a racquet—or nine or ten—made to suit every conceivable type of player. But to an uninitiated consumer, the tremendous array of racquets in a typical sporting goods store can be an overwhelming sight.

Although there are no official specifications for tennis racquets, most are about 27 inches long (except the oversize Prince and its competitors) with strung, oval heads. Where racquets vary is in frame material, weight, grip size, balance, stringing material, string tension, and price—they run the gamut from $8.99 for a prestrung import to more than $200 for some of the fancier composite models. Most cost between $40 and $100, with many excellent racquets at the lower end of that range.

Fig. 2-2

The racquet frame may be constructed of laminated wood (between eight and twelve thin layers), steel, aluminum, or fiberglass, or it may be a composite—the newest major development in racquets—a combination of two or more dissimilar materials, among them any of those already mentioned and/or plastic, boron, titanium, graphite, and other expensive space-age substances, joined to unite specific qualities, such as durability and flexibility.

It is the degree of flexibility that will make the most difference in how a racquet "plays" and a knowledgeable salesperson should be able to tell you whether a particular frame is flexible or stiff. In general, a stiff racquet adds control, making it a good choice for an accomplished, hard-hitting player—but not for one who suffers from tennis elbow, as an unyielding frame is likely to aggravate the condition. A more flexible frame, which "flings" the ball off the strings, enhances power and is more appropriate for the average player.

Racquets come in three weights: light (12–12¾ ounces), medium (12¾–13½ ounces), and heavy (13½–14¾ ounces). Most women find that light racquets suit them best, while men tend to prefer medium-weight

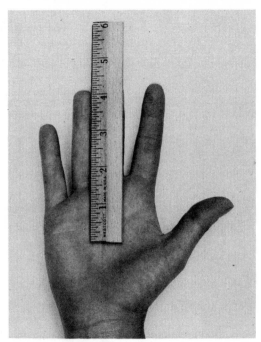

Fig. 2-3 Determining your grip size

racquets. (There are also junior racquets for children; they weigh 10 ounces and are an inch or two shorter in the handle than standard.) Choose a racquet whose weight is appropriate for your size and strength. A difference of an ounce or two can be critical: a racquet that is too heavy or too light will hamper your game and may also leave you with a tired or even sore hand, wrist, or arm.

Racquet grips, which vary in shape from one manufacturer to another, are generally leather-covered and range in size from four to five inches, in ⅛-inch increments. To determine your grip size, place a ruler between the ring and middle fingers of your playing hand and measure the distance from the tip of your ring finger to the lower of the two creases that run across your palm. If you find that your present grip is too large or small (either will put extra strain on your arm), the grip base can be sanded down or built up with tape at a pro shop or sporting goods store.

Racquets may be head-heavy, head-light, or evenly balanced. A racquet's balance can be determined by seeing which way it tips (strung, or with an equivalent weight attached to the head) when it is supported by one finger at its longitudinal midpoint. An evenly balanced racquet will not tip one way or the other, while on a head-heavy racquet the head will dip, and on a head-light one it will rise. A racquet that is head-heavy can add power to your shots, but it will also be more tiring to use. A head-light racquet will permit a quicker swing, which is especially useful at the net.

The average player will probably be happiest with a racquet that is evenly balanced or slightly head-light.

Racquets may be strung with either gut or nylon. Most quality racquets are sold unstrung so that the buyer can select his own stringing material. Gut—the processed intestines of lamb, sheep, or cattle—is more expensive ($25–$35) and less durable than nylon, but it is also more sensitive and resilient, and nearly all experienced players prefer it. The thicker the gauge of the gut, the more durable but less lively it will be, although most club players would probably be unaware of the difference and are better off with the relatively thick 15-gauge (about one-fifteenth of an inch in diameter) rather than 16- or the unusually thin 17-gauge. All gut is extremely susceptible to the elements. A racquet strung with gut should be kept away from temperature extremes—for instance, the trunk of your car on a hot, sunny day—and in a waterproof cover to protect it from dampness, and it should never be used with wet balls.

Nylon stringing—unaffected by moisture, less expensive ($10–$15), and longer-wearing than gut—is a better choice for a beginner. Like gut, it comes in several gauges, the thinner gauges being more sensitive and resilient but less durable.

"Synthetic gut" strings—actually nylon fibers that have been twisted or braided together—fall somewhere between bona fide gut and standard nylon strings in resiliency, price, and durability.

String tension is an important variable. Low tension—looser strings—will give you more control; tight strings will give you more power—and more vibration up your arm, which can aggravate tennis elbow. Average tension is between 55 and 65 pounds.

Quality tennis racquets are extremely well-engineered, well-constructed implements, and with a small amount of care they should give years of service. Keep you racquet away from dampness and extremes of temperature, and use a waterproof cover. In the past it was felt that a wood racquet should be kept in a press when it wasn't being used, but most racquet manufacturers now agree that a press is not necessary because modern wood racquets are strengthened with fiberglass or graphite overlays, which reduce their tendency to warp. Store your racquet either on wall pegs or by standing it on its butt end against a wall. And treat it gently; it may help to keep in mind that when you flub a shot, it's not your racquet's fault!

Finally, a few words of warning: try before you buy. Many of the new racquets on the market command fairly hefty prices, and while the majority of them represent genuine innovations in racquet design, some are just fads designed for those players looking for miraculous developments in equipment that will transform them from C players to touring pros. Try out as many store demonstration models or friends' racquets as you can, because even perfectly legitimate designs and materials are better suited to some players than to others.

BALLS   Tennis balls, which are made of felt-covered rubber, are about 2½ inches in diameter and weigh about 2 ounces. When dropped 100 inches onto concrete, a tennis ball should bounce between 53 and 58 inches. At one time, balls came in only one color—white—but now "optic yellow" balls are much more popular because under most conditions they are easier to see. Almost all of the dozen or so brands of balls on the market are pressurized and come in vacuum-packed cans of three, though there are a few companies making pressureless balls, which are longer-lasting but less lively; the best-known is Bancroft/Tretorn. Most players prefer the liveliness of pressurized balls.

Look for "USTA-Approved" or words to that effect on the can to insure quality control. Reliable sporting goods stores will exchange a newly opened but "dead" can of balls.

Balls should last between three and five sets for experienced players and somewhat longer for beginners—but even beginners should try to use lively balls that have a good nap. They will last longer if they are kept dry and away from temperature extremes. A ball restorer or preserver can extend their life by a set or two.

There are different balls made for different surfaces. "Championship" or "regular" balls are designed for use on soft courts; "heavy duty" or "extra duty" balls, which have a more durable covering, are for hard courts. There are also balls made especially for play on grass courts, and "high altitude" balls, which have a lower internal pressure to reduce their liveliness. Nonpressurized balls are also suitable for high-altitude play.

DRESS AND ACCESSORIES   Standard tennis attire is shorts and shirt for men, shorts or a skirt and shirt, or a one-piece tennis dress for women. But within these general guidelines there is a great deal of latitude. In recent years a number of new lines, new labels, and high-fashion designers have joined the established active sportswear manufacturers in the tennis apparel market, and today tennis clothes come in all colors, dozen of styles, and every price range. Whether you prefer your tennis duds plain or fancy, domestic or imported, traditional or avant-garde, your choices should be guided primarily by considerations of comfort and practicality. The fabric should be a cool, comfortable, absorbent, and easily laundered one, such as cotton or a crease-resistant blend of cotton and polyester. If you prefer the look of colorful tennis clothes, the rainbow is the limit; if you find the wide assortment of colors bewildering, it may help to remember that the traditional white (or white with a small amount of colored trim) is always right—cool and the least distracting to other players—and at a few clubs still required.

Tennis shoes have come a long way since sneakers. They vary in design, quality, and price—up to $40 for many of the leather models. Buy the best-quality tennis shoes you can afford; they are your most important purchase where comfort and safety are concerned. When you go to buy tennis shoes, bring along the kind of tennis socks you ordinarily wear to play, and simulate running, jumping, stopping, and starting in the store to see that the shoes fit properly. Make sure that your toes have enough room and that your heels don't slip around.

Shoe uppers come in leather, vinyl, canvas, duck, and nylon. Leather, the most expensive, and vinyl, which costs somewhat less, provide the most support and durability; vinyl shoes should have holes for ventilation. Canvas, duck, and nylon uppers are lightweight, reasonably durable, and generally less expensive than either leather or vinyl. In nylon shoes, look for a wide mesh so that your feet can breathe.

Soles are made of either rubber or polyurethane. Rubber is a better shock absorber. Urethane is more durable, but it is harder on your feet and legs and also hotter underfoot. Many brands of tennis shoes can be resoled for about $15, though not with urethane.

There are two basic tennis shoe lasts: the V-vamp, best for people with narrow feet, and the lace-to-toe vamp, which can be easily adjusted for various foot widths.

Tennis shoes should have absorbent linings, such as terry cloth, and some padding inside for comfort—but shoes with two much padding won't give enough support.

Tennis socks come in wool, cotton—the traditional fabrics—and easier-to-care-for acrylic, nylon, and various blends. Some players wear a thin pair under a thick pair for greater absorbency.

Optional dress and accessories include warm-up suits for before and after play—available in a wide assortment of fabrics and colors—head and wrist sweatbands, tennis hats, and tennis gloves, which some players wear to prevent blisters and to keep the racquet from slipping in their hands.

METHOD OF PLAY Tennis can be played by either two players—singles—or by two pairs of players—doubles—with most of the rules the same for both forms; the major differences between the two will be noted in the description that follows. See pp. 211–224 for complete singles and doubles rules.

A tennis match is scored in points, games, and sets. Either the server or the receiver may win points; the server's score is always stated first. Each player begins with 0, called "love." The first point of the game is 15 (often informally shortened to "5"), the second is 30, the third is 40, and the fourth is game—except that if the score reaches 40 all, called "deuce," a player must win two points in succession to win the game. One point above deuce is called "advantage *player's name*," or more colloquially "my ad" or "your ad." If the player who has the advantage wins the next point, he wins the game; if he loses it, the score returns to deuce and the game continues until one player does win two consecutive points. (Occasionally, "No-Ad" scoring is used; see p. 223.) The first player to win six games wins the set, as long as he is ahead by a two-game margin—for example, 6–4 or 7–5—unless at 6 all a tiebreaker is played (see p. 222). A match is usually the best three out of five sets for men, the best two out of three for women.

The ball is put into play with the serve. The usual method of deciding who serves first is by spinning the racquet: one player places his racquet head-down on the ground, spins it by the grip, and lets it go, while his opponent calls on which side it will land (for instance "up" or "down," referring to the position of the racquet logo on the handle). In some tournaments, a coin is tossed. The winner of the call may choose either to serve the first game or to receive serve, or he may choose to begin playing from a particular end of the court. One player serves an entire game; opponents change ends after every odd-numbered game.

In doubles, the two teams alternate serving games. At the beginning of a set, each team decides which partner will serve first. The first server on Team A serves the first game, the first server on Team B serves the second game, then the second server on Team A serves a game, then the second server on Team B, and so on. On the receiving team, partners alternate returning the serve. Teams may change their serving and/or receiving order at the start of each new set.

To put the ball into play, the server takes a position behind the baseline, tosses the ball into the air, and hits it before it touches the ground. He sends the ball in a diagonal path so that it bounces into the opposite service court beyond the net. He alternates serving from the right (deuce) and left (ad) courts.

The server is allowed two tries on every point to hit a legal serve. If the first serve is not good, it is called a fault and the server tries again. The most common faults are serves that go into the net, serves that land outside the correct service court, and footfaults (serves made while the server's foot is on or over the baseline). After two consecutive faults—called a double fault—the point goes to the receiver.

If the served ball touches the net and then lands in the correct service court, it is called a let. Lets are replayed; that is, if the first serve is a let, the server "takes two"; if the second serve is a let, he "takes one." A let is also called if the server serves before the receiver is ready, or if a player is interfered with by anything beyond his control during a point, such as an errant ball from a neighboring court.

After the served ball has bounced in the correct service court, the receiver returns it over the net into any part of the opponent's court. Once the return of serve has been made, the players may hit the ball either on the fly or after one bounce, and this back-and-forth rally continues until a point is scored when one player fails to make a good return—by hitting the ball into the net or out of bounds, or by failing to hit the ball at all before it has bounced twice. The ball may be struck only once on each return, and it may not touch a player or his clothing while it is in play.

A ball that bounces on any of the court lines or touches the net or one of the net posts is still in play. Even if it passes outside a post, it is still good if it then bounces within the sideline on the correct side of the court.

GRIP Getting a good grip on the racquet is essential if you want to hit powerful, controlled, solid strokes. There are three basic grips in tennis: the Eastern forehand, the Eastern backhand (so named because they first came into widespread use on the East Coast), and the Continental. The Eastern forehand and backhand are used to hit groundstrokes—shots made after the ball has bounced. The Continental is for serves, volleys (balls taken on the fly), and overheads (balls hit in the air above the head).

To find the Eastern forehand grip, hold your racquet at the throat with your free hand so that the face is perpendicular to the ground. Lay the palm of your playing hand flat against the strings, then slide it down to the handle and close your fingers around it, as if to shake hands with it. The V formed by your thumb and index finger should be on the top bevel of the handle, and the butt of the handle should rest comfortably against the heel of your hand. Separate your index finger slightly from the others for greater control. (Fig. 2-4)

For the Eastern backhand grip, give your hand approximately one-quarter turn to the left from the Eastern forehand, so that the V between your thumb and index finger is on the flat plane on the left of the handle. Your thumb can lie diagonally across the back of the handle

 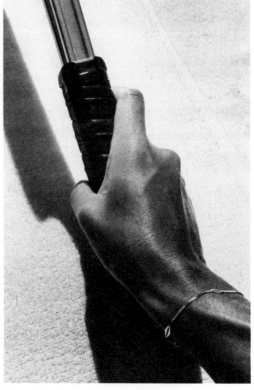

Fig. 2-4   Eastern Forehand Grip   Fig. 2-5   Eastern Backhand Grip

to help brace the racquet at impact or it can be wrapped around the handle, but it should definitely *not* be straight up. Again, separate your index finger slightly from the others. (Fig. 2-5)

Use the forehand grip for balls that come to your dominant, racquet-holding side, and the backhand grip for balls to your other side. The reason for changing your grip is to keep the racquet face perpendicular to the ball's flight for shots on both sides of your body. If, for instance, you were to use the forehand grip for backhands, you would pop the ball up in the air on your backhand side. Switching from one grip to the other should be a smooth and reflexive motion. Get in the habit of supporting your racquet lightly at the throat with your free hand between shots. As soon as you see to which side the ball is coming, the very first thing you should do is slide your racquet hand around to the correct grip.

The Continental grip, which originated on the dirt courts of France, is midway between the Eastern forehand and backhand. Some players use it for all their strokes, but this takes more than average wrist strength as well as superior timing, and for most players the grip is really best limited to

Fig. 2-6 Continental Grip

Fig. 2-7 Good Ready Position: Feet shoulder-width apart, weight forward, racquet out in front, eyes glued to the ball.

serves, volleys, and overheads. Find it by holding your racquet with the forehand grip and giving your hand one-eighth turn to the left, which will put the V between your thumb and index finger just to the left of the handle's top bevel. Once again, your index finger should be separated slightly from the others. (Fig. 2-6)

Whichever grip you are using, make sure to squeeze the handle firmly—though not in a death grasp—when you are stroking the ball, and to relax your grip between shots in order to avoid tiring your hand and arm.

READY POSITION Ready position is the best stance to assume after every shot you hit, while you're waiting for your opponent to return the ball. It is the position that will enable you to get the quickest, most controlled start in any direction, so that you can reach the ball in time to set up properly and make a good shot—or at least get your racquet on a ball that might otherwise be completely out of your range.

Face the net, feet about shoulder-width apart and knees flexed, with your weight forward on the balls of your feet and your heels just slightly off the ground. Hold your racquet directly in front of you, using the forehand grip, with the head about waist-high; support it at the throat with your nonplaying hand. You should feel relaxed, alert, and ready to take off the instant the ball comes off your opponent's racquet.

COURT POSITION

As soon as you've hit the ball, always return to the best court position that time allows. With a good ready position and a solid court position, you'll be able to cover the court efficiently and retrieve most of your opponent's shots.

There are actually two strategic positions on the tennis court, one for the back court and one for the net. When you're playing in the back court, your base of operations, the spot to which you should return after every shot, is the center of the baseline—actually a few steps behind it, because it's easier to move forward quickly than backward.

When you're playing at the net, your best position between shots is straddling the center line, 6–9 feet away from the net. Your particular optimum distance from the net will depend on the level of your net game—the closer you are to the net, the faster the action and so the sharper your anticipation and reflexes must be.

Where you want to *avoid* waiting for your opponent's shots is in the area between the baseline and the service line. This no-man's-land—too far from the net to allow you to volley, and not back far enough to allow you to hit a groundstroke—is the place where you would be most vulnerable to a ball hit at your feet.

Sometimes, alas, proper court position is an unattainable ideal. The fact is that you have to play the ball, not the court, and there will be times when you must sacrifice perfect position in order not to be in motion while your opponent is playing his shot, so that you don't get caught going the wrong way. After making your shot, immediately move toward the center of the forecourt or the back court, but just before your opponent hits the ball, stop where you are and set up in ready position, distributing your weight evenly on both feet. If you were on the run while your opponent was hitting, or even if just your weight were committed in one direction or another, you would be inviting him to aim behind you, to the area you're leaving. He could send the ball within three feet of you, but if you were committed in the wrong direction, it might as well be a mile.

For court positions in doubles, see Doubles (p. 57).

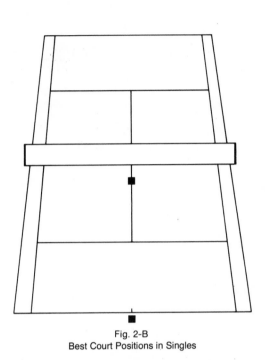

Fig. 2-B
Best Court Positions in Singles

**Fig. 2-B Best Court Positions in Singles:
Return to the center between shots, whether
you're on the baseline or at the net.**

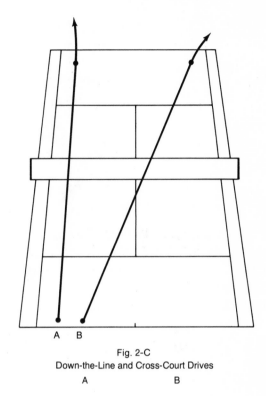

A   B

Fig. 2-C
Down-the-Line and Cross-Court Drives

A   B

Fig. 2-C

STROKES The basic strokes in tennis are forehand and backhand drives—hard-hit
shots that are generally played from the back court. The forehand is used
to return balls that come to your dominant, racquet-holding side; the
backhand is for balls to your other side. All drives can be hit either
cross-court (diagonally across the court) or *down the line* (parallel to and
near one of the sidelines). (Fig. 2-C) In the course of a match you will
probably hit more forehand and backhand drives than all the other strokes
combined; they are the cornerstone of the game.

When broken down for instructional purposes, all tennis strokes have
three basic components—backswing, swing, and follow-through. In
practice, though, your motion for each stroke should be smooth and
continuous, a fluid gathering and releasing of momentum.

Forehand. (Figs. 2-8) As soon as you see that the ball is coming to your
right, pivot out of ready position and, if necessary, move to the ball with
quick steps. When you are within one stride of it, plant your back foot
(right if you're right-handed) so that you can lean your weight into the
shot as you swing. While you're moving to the ball, you should also be
taking your racquet back at about waist-level; at the peak of your

Fig. 2-8 Forehand. 1. Player pivots out of ready position and turns sideways to the net, as he begins to take his racquet back.

2. He awaits the oncoming ball with his racquet back, his knees flexed, and his eyes riveted on the ball.

backswing, the racquet should point toward the back fence, with the face perpendicular to the ground. Your body should be in an open stance—feet placed at approximately a 45-degree angle to the baseline. Your knees should be flexed, your torso rotated back, and your eyes riveted on the oncoming ball.

Time the stroke so that you meet the ball when it is about waist high and even with your front foot. Keeping the face of the racquet perpendicular to the ground, stroke through the ball with a firm wrist. As you swing, let your arm and elbow straighten and shift your weight forward. This forward transfer of body weight is a key element of the stroke; it is in fact the main source of your power. Hitting "off the back foot," a common error, is what keeps a great many players from achieving the pace and depth necessary for effective drives. The cause of the problem is most often a late backswing, which throws off the timing of the entire shot.

After you've hit the ball, follow through smoothly by continuing the stroke up and out after impact, in the direction of the ball's flight. The racquet should finish slightly above shoulder level, with most of your weight on your front foot.

3. He meets the ball out in front of his body as his weight comes forward. Open racquet face indicates that player will put slight topspin on the ball.

4. His follow-through is high, in the direction of his shot. His knees remain bent, his head down.

To hit a low-bouncing ball, get down to it by bending more at the knees; don't just lower the head of your racquet and "scoop" the ball. For a high-bouncing ball (but not high enough to return with an overhead), it is best to back up so that you can still meet it when it is waist high and in front of you, but if you don't have time to move back, take a higher backswing and, if necessary, extend your body upward.

Backhand. (Fig. 2-9) Perhaps because it entails a less familiar motion than the forehand, the backhand is frequently the bane of the beginner's and even the advanced beginner's game. Typically, if he has enough time, he runs around it; if not, he winds up, flails, and prays; his shot is at best defensive. However, with some know-how and practice, a player at any level can develop as much proficiency and confidence in his backhand as in his forehand. In fact, many top players prefer hitting backhands; the stroke is potentially more efficient and powerful, because you are swinging away from, rather than across, your body.

Early preparation is essential to the success of the stroke. The moment you see that your opponent has hit to your backhand, adjust your grip. Guiding it with your free hand, begin to take the racquet back across your body, keeping your elbow in close. At the same time, begin to move into

Fig. 2-9 Backhand. 1. As he turns to move to the ball, player begins to take his racquet back, cradling the throat with his free hand.

2. Just before impact. Note that player's shoulders are rotated so that his back is half-turned to the net.

position. The backhand, unlike the forehand, requires a closed stance—body facing the left sideline and feet roughly parallel to the baseline. By the time you've reached the ball, your racquet should be all the way back, your torso should be rotated so that your back is half-turned to the net, your knees should be flexed, and your right shoulder should be lower than your left. As always, you should be watching the ball intently.

Leading the stroke with the racquet (not your elbow), meet the ball between hip- and waist-high, when it is a foot or so in front of your right foot. As you swing, keep the face of the racquet perpendicular to the ground, let your arm and wrist straighten, and shift your weight forward. Follow through along the path of your shot, as if you were going to sail the racquet over the net. The racquet head should finish at about shoulder level.

Thanks to the spectacular success a number of top players have had with it—including Jimmy Connors, Chris Evert Lloyd, and Bjorn Borg—the two-handed backhand has become an extremely popular stroke for players at all levels. Average players find that the extra power provided by the additional hand makes it an easier stroke to master than the conventional

3. He meets the ball out in front of his body with a straight arm and a locked wrist.

4. His follow-through is in the direction of the ball's flight, but his knees are bent and his head is down.

one-handed backhand. For advanced players, the two-handed stroke facilitates putting spin on the ball, as well as disguising the direction of the shot. For all players, however, the stroke has one disadvantage: it reduces your reach. If you elect to use it, you must compensate by getting to the ball more quickly.

For the two-handed backhand, your right hand holds the racquet with the Eastern backhand grip; your left hand, placed just above it on the handle, uses the Eastern forehand grip. Both hands hold the racquet equally firmly. Get into position as early as possible—preferably before the ball crosses the net to your side of the court—taking your racquet back slightly lower than for the one-handed stroke. Contact the ball when it is waist high and just in front of your front foot as usual, but swing in a more upward direction, keeping your wrists firm. Follow through high over your right shoulder.

Spin. Spin, which is the ball's forward, backward, or sideward rotation in flight, influences the ball's curve, its pace, and whether it will bounce high or low, to the right or left. The forehand and backhand strokes just described are all *flat.* At the moment of impact, the racquet face is perpendicular to the ground and the ball travels with little spin. Actually, every shot you hit carries some spin, even when it hasn't been

Fig. 2-10 For the two-handed backhand, the backswing is closer to the body and a little lower than for the conventional one-handed stroke.

intentionally imparted, but the deliberate application of spin is extremely useful in tennis for the control, variety, and deception it can add to your game. One kind of spin or another can be put on almost every shot; where it is particularly advantageous to do so, this will be noted in the text.

There are basically three types of spin: *topspin, backspin,* and *sidespin.*

Topspin accentuates the ball's *forward* rotation. A ball that is hit with topspin will travel in a rounder arc, then drop sharply and take a high, sudden bounce, crowding your opponent with a difficult-to-return chest-high ball. Because it brings the ball down more steeply, topspin allows you to hit harder and aim higher over the net and still keep the ball in the court. Thus topspin is considered the more offensive spin; indeed most of tennis's top players "top" the majority of their drives. To impact topspin, you swing from low to high. On the backswing, drop your racquet head about a foot lower than your intended point of contact. At the same time, bend your knees more so that you can lower your racquet head, hand, and wrist all together, and so that your whole body, not just the

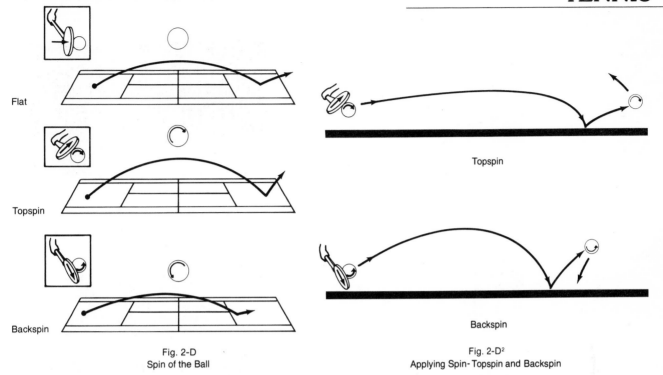

Flat

Topspin

Backspin

Fig. 2-D
Spin of the Ball

Topspin

Backspin

Fig. 2-D²
Applying Spin- Topspin and Backspin

Fig. 2-D A ball hit with topspin travels in a more rounded arc and takes a steeper bounce. One hit with backspin takes a lower, flatter path and a shallower bounce.

Fig. 2-D² Applying Spin. For topspin, swing from low to high, keeping your racquet face perpendicular to the ground as usual. For backspin, swing from high to low with an open racquet face.

racquet, goes from low to high. Swing upward through the ball, but keep your racquet face perpendicular to the ground as usual. The follow-through is high, a continuation of your rising swing.

Backspin, which is also called underspin, chop, or cut, makes the ball rotate *backward* as it travels forward. A ball hit with backspin rises in flight and tends to "float" longer in the air; then it takes a low, shallow bounce, forcing an opponent who is deep in his back court to race in to reach it, and to hit upward to clear the net. However, backspin is generally less offensive than topspin because it tends to slow the ball down; it is used primarily as a change of pace or to force your opponent into error. To put backspin on the ball, you swing from high to low. Take a high backswing, opening the face of your racquet, and swing downward, sliding the racquet under the ball by rolling your wrist under a bit.

Sidespin, or slice, puts a *horizontal* rotation on the ball. It spins in flight to the right or left, then abruptly changes direction after bouncing. This spin is used mainly on the serve, where it also adds control by causing the ball to drop more sharply into the court. To apply slice, you pass your

Fig. 2-11 Bending for a low forehand volley. Note the locked wrist and open racquet face. Because the ball is wide, player has crossed his outside leg in front of his body for better "reach."

Fig. 2-12 Backhand Volley: This player, too, has stepped across with his outside leg. He meets the ball well out in front of his body.

racquet face around the outside of the ball—the side farthest from your body—as you swing forward. Slice, and other service spins, will be covered more thoroughly in the section on the serve.

Volley. A volley is a shot that is hit before the ball bounces. Most volleys are made from inside the service line, near the net. Because the ball reaches you in half the time in the front court, and is traveling much faster than after it bounces, volleying demands excellent anticipation and quick reflexes.

Straddle the center service line in ready position, letting your distance from the net depend on your ability: the closer you are to it, the sharper the angles you can hit, but the faster the action is and the more vulnerable you are to a shot hit over your head. Usually, average players find that they are most comfortable standing between six and nine feet away from the net.

The Continental grip is preferred for volleying because you can use it for both forehand and backhand volleys; the action at the net is usually too fast to change grips. Between volleys, cradle the racquet throat with your free hand, which you can also use to guide the racquet back. Keep your elbows out in front of your body to facilitate meeting the ball well in front of you.

The volley stroke is essentially the same on both sides of your body—a short, compact, forward punch, with almost no backswing. As soon as you

Fig. 2-13 Half-Volley: You may have to put your racquet—or your knee—on the court to hit this defensive shot. Whenever possible, keep your racquet head higher than your wrist.

determine to which side your opponent's shot is coming, pivot your shoulders and upper torso to the right or left so that they are more or less sideways to the oncoming ball. Take your racquet back only as far as your shoulder, with the face slightly open. Don't wait for the ball to come to you. Keeping your wrist locked and your grip firm, and leaning your weight into your shot, attack the ball well in front of your body, when it is between waist- and shoulder-high. Take a short follow-through, then recover quickly to the center and get set for the next one.

Always try to volley the ball when it is higher than the net so that you can punch downward on it aggressively. For low, defensive volleys, bend more at the knees to get down to the level of the ball, and open the face of your racquet more to lift it over the net. (Fig. 2-11–12)

Half-volley. The half-volley is a stroke made by hitting the ball immediately after it has bounced, when it is just off the ground. It is generally a defensive shot that your opponent has forced upon you by aiming the ball at your feet.

Immediately bend your knees and crouch low. Take only a short backswing, with your racquet face open and your racquet head up. Swinging upward in order to clear the net, and keeping your wrist and forearm firm, contact the ball slightly in front of you, immediately after it comes off the ground. Take a short follow-through in the direction of your shot, making the stroke as fluid as possible. (Fig. 2-13)

Fig. 2-14 To hit a lob, player gets his open-faced racquet under the ball.

Lob. The lob is a stroke that sends the ball high into the air. It is generally used defensively—to gain time when you are out of position, either outside the sideline or deep behind the baseline. However, it can also be used offensively—hit over the head of an opponent who is hugging the net, usually when you are inside your baseline. The defensive lob is slower and has a higher trajectory than the offensive lob, which should sail just out of reach of your opponent's outstretched racquet.

A lob will be most effective if you can disguise it by starting off with the same backswing as for a drive. Just before impact with the ball, open the face of your racquet to apply more lift, and follow through in a more upward direction. (Fig. 2-14) Generally place your lobs deep—near your opponent's baseline—and on his backhand side.

An offensive lob can be hit either flat or with slight topspin; topspin will bring the ball down more quickly, giving your opponent less time to retrieve it. A defensive lob is best hit with backspin, which will hold the ball in the air longer and give you additional time to recover a solid court position.

When you play tennis outdoors, be conservative with your lobs if there's a breeze; it will affect your slow, high shots more than the others. Also keep in mind that when your opponent is on the sunny side, you can

Fig. 2-15 Overhead: As soon as your opponent sends up a lob, turn sideways and cock your racquet back. "Sight" the ball with your free hand.

cause him considerable difficulty by lobbing; in fact the title of the great Australian coach Harry Hopman's book on tennis is *Lobbing into the Sun.* When you play tennis indoors, you may have to tone down your lobs to avoid losing the point by hitting the ceiling or suspended lights.

Overhead smash. The overhead, which is hit when the ball is in the air above your head, is the shot that makes your opponent regret having lobbed. It's one of the most satisfying shots in the game, a wonderful opportunity to give the ball a good healthy crack and put it away. Among club players, however, the overhead is the shot that is most frequently flubbed, either because they panic, fail to prepare properly, or try to do too much with it. What is really at the root of all these errors is the fact that it is the least-practiced stroke in tennis.

As soon as you see that your opponent has sent up a lob, turn sideways to the net, cock your racquet behind your right shoulder in the "backscratching" position, and begin moving back. It's important that you get your racquet cocked immediately; otherwise timing the stroke will be exceedingly difficult. If the lob is a short one, skip backward quickly with short, crossover steps. If it's a deep lob—one that will land near the baseline—there's no time for skipping; turn your back to the net and *run,* keeping the ball in sight over your shoulder.

Get in position so that the ball is descending above your right shoulder and slightly in front of you. Watch it carefully; "sight" it by pointing at it with your free hand. This will help you to get your weight into the shot as well as to gauge the speed and trajectory of the ball. Don't let it get behind you. Better to go back too far than not far enough—it's easier to adjust forward than backward.

When the ball is within reach, swing up and forward, with your arm and body fully extended on impact and your weight leaning into the shot. Really pound the ball, but forget about fancy spins for this shot; just hit it deep or at a sharp angle. Follow through down and to the left. (Fig. 2-15)

Generally speaking, it's better to play your overheads on the fly, to give your opponent less time to get set for his return. When confronted with a *very* high lob, though, it's often advisable to let the ball bounce first. For one thing, it may go out, especially if there's a breeze; for another, timing your shot will be easier after the court has absorbed some of the ball's momentum. Just make sure you back up far enough so that the ball isn't behind you after it bounces.

The very deepest lobs—those that bounce near the baseline—should generally be returned with another lob rather than smashed back; a deep, effective overhead is extremely difficult to hit from that distance.

Drop Shot. The drop shot is a stroke hit with a soft, deft touch, to make the ball drop right over the net and bounce no more than a few feet beyond it. It is most effective when your opponent is deep in his back court and either expecting a short ball or simply incapable of running one down because he is tired or slow.

The shallower your opponent's shot, the easier it is to hit a drop shot; in fact most players shouldn't even attempt it when they are back on the baseline. To disguise your shot, take a normal backswing, as if you were going to hit a drive, then at the moment of impact open your racquet face slightly, relax your grip, and hit under the ball to apply backspin, using a gentle but firm lifting motion—as if you were hitting the ball to a child standing in the forecourt. There's no need to skim the net; the ball should clear it by two or three feet. Take a short follow-through in the direction of your shot.

Drop (or stop) volley. A drop shot played on the fly is called a drop volley (or stop volley). It is an advanced shot that requires great "touch," and one that should be sparingly used. It is most effective on soft surfaces, where the ball will stay low to the ground after bouncing. Stroke it like a normal volley, but with pronounced backspin, which is applied by getting your racquet head underneath the ball and rolling your wrist under as you hit. Take almost no follow-through. (Fig. 2-16) Aim the ball short and angle it sharply away from your opponent.

Lob volley. The lob volley is another difficult "touch" shot, a lob hit on

Fig. 2-16 Drop Volley: Instead of following through, player turns his wrist so that the face of his racquet comes up under the ball. The resulting backspin will make the ball die when it bounces.

the fly from a position near the net. Its use is mainly confined to doubles, when all four players are engaged in rapid-fire volleying at the net and you want to drive your opponents back to their baseline.

To be effective, the lob volley must be disguised until the last moment. Take a short backswing, as for a normal volley, then on the forward swing open your racquet face and hit up from underneath the ball. Be sure to aim high and deep enough; if you don't get the ball up out of your opponent's reach, duck!

SERVE Because it is the one time you have two chances on one point to hit an offensive shot from a stationary position, the serve is the single most important shot in tennis. A strong serve—deep, hard, and to your opponent's weaker side—can win you the point outright, or set up a winner on your next shot. A weak serve, on the other hand, can not only neutralize your offensive advantage but actually turn it over to your opponent. As you can practice your serve without a practice partner—all you need is an empty court and a bucket of old balls—there's really no reason why it shouldn't be your strongest, most reliable shot.

Fig. 2-17 Serve. 1. Player starts with the racquet and ball in front of him.

2. As he begins his toss and backswing, he lets his weight rock back.

3. He tosses the ball high enough so that he will be fully extended when he hits it. At the same time, he takes his racquet back behind his right shoulder. He is ready to release all his power into the stroke.

Most players use the Continental grip for serving because it allows them maximum wrist snap and gives them the greatest flexibility in applying spin. Beginners, however, are better off learning with the more familiar Eastern forehand grip and changing over to the Continental when they have become comfortable with the serving motion itself.

In singles, stand near the center mark to serve; this will put you in the best position to deal with your opponent's return. (For serving position in doubles, see p. 57). Line up your toes toward the service court into which you are aiming, with your left foot at approximately a 45-degree angle to the baseline and a few inches behind it—to avoid footfaulting—and your right foot about a shoulder width further back, roughly parallel to the baseline. Your body will be almost sideways to the net.

The service toss and swing should be simultaneous, coordinated motions

4. Player has just hit his serve. His weight continues to come forward . . .

5. . . . as he follows through, down and across his body, to the left.

that are carried out smoothly and without a hitch in order to achieve as much momentum and power as possible. Begin with the ball and racquet in front of you about chest high, with the racquet pointing toward the service court for which you're aiming. Hold the ball against the strings in the fingers (not the palm) of your free hand. As you let your weight rock forward, drop both arms together; then, as you raise your tossing arm up, swing the racquet down past your right leg and in a large arc up into the backscratching position behind your right shoulder, with your elbow pointing up. As you take the racquet back, let your weight shift onto your rear foot. Your back should be arched, your wrist cocked, and your knees bent. Your body is coiled, ready to release its power into the stroke.

As the racquet swings into the backscratching position, your other hand releases the ball gently when it is about shoulder level, placing it about two feet in front of you, one foot to your right, and as high as you can reach when your racquet, arm, and body are completely outstretched. After you've released the ball, let your tossing arm continue its movement upward; this will help you place the ball accurately.

As the ball reaches the peak of the toss, "throw" your racquet up and forward; try to get over the top of the ball with your racquet. Lean your weight into your serve, and uncock your wrist on impact. Follow through down and cross your body to the left.

There are two basic variations on the flat, spinless serve that has just been described: the *slice* and the *American twist*. The key to both is in the toss. By placing the ball in different spots above your head and compensating with your swing, you can vary the spin of your serve, thereby altering its curve and bounce. Relatively few top players rely primarily on the flat serve, because it must be hit with a great deal of accuracy, depth, and pace to be effective; it leaves precious little margin for error. A serve hit with spin, on the other hand, is safer, more easily controlled, and in addition gives most receivers more trouble than all but the very fastest flat serve.

Most players hit their basic serve with slice (sidespin). By making the ball drop more sharply into the court, sidespin increases control; it also causes the ball to skid when it bounces and to curve from the receiver's left to his right, so that it veers away from his body on the forehand side or into his body on the backhand side. The basics of the stroke are essentially the same as for the flat serve, with the sidespin applied by tossing the ball up slightly more to your right and brushing across its outer edge on contact. The follow-through is down and to the left as usual.

The American twist serve, hit with heavy topspin and slight sidespin, travels in a high curve over the net and takes a high, kicking bounce to the receiver's left. It is the most difficult serving motion to master, but for advanced, physically strong players it is a safe and effective serve, one that is most often used in doubles and as a second serve. For the American twist serve, the toss is above your *left* shoulder and the racquet moves sideways from left to right and up over the ball. In order to get your racquet around and over the ball from the left, you must arch your back a great deal on the backswing, and on contact with the ball you need an especially sharp wrist snap. The follow-through is down and to the *right*.

A few more words about the ball toss: *Practice it*. A consistent toss is absolutely fundamental to developing a steady, effective serve because you can't "groove" your swing if the ball is in a different spot in the air each time. However, everyone occasionally puts up a bad toss—too far forward,

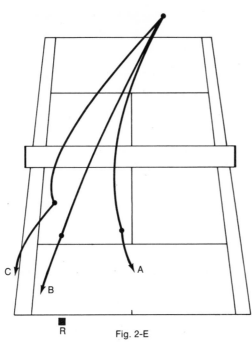

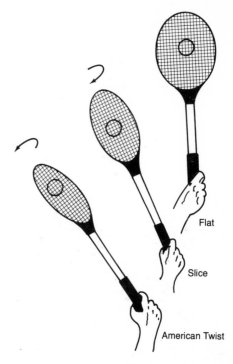

Fig. 2-E

Fig. 2-E The Three Basic Serves. The slice serve (A) travels low over the net and curves to the receiver's right; the flat serve (B) comes in harder and almost straight; the American twist serve (C) crosses the net higher and kicks to the receiver's left.

Fig. 2-E²
Putting Spin on Your Serve

Fig. 2-E² To hit a slice serve, contact the ball on its outside edge; for an American twist, come over the ball from the left.

too far behind, too much to one side. You don't have to swing at a bad toss; you can—and should—catch the ball and begin again. As long as your racquet hasn't made contact with the ball, it's perfectly legal.

If you play outdoors, no doubt you're familiar with the vexing problem, on those gloriously sunny days, of the disappearing ball. You toss it up, barely manage to keep it in sight in the brilliant light to make contact, and then instead of your opponent's return, you see spots. Obviously, some accommodation is necessary. Sunglasses, a brimmed hat, or a visor will help somewhat, but adjusting your toss—moving it to the left or right, or lowering it—or serving from a different position behind the baseline will probably be more effective.

RETURN OF SERVE If the serve is the most important shot in the game, the return of serve is a close second; it is the receiver's best chance to neutralize his opponent's offensive advantage. True, the serve is the hardest-hit shot in the game; a speed of ninety miles per hour is not unusual for a good male club player. In addition, the ball can curve right or left, kick high, or bounce into you.

But the receiver has a few things going for him, too: he has time to get ready—"quick-serving" is illegal—he is stationary, and he knows approximately where the serve will land.

Wait for the serve in ready position—concentrating, alert, and prepared to adjust the moment the ball leaves the server's racquet. There is no one correct spot in which to stand. As a general guideline, you should be more or less on an imaginary line drawn from the server through a midpoint deep in the service court—which will put you midway between the ball's possible lines of flight—and somewhere around the baseline—a few feet behind it against a strong server, a few feet inside it against a weak one. If you're playing against a new opponent, it may take some trial-and-error work before you know how close to the service line you can safely stand. In any case, move in a step or two for the second serve, which will have less speed and depth.

Concentrate on watching the ball rather than the server. This will help you to get into position more quickly once the ball has left his racquet. Note particularly the placement of the toss: if it is directly overhead, you can expect a flat serve; if it's to his right, a slice; if to his left, a twist.

As soon as you can see to which side the ball is coming, get your racquet back and move into position so that you can meet the ball out in front of you and lean your weight into the shot. To return a hard, flat serve, shorten your backswing and simply block the ball back, getting your pace from the serve itself. A slice or twist serve requires a more complete swing and an extra-firm grip in order to redirect the spinning ball.

SINGLES TACTICS As noted, the server has a significant offensive advantage. Therefore, with your first serve, you can and should take more risks—in other words, hit the ball harder, but not so hard that your chances of hitting a legal serve are slim. A rule of thumb: if you're not getting your first serve in at least 70 percent of the time, ease up on it, because when you miss your first serve, you lose a significant offensive advantage; on your second serve your opponent will be closing in both literally and psychologically. It's also far more tiring, over the course of a match, to have to serve twice for many of the points.

The best spot to aim your first serve is *deep to either corner of the service court.* A serve to the outside corner will pull the receiver out of position and open up the court for your next shot; a serve to his backhand side will draw a weak return. Aim for other points occasionally—hit deep and directly at your opponent, for instance—and mix up the speed and spin of your serves to keep him guessing.

If you do serve a fault, avoid rushing your second serve. Relax, take a deep breath, and play it safer by slowing down a bit and controlling the ball with more spin. The best placement for your second serve is *deep to your opponent's backhand corner,* which will increase the likelihood of drawing a weak return. Again, move the ball around some and vary the spin and speed to throw the receiver off balance.

The receiver, who is very much on the defensive, should concentrate first and foremost on keeping the ball in play. It has been shown statistically that simply by getting the ball back, he will practically even his chances of winning the point. Naturally, if the server gives you the gift of a "fat" serve—shallow and high—by all means move in on it and slam it back hard, but in general, aim your returns at least three or four feet over the net and well within the lines. If possible, place your return where it will give the server difficulty. Against a server who rushes the net, hit your return low and shallow to force him to volley up defensively from below net level. Against a server who stays back on the baseline after serving, return the ball deep—within ten feet of the baseline. The server can't do much damage from back there and you might draw a shallow shot that you can attack. An occasional drop shot return—easier to hit off a second serve—can be an effective surprise against a server who stays back.

In tennis *the* offensive position is at the net; when you come to the net, the action is faster and the points are more quickly won—or lost. In the past, net-rushing was a maneuver largely confined to play on fast courts such as grass, but these days the topflight players (and the amateurs who imitate them) are rushing the net—using fast-court tactics, in other words—even on clay. On any surface, a successful net-rusher needs fast feet, fast reflexes, and of course, a reliable volley and overhead.

If you were to attempt to come in to the net on just any old shot, chances are you would be quickly passed or lobbed over: end of point. If you want to play the net, first you have to hit a forcing shot—a shot that will draw a weak return and allow you to come in. This might be—and most commonly is—a deep, strong serve; it could also be a deep drive hit off your opponent's short ball, or perhaps an offensive lob. A shot that allows you to come in during a rally is called an approach shot.

As soon as you've made your approach shot, run in as quickly as you can, essentially along the path of your shot but a few feet closer to the center of the court. Try to get at least to the service line for your first volley, but wherever you are, stop moving when your opponent plays his return so that you can observe the direction of his shot and avoid getting caught going the wrong way.

The first volley can be a tough one to make, because it often has to be hit on the run or from an awkward, off-balance position. Don't try to do too much with it—but do try to send it deep and, if possible, to a corner or to your opponent's backhand. Then continue in quickly to the volleying position—six to nine feet away from the net—where you can often volley the ball away to open court immediately. If you don't have a clear opening, keep your volleys deep until you do, to prevent your opponent from passing you.

Some players prefer to slug it out from the baseline rather than rush the net, especially on slow surfaces such as clay. Points are generally longer when they are played out from the baseline, and usually it is the steadier, more patient player who wins them. Even among top players, tennis matches are more often won on errors than on winners. Steadiness, which is the ability to keep the ball in play by hitting "percentage shots"—shots that clear the net and the lines by a safe margin—is at all levels of proficiency a key asset, particularly in baseline play. The steady player waits for a clear-cut opening before he tries to put the ball away; he lets his opponent make the errors.

But beyond the beginner's level, outsteadying your opponent, while essential, is not enough. Apart from consistency, the most important key to successful baseline play is *keeping the ball deep.* Few players can hit really offensive returns off deep shots. By aiming the ball within a few feet of your opponent's baseline, you can usually force him to give you a short ball eventually, enabling you to come to the net or win the point immediately.

The best way to draw that short ball is by running your opponent all over the court; this will keep him off balance until you extract a weak return or an outright error. There are any number of ways in which you might do this: You can hit deep drives alternately to the left and right corners—establishing a pattern that leads your opponent to begin running hard to the other side immediately after making his shot—and then hit two drives in a row to the same side; the second will be behind him and virtually irretrievable. Or you can hit several deep cross-court drives to the same corner, each one more sharply angled than the last, to force your opponent further and further out of position; then drive one hard down the line—an almost certain winner. Or, one of the most effective patterns of all, you can alternate lobs and drop shots; there is nothing more tiring or exasperating than chasing them down.

If your opponent rushes the net, keep your shots low (except for lobs!) to force him to volley up from below the level of the net. What you are waiting for, again, is a short ball—one that bounces within a few feet of your service line at the most. That's your chance to try to end the point, either with a *passing shot*—a cross-court or down-the-line drive hit out of his reach—or, if he is camping on the net, with an offensive lob.

Whether baseline player or serve-and-volleyer, it's important to be able to assess the strengths and weaknesses of your opponent's game. If you play against the same person every week, chances are you know just as well as he does how his forehand stacks up against his backhand, what his favorite shot is, how he deals with a sudden change of pace, whether he can run down your drop shot, and so on—and you probably play him accordingly. But when you come up against a new opponent, you have to learn quickly. Start evaluating his game while you're warming up together. Try out a variety of shots, spins, placements, and speeds to see how he handles your game. Is his forehand stronger? Play his backhand. Does he have a weak net game? Hit short shots to tempt him to come in. Does he prefer a fast pace? Hit softly and use spin. Of course, none of your findings should be written in stone; maybe your opponent just needed a few of your lobs to get that overhead going, for example.

You should also be alert for weaknesses that develop during the course of the match. That seemingly indefatigable retriever of the first set may look like a completely different (and slower) player by the time it's one set apiece; that's the time to start "drop shotting" him.

In general, though, don't overplay your opponent's weaknesses, or you may give him so much practice that they become strengths. Varying your shots is the best way to keep him guessing, especially if you can also disguise them by beginning your strokes the same way whenever possible.

DOUBLES True, it's played with the same equipment, on only a slightly larger court, and with most of the same rules, but from a tactical standpoint doubles is a completely different ball game. Just go down the roster of some of today's top doubles teams—McMillan-Hewitt, Fibak-Okker, Smith-Lutz—they're made up of players who often don't make it past the first few rounds in singles tournaments.

What's so different about doubles? Above all, it's a game of position—*net* position. Getting to the net is essential in doubles; it's where a full 80 percent of the points are won. In a good doubles game, both teams are constantly trying to come to the net and stay there, retreating back to the baseline only when forced, and then immediately striving to come in again. Because the emphasis is on net position, the net strokes—volleys and overheads—are more important than they are in singles, and more important than are groundstrokes. And while there is less running than in singles, the doubles game is faster-paced, with a premium on reflexes and anticipation.

If one partner has the better serve, he should serve first for the team,

Fig. 2-18   Between 1968 and 1979 the great
doubles team of Bob Lutz and Stan Smith
never lost a Davis Cup match.

because in a close set, he may get to serve an extra, decisive game. The best serving position in doubles is midway between the center mark and the doubles sideline; this will give the server the shortest route to his net position. His dual objectives are to get his first serve in—a good doubles player gets his first serve in at least 80 percent of the time and *never* double-faults—and to follow it in to the net.

In doubles, the most effective serve is hit with about three-quarters power and considerable spin. Such a serve, relatively slow and spinning, is safe and easily controlled; it also gives the server more time to get to the net for his first volley. Most top doubles players use the American twist; if this rather difficult serve isn't in your repertory, rely on the slice.

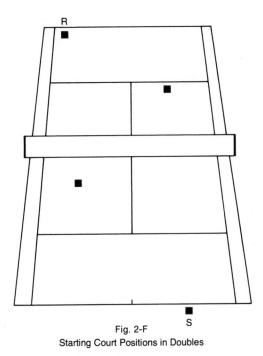

Fig. 2-F
Starting Court Positions in Doubles

Fig. 2-F The server stands midway between the center mark and the doubles sideline; his partner is six to nine feet from the net. The receiver is just inside the baseline and his partner just inside the service line.

Whatever serve you use, the majority of both first and second serves in doubles should be directed *deep to the receiver's backhand* in order to draw a weaker return. As in singles, mix up the placement, pace, and spin of your serve a bit to keep the receiver guessing.

The server's partner begins the point standing six to nine feet away from the net, slightly closer to the center service line than to the far sideline, but ready to spring quickly over to his alley should the return be hit down the line. He must also be alert for cross-court returns that he can intercept and for lob returns hit over his head, for which he'd have to retreat.

The return of serve is the most difficult and also perhaps the most important shot in the doubles game. In order to win a set, a side must get at least one service break. Holding serve is much easier in doubles than in singles: the serving team has the initiative and there are two players to cover the return. If the receiving team is to have a chance in the game, both partners had better have strong returns.

When a team is receiving, the player with the stronger game should return serve in the ad (left-hand) court; that way shots down the middle—where most are hit—are covered by his forehand (assuming he is right handed); in addition, in close games it is the ad court player who returns the serve on the most crucial points—ad in or out. If one partner is left-handed, he should probably take the deuce court side, which will put his forehand in the center.

Because the receiver can expect the serve to be slower than in singles, he should stand a few steps closer to the net in doubles—inside the baseline if possible—and move in even closer for the second serve. His objectives are first, to get the ball back, and second, to force a weak shot in return so that he can come to the net. A carelessly placed return in doubles is usually tantamount to giving away the point; the opposing net player, who is directly opposite the receiver, is just waiting to volley away any shot on which he can get his racquet. More vulnerable is the server, who is busy rushing the net.

The most effective return of serve in doubles is a low, slow, shallow cross-court drive, hit out of the opposing net player's reach. This shot will force the in-coming server to volley up from below net level and give the receiving team a rising ball to attack. You can vary this return by sailing a lob over the net player's head occasionally, or by driving the ball hard down his alley—either of these returns should make him think twice about leaving his position to intercept your cross-court return. You can also hit an occasional hard, deep, cross-court drive to catch the incoming server off guard. Whenever your return does succeed in drawing a weak, defensive shot, seize the offensive: come in quickly and join your partner at the net.

The receiver's partner starts out in a modified net position—on or just inside the service line—and slightly closer to the center line than to the far sideline. His role is to cover weak first volleys hit within his range by either the server or the net player. When his partner's return of serve is strong enough to put the serving team on the defensive, he should move in closer to the net to a more offensive position so that he can intercept the volley and return it at one of his opponents' feet.

We left the server in the act of serving deep to the receiver's backhand. Immediately after serving, he must follow his serve straight in toward the net, but he should be prepared to change direction if necessary around the service line in order to reach the return and make his first volley. If the receiver *doesn't* come in on his return, the server should hit his first volley cross-court, as deep as possible. If the receiver *does* come in, the server should aim this volley at his feet. In either case, the server should then come in quickly the rest of the way to the net, where he joins his partner, each player in the center of his half of the court and about eight feet away from the net. As in singles, the team's best distance from the net will depend on their heights, reflexes, and ability to anticipate: the closer they are to the net, the sharper their downward volleys and angle volleys can be, but the more vulnerable they are to offensive lobs.

If an opponent does lob when your team is at the net, one partner should call the shot—"Mine!"—and if possible smash it back to open court; the partner with the better overhead should take as many of these as possible. Often two overheads are necessary, one to open up the court by drawing your opponents out of position and one to end the point. The first can be hit down the center and the second angled away, or vice versa.

Doubles, of course, is a team sport. A good doubles team consists of two compatible players who have complementary games, confidence in each other's ability, and a spirit of cooperation. Developing a seasoned, smoothly functioning team also requires experience playing matches together as well as practice sessions devoted to problem areas. Quite a tall order; but fortunately there are some key aspects of teamwork that can be brought to bear immediately—between brand-new partners or even utter strangers.

One of the most important is communicating during play with brief instructions, a habit that can save the day in confusing situations. In addition to "Yours!" and "Mine!" among the most useful are "Bounce it!" if you think the ball your partner is about to hit might be on its way out, and "Switch!" if you're crossing over to take a shot in your partner's territory. Make your calls loudly, clearly, and quickly.

It's a good idea to prearrange which of you will take what shot when you are both at the net and the action is too fast to call each shot. If an opponent hits the ball down the center, for example, it generally works out best for the player who made the last volley to take it, because he's more in the rhythm of the point; if an opponent drives the ball cross-court, it is the player on the opposite side from where the shot was made who should take it, because he has more time and a more comfortable angle.

Poaching—playing a ball in your partner's territory—is an important maneuver in doubles. Most poaching is done when the net player cuts off a cross-court return of serve hit to his partner. By virtue of his position, the net player can hit more offensive shots than his teammate, who is in the back court or rushing the net; in fact, the net player's unexpected move will often put an immediate end to the point by catching the opposing team by surprise. Some poaches will be the result of spur-of-the-moment opportunities, but for planned poaching it is advisable to work out behind-the-back hand signals in advance. An open hand, for example, could mean "I'm not going to poach"; a closed fist could be "I'm going to poach, so get ready to cover my side in case the ball comes back"; one finger up might mean "I'm going to fake a poach with a head feint or a little movement to tempt them to hit down my alley, but I'm not really going, so stay on your side." Poaching is almost always done with

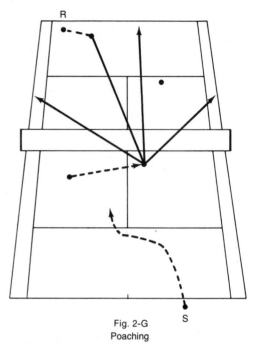

Fig. 2-G
Poaching

Fig. 2-19 Poach. Net player has stretched across to intercept a ball hit to his partner, who moves to cover the open territory.

Fig. 2-G Poaching: The net player intercepts the cross-court return of serve. He should angle the volley to either sideline or volley down the middle.

the intention of ending the point outright, which means that the poacher must have a reliable put-away volley and excellent timing; if he goes across too soon, the striker can hit down his alley; if he goes too late, the ball will be gone. The time to make your move is the moment your opponent has committed his shot.

Both teammates must do their best to keep up team morale, primarily by neither yelling, muttering, groaning, nor glaring at each other. This is not only common decency but practical advice as well, as none of these reactions ever succeeds in making anyone play any better.

Learn to identify and exploit the chinks in your opponents' games. Probe for weak strokes, and look for weak positions and faulty teamwork, neither of which is terribly uncommon in average club doubles. Perhaps one net player leaves his alley open, even though he's incapable of moving quickly to cover it; perhaps the team stands too far apart at the net, leaving a hole in the center; perhaps they crowd the net, inviting an offensive lob. Once you've spotted a weakness, however, don't overplay it, or they'll soon correct it; use it only when you need a point.

Don't forget the lob, which is a particularly useful shot in doubles. A high, deep defensive lob when your team is in trouble will give you time to regain a stronger court position; a lower, faster, but still very deep offensive lob sent over either opponent's backhand side when they are camping too close to the net will force a retreat and allow you to come in on the weak return.

Finally, when you don't know what else to do, the safest shot in doubles is down the center, where the net is lowest; it may even win you a point outright if your opponents have trouble deciding who should take the shot.

TENNIS CHECKLIST

1. Keep your eyes on the ball. The sooner you know where it's heading, the sooner you can get to it and set up for your shot.
2. Whenever your opponent is hitting, try to be stationary and in ready position; whenever *you* are hitting, try to be stationary and turned sideways to the net.
3. Take your racquet back as early as possible.
4. Contact the ball in front of you, leaning your weight into your shot.
5. Vary your shots. Place them with the purpose of making your opponent move.
6. Try to anticipate your opponent's shots by paying attention to his hitting habits.
7. Play a steady game; let your opponent make the errors.
8. Especially in doubles, try to get to the net; that's where the points are won.

Fig. 3-1

SQUASH

ABOUT SQUASH   In about 1850, schoolboys at England's famous Harrow School, while waiting their turn for the school's one rackets court, took to knocking a ball around in the confined space adjoining it. Because this area was smaller, they used a softer, slower india rubber ball, which made a "squashy" sound instead of the loud report of the rackets ball when it hit the wall. And thus did squash racquets—or simply squash—and its onomatopoeic name originate.

The slower ball made for longer rallies and an easier game, and soon more Harrovians were playing squash than rackets. The accommodating school installed the first four official squash courts in 1864. The game's popularity spread quickly to other swank English boarding schools, and in a short time it had become *the* game among England's moneyed sportsmen, many of whom had courts built at their country estates. In addition, hotels, exclusive gentlemen's clubs in London, and even, in the early 1930s, five ocean liners, had squash courts installed. Courts were built at British military outposts, spreading the game throughout the Empire. It is still extremely popular in India, Pakistan, Egypt, and especially Australia, where it is played by one-sixth of the population.

Squash reached the United States in the early 1880s; the exclusive St. Paul's School in Concord, New Hampshire, led the way. As had happened in England, other private boys' boarding schools in the Northeast were quick to follow. Naturally, the graduates of these schools took the new game to their colleges and universities, and by the turn of the century it was being played at posh private athletic clubs in Philadelphia and Boston. (In the New York area, another game, squash *tennis,* was all the rage at the time; squash racquets didn't begin to catch on there until around 1915.)

Because the rules and the size of the court weren't standardized in England until 1929, the United States Squash Racquets Association, formed in 1920, established its own standards. The upshot was that the North American court was—and still is—two and a half feet narrower than the English (International) court and the ball used in the North American game is harder and faster. As a result of these and several other differences, North American or "hard ball" squash stresses quick reflexes and put-away shots, while International or "soft ball" squash puts a greater premium on physical endurance. An International squash match can last over two hours—twice as long as a typical North American match.

The differences between the two games are significant enough to discourage widespread competition between players from the United States, Canada, or Mexico and those from the rest of the world. However, the tournament scene within the United States itself is extremely lively, with more than a hundred sanctioned tournaments in a seven-month season (October–April), highlighted by the North American Open in January and the United States Singles Championships in February.

GOVERNING BODY
United States Squash Racquets Association
211 Ford Road
Bala-Cynwyd, PA 19004

Official Newspaper: *Squash News*

COURT
A North American singles squash court is 32 feet long, 18½ feet wide, and 16 feet high at the front wall. The side walls must be 16 feet high extending back at least 22 feet, from which point they may be as low as 12 feet to accommodate gallery space. The back wall is 6½ feet high.

Six and a half feet above the floor on the front wall is the front wall service line. Running along the base of the front wall is a strip of sheet metal 17 inches high called the telltale, or tin. When it is struck by the ball, it produces a flat metallic clang, signifying that a shot is out of play. There are also out-of-play areas at the top of all the walls, above the play lines.

Ten feet from the rear wall on the floor is the short line, or floor service line. A center line divides the rear 10 feet of the court into two service courts, and in each of the outer front corners of the service courts is a quarter circle "service box," with a radius of 4½ feet.

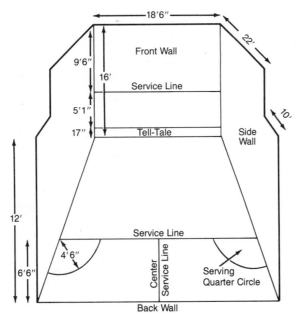

Fig. 3-A
North American Squash Court

Access to the court is through a door located in the center of the back wall; its hardware must be flush with the playing surface.

Squash courts are painted white with red lines. Traditionally, they have wood walls and wood floors, though recently plaster, plastic laminates, precast concrete, and glass walls have become available.

RACQUET A squash racquet is 27 inches long and has a circular head with an outside diameter of not more than 9 inches. The frame may be of wood or any other material approved by the United States Squash Racquets Association, and it may be strung with either gut or a substitute such as nylon. Metal stringing is prohibited. Racquets range in price from about $10 to $40; the more expensive ones are purchased unstrung so that the buyer can have it strung to his or her own specifications.

Though squash racquets are the same length as tennis racquets, they are very much thinner and lighter. And since the new official ball is smaller and lighter than the previous ball, racquets are now being made lighter than ever; the new models range from 7 to 8½ ounces—plus about half an ounce for strings.

Racquets vary in balance point. A head-heavy racquet will provide more power; a head-light racquet will give more control.

Fig. 3-2

They also have different degrees of flexibility. Hard hitters usually prefer stiff racquets; control players tend to select more flexible ones.

Grips range from 3½ to 4¾ inches and come in various shapes—round, oval, square, or octagonal. Unlike tennis racquets, each squash racquet model is generally available in only one grip size. Choose a grip that is large enough not to slip in your hand but small enough to allow the wrist snap that is so important in giving power and control to squash strokes. Some grips come covered with toweling—best for absorbing perspiration; others are covered with leather, which is less likely to cause blisters.

Squash racquets are generally strung with nylon or gut at between 30 and 40 pounds of tension. Nylon stringing is more durable; gut is more resilient and gives better "touch." Gut stringing is definitely a luxury—both more costly and more perishable than nylon; to prolong its life, protect it with a racquet cover and keep it away from dampness—including the sweaty contents of your gym bag after the game.

If you're buying your first racquet, choose one that simply feels comfortable to swing. You are probably better off with an evenly balanced racquet that is prestrung with nylon, on the heavy side, and inexpensive: racquets are fairly fragile and not guaranteed, and new players have a tendency to hit the walls.

BALL Squash balls are made of hollow, nonpressurized rubber. The official North American singles ball is the 70-+. This recently introduced and easier-to-play-with ball—so called because, unlike the old ball, it does not get too hot and thus too fast when the temperature of the court rises above 70°F (21°C)—is 1.56–1.63 inches in diameter. It comes in two versions. The slower blue-dot ball, made for play in temperatures of 60°F (15°C) and above, should rebound 15–19 inches when dropped from 100 inches at 68°F (20°C); the faster white-dot, for colder temperatures, should rebound 20–24 inches under the same conditions.

A different ball is used for doubles. It is slightly harder and livelier than the singles ball.

A squash ball gets livelier as it warms up, but the rules expressly forbid heating or chilling it; the players' before-play practice period also serves to warm up the ball.

Balls are relatively expensive—about $3 apiece—but they are extremely durable, usually lasting at least twenty-five or thirty games before breaking.

DRESS Clothing and accessories for squash are essentially the same as for tennis (p. 30), although for casual games dress is typically more informal, with gym shorts and T-shirts the norm.

METHOD OF PLAY There are two forms of squash—singles and doubles. The rules for doubles, which have not been included because doubles is so rarely played, may be obtained from the USSRA. See pp. 225–228 for complete singles rules.

In North American squash, either the server or the receiver may score points. The first player to win 15 points wins the game, except if the score becomes tied at 13 all; then the player who lost the tying point may either

- set the game to 5 points, making the game 18 points;
- set to 3 points, making the game 16 points; or
- elect "no set," in which case the game remains 15 points.

If the game has *not* been tied at 13 all, but *becomes* tied at 14 all, the player who lost the tying point may either

- set to 3 points, making the game 17 points; or
- elect "no set."

The choices are strategic ones; in general, a player who feels that he is stronger than his opponent will set a longer game.

A match is usually the best three out of five games.

At the start of the match, the players spin a racquet (see p. 32); the winner may choose either to serve or to receive first in the first game. During the game, the player who has won the previous point serves the next point and continues serving until he loses a point. The winner of a game has his choice of serving or receiving first in the next game.

Each time there is a new server, he may deliver his first serve from either service box, but from then on he must alternate service boxes until he loses his serve. The server must keep at least one foot within the service box—not touching the lines surrounding it—until the ball has left his racquet. He may hit the ball either on the bounce or on the fly. The served ball must travel directly to the front wall, without first touching another wall or the floor, and strike it above the service line and below the sixteen-foot line. On the rebound, it must bounce behind the floor service line in the opposite service court, unless the receiver chooses to play it on the fly. Before bouncing in the appropriate service court, the ball may hit any other wall or walls.

The server is allowed two tries. If his first serve does not meet all the above requirements, it is a fault and he may try again. After two consecutive faults, he loses the point and the right to serve.

To return the serve, the receiver stands in the service court on his side. The return of serve and all subsequent shots may be struck either on the fly or after one bounce, as long as the ball reaches the front wall on the fly above the telltale and below the sixteen-foot line. The ball may touch any wall or walls either before or after reaching the front wall. It may be struck only once on each return.

Players alternate hitting the ball until one of them fails to make a good return and loses the point—unless a let or let point occurs.

A let is the replaying of a point, ordinarily granted when one player obstructs another. Sportsmanship and safety have always been primary considerations in squash, and the rules concerning the players' rights to play the ball are quite detailed. Basically, a player is obligated to get out of his opponent's way, allowing him to see, reach, and/or strike at the ball, even if by so doing he must put himself at a disadvantage. He must also allow his opponent to play the ball to any part of the front wall, or to either side wall near the front wall. If a player who is unintentionally obstructed *could otherwise have made a good return,* he may request a let, and if the referee concurs, the point is replayed. If a let is not awarded, the player who requested it loses the point. In refereed matches, if the referee feels that the obstruction was avoidable (though not necessarily intentional) he may award a point *(let point)* to the obstructed player instead of having the point replayed. When there is no referee, a player who feels that he was hindered requests a let from his opponent; the rally stops, and the point is replayed.

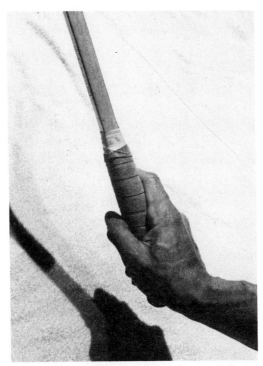

Fig. 3-3 Most players use the Continental grip for all shots. The V between thumb and forefinger should be just to the left of the center of the shaft. Your grip should be firm, but not tense.

The rules concerning being touched by a ball in play are quite detailed in order to cover all possible situations (see p. 226), but in general, if the ball touches either player, or anything he wears or carries (other than the racquet of the striker), he loses the point.

GRIP Since time between shots in squash is usually extremely short, most players use the same grip—the Continental—for all strokes. Find it by holding your racquet in front of you at the throat with your free hand, with the face perpendicular to the floor, and "shaking hands" with the handle. The V formed by your thumb and index finger should be on the ridge just to the left of the top of the handle; the end of the handle should extend slightly beyond your hand. Separate your index finger slightly from the others for added control. (Fig. 3-3)

Hold your racquet firmly when you are stroking the ball, but when time permits, relax your grip between shots; keeping a tight grip continuously throughout two or three games would be extremely fatiguing.

Fig. 3-4 On the T and ready to go: Body alert and in a crouch, knees well bent, weight forward, racquet waist-high in front of her.

READY POSITION   In squash, it is often a challenge simply to *get* to the low-bouncing ball before it has touched the floor twice and is out of play—to say nothing of hitting a controlled, powerful, well-placed shot. Therefore a good ready position, one that will allow you to get a quick start in any direction, is absolutely essential.

Face the front wall, with your feet about shoulder-width apart, your knees flexed, and your weight forward and evenly distributed on the balls of your feet. Because the ball is generally hit between ankle and knee height, your body should be in a somewhat lower position than for tennis. Get down in a crouch by bending your knees more and leaning your body forward slightly, keeping your back straight and your head up. Hold your racquet in front of you, supporting it with the fingertips of your free hand, with the head well above your wrist. Keep your elbows in close to your body. And—very important—cock the wrist of your playing hand to form a right angle with your forearm so that you don't have to waste time cocking it after your opponent makes his shot.

As in all sports, it's important to keep your eyes on the ball at all times. When your opponent is playing the ball behind you, though, your body should remain facing the front wall. Rather than turning to face your opponent directly, which would not only be dangerous but a waste of time, keep him in view by turning your head slightly and looking over your shoulder, using peripheral vision. You can raise your racquet head in front of your face for added protection.

Your position on the court is crucial. The most advantageous spot is the so-called T, where the center line meets the floor service line (see "Tactics," p. 92).

STROKES *Forehand.* The motion of the forehand stroke in squash is similar to throwing a baseball sidearm. It is a wristier action than a tennis forehand, but in all other respects it is more restrained; a full, roundhouse swing would be both unnecessary and dangerous on a squash court.

Pivot out of ready position on your right foot and turn to face the right sidewall, remaining in a crouch. As you turn sideways, take your racquet back, holding it perpendicular to the floor with the head slightly above the level of your own head. Your elbow is tucked in close to your body; your wrist is cocked all the way back; your right shoulder is higher than your left.

Stay in a crouch as you move quickly behind the ball. As it approaches, bend your knees even more deeply, and step toward the ball with your left foot, planting it at about a 45-degree angle to the front wall—this will get your weight moving forward into the shot. Time your swing so that you make contact with the ball when it is slightly in front of your front knee. Dropping your right shoulder lower than your left, lead the stroke with your elbow, but at the last moment whip your wrist through in order to give your shot more power. Keep your racquet face open and swing slightly downward to apply backspin, which will make the ball drop more quickly to the floor.

Keep your body and racquet low as you follow through forward, straightening your arm as if reaching for the front wall. (Fig. 3-5)

Backhand. The backhand, used when the ball comes to your non-dominant side, is potentially a more powerful, versatile, and easily disguised stroke than the forehand. To hit it, pivot so that you are facing the left side wall, and simultaneously take your racquet back across your body to the left, keeping your forearm parallel to the floor. Your elbow is in close to your body, which is in a crouch, and your right shoulder is lower than your left. Your wrist is cocked back as far as possible.

Fig. 3-5 Forehand. **1.** Player faces the side wall, racquet up and back, knees bent, wrist cocked.

2. He positions himself behind the oncoming ball, knees bent even more for a better weight transfer. Leading the stroke with his elbow, he contacts the ball when it is slightly in front of his front knee.

Fig. 3-6 Backhand. **1.** As the ball approaches, player is sideways to its flight, with his racquet diagonally across the back of his neck and his wrist cocked.

2. He steps in with his front foot and prepares to meet the ball ahead of him.

3. After impact. Player's forearm has come through, his wrist has snapped.

4. He follows through forward, his body remaining low.

3. Player's arm and the racquet form a straight line on impact, giving direction to his shot.

4. For the follow-through he remains in a crouch, with his racquet pointing toward the front wall. He finishes with his racquet head in the air.

Staying low, move quickly behind the ball. As it approaches, raise your racquet up higher, until the handle is diagonally across the back of your neck; this will twist your shoulders and hips further around to the left and enable you to release more power into the shot. Time your swing to meet the ball when it is about six inches ahead of your front knee—slightly further in front of you than for a forehand. As the ball comes into hitting range, bend your knees more deeply, then step toward it with your right foot to get your weight moving forward. Lead the stroke with your elbow, which is bent initially but which straightens as you swing so that on impact your arm and the racquet form a straight line. Just before impact, begin to snap your wrist sharply, whipping the open-faced racquet through in a slightly downward direction to impart backspin.

For the follow-through, your body remains facing the side wall in a crouch, with your shoulders down and your knees bent. Finish with your racquet head in the air. (Fig. 3-6)

Spin. Most squash shots are hit with backspin, sidespin (slice), or a combination of both. Backspin makes the ball die quickly; sidespin makes it hug the walls. To apply backspin, open the face of your racquet and swing forward at a slightly downward angle. Apply sidespin by drawing the strings across the ball from right to left for a forehand, from left to right for a backhand.

Volley. The volley is usually an attacking stroke in squash. By returning your opponent's shot on the fly, you prevent him from taking a momentary rest, and also rob him of precious seconds in which to retrieve the ball. Your volley, in other words, puts extra pressure on him, and it makes good sense to move in and volley the ball rather than waiting for it to bounce whenever you have the opportunity.

Volleying requires quick reflexes. Just as your opponent has less time to reach your volley, you have less time to execute it. For this reason, it is important that you start out in a good, alert ready position—weight forward, wrist cocked, racquet head up—to enable you to get to the ball quickly and meet it solidly and crisply out in front of your body.

To save time, don't turn sideways or take your racquet back. Just move quickly behind the flight of the ball and take a short, quick step toward it with your outside foot (left for a forehand, right for a backhand), which will get your body weight moving forward and bring your shoulders and hips halfway around to the appropriate side wall. Begin your swing early enough to attack the ball well out in front of you—further ahead of you than for a ground stroke. Your wrist leads the stroke and snaps sharply at the last moment, bringing your open-faced racquet through in a slightly downward direction for backspin. Take a short, low follow-through toward the front wall, as if you were going to throw your racquet at it.

Always keep your racquet head higher than your wrist when you volley.

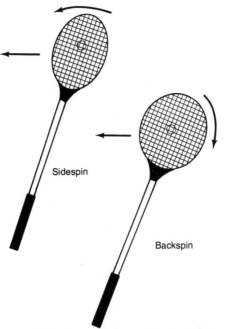

Fig. 3-B Spin. To impart backspin, open the face of your racquet and swing downward slightly. For sidespin, draw the strings across the ball from right to left for a forehand, from left to right for a backhand.

Fig. 3-7 A Backhand Volley: Player meets the ball well in front of him, his wrist firm.

For low shots, bend more deeply at the knees and waist rather than simply dropping your racquet head lower.

If the ball is traveling higher than your shoulders when it comes off the front wall, let it go by you and take it off the back wall instead of volleying it. An effective volley is extremely difficult to make at that height, whereas you may get a setup off the back wall.

Don't make the mistake of trying for a pinpoint placement with your volleys; you'll probably hit the tin. Aim at least one foot above it to allow a good margin of safety.

Half-volley. The half-volley, hit when the ball has just bounced, can be either a defensive or an offensive stroke in squash. Often you have no choice: the ball has bounced at your feet and hitting it just as it comes off the floor is the only way you can keep it in play. On the other hand, when the ball bounces in midcourt, by moving in and hitting a half-volley instead of a normal ground stroke you can often succeed in rushing your opponent just as well as with a volley.

Again, for maximum control, don't turn sideways, and don't take any

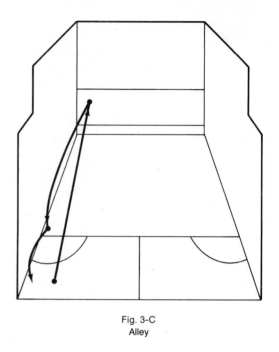

Fig. 3-C
Alley

backswing. Quickly move behind the ball's flight and, if you have time, step toward it with your outside foot in order to turn your body partly sideways. Bend your knees deeply to get down to the ball, keeping your racquet head higher than your wrist if possible. Shifting your weight forward, meet the ball well out in front of your body, just after it has bounced. Make sure to keep your wrist locked for better control. Take a short, low follow-through.

Aim the half-volley, like the volley, safely above the tin.

Shots. Squash shots fall into two general categories—the deep shots, which are used to send the ball into the back court, and the short shots, which die in the front court.

The deep shots are *drives* and *lobs,* both designed to send the ball past your opponent into the back court. Both can be hit either cross-court or down the line.

Tactically, drives are used either to force your opponent off the T so that you can move to it and control the rally, or to win the point outright if he is already out of position. They are executed with the basic forehand or backhand stroke that has already been described. (pp. 73–76) A

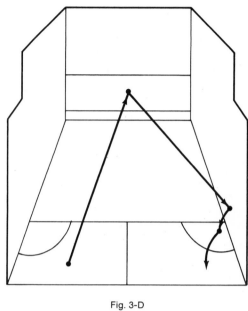

Fig. 3-D
Cross-Court

Fig. 3-8 The front court player is in position to hit an offensive drive down the side wall—an alley.

down-the-line drive, also called an *alley* or a *rail,* is hit along the nearest side wall; it is the game's bread-and-butter shot. When you are hitting an alley to gain the T, aim the ball 3 to 5 feet above the tin for length (depth), so that it comes back to bounce at the service line and bounces again before reaching the back wall. (Fig. 3-C) When you are in a position to hit an alley for a winner—usually when your opponent is out of position in the front court, or when his too-hard or high cross-court drive pops off the back wall and pins him along the side wall—hit harder, use slightly more backspin, and aim much lower—just a few inches above the tin. When that shot comes off the front wall, it will be traveling too fast and too low for all but the most agile opponent to return.

A cross-court drive is hit from one side of the court to the approximate center of the front wall. To direct the ball cross-court, you must snap your wrist a bit earlier than for an alley. The ball will rebound low on the far side wall near the floor service line, then continue back. A cross-court drive hit to force your opponent off the T should be aimed 3 to 4 feet above the tin. (Fig. 3-D) When he is out of position and you drive the ball cross-court, again, use slightly more backspin and aim just a few inches above the tin.

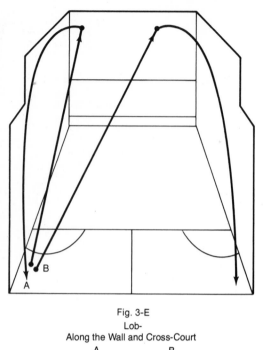

Fig. 3-E
Lob-
Along the Wall and Cross-Court
A   B

Fig. 3-9 Player in front stretches to retrieve a short ball, his racquet face open to send the ball high. A lob will give him time to get in better position.

High, slow lobs, like drives, can be hit to move your opponent off the T and into the back court, but unlike drives, they are rarely used as attempted winners, because of all the shots in the game they give your out-of-position opponent the most time to reach the ball. However, when *you* are on the defensive, always lob; usually it's the only way you can keep yourself in the point when you are out of position but can reach your opponent's attempted put-away shot. Your lob will be almost impossible for him to attack, and it will also give you time to gain a better court position. The lob is hit with the same stroke as the drive, except that you must get your racquet under the ball, swing in an upward direction, and follow through high to send the ball up in a high, slow arc (Fig. 3-9); it should still be ascending as it strikes well up on the front wall, and it should travel back at a great enough height to bounce near the service line, so that your opponent cannot volley it from midcourt. When you are lobbing to force your opponent to give up the T, you can use either a cross-court or an alley lob (Fig. 3-E), depending on your opponent's expectation. Keep your wrists firm for this shot. A defensive, desperation lob—hit when you're struggling to retrieve your opponent's attempted deep put-away shot—should always be hit down the alley, as this is the

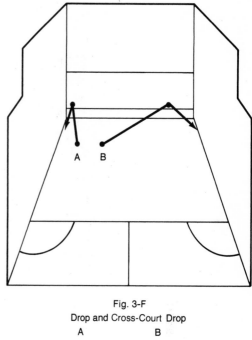

Fig. 3-F
Drop and Cross-Court Drop
A   B

op shot can end the
onent is deep in the

ensive lob is not stroked; it is hit only with wrist snap for

ch" shots, which die in the front court, are usually hit
further forward (with two exceptions—see end of
e short shots, hit when you are in good position in
r opponent is further back, are used either to move your
out of position into the front court so that you can hit a
deep winner, or to win the point outright. Defensive short shots are used
to "dig out" your opponent's attempted short put-aways.

Retrieving a ball that requires forward movement calls for a slightly
different technique from that used when you are moving to the side or
back: Don't turn sideways or take your racquet back first, but instead run
directly to the ball with your racquet in front of you. Then, if you have
time, turn sideways and take your racquet back just as for a deep shot; if
you don't have time, simply get your racquet under the ball and flip it
upward with a flick of your wrist.

There are four basic short shots hit from center or front court—the *drop
shot,* the *cross-court drop,* the *corner,* and the *reverse corner*—and two

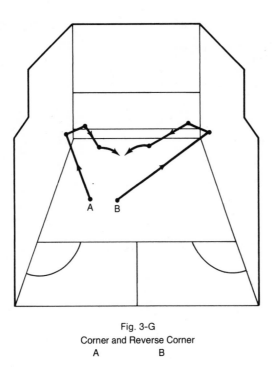

Fig. 3-G
Corner and Reverse Corner
A   B

that are hit from the back court—the *three-wall* and the *roll corner*.

The drop shot is a slow, low alley hit softly but crisply with both backspin and sidespin to keep the ball low and near the wall. (Fig. 3-10) Aim it about three inches above the tin and a foot or so from the nearest corner, so that the ball bounces near the side wall after dropping off the front wall; ideally, it will nick in the crack between the side wall and the floor. For an offensive drop shot, use no wrist snap. For a defensive drop, use *only* wrist snap, getting underneath the ball and flipping it upward softly.

The cross-court drop shot (Fig. 3-F) is rather more difficult to execute than a straight drop, and it is only used offensively, as a surprise. As for the drop, hit the ball softly but crisply, aiming about three inches above the tin, but when hitting a cross-court drop aim slightly further from the (far) side wall. Use only slight sidespin.

The corner and the reverse corner both hit a side wall first and then die off the front wall. The corner is hit with heavy sidespin up to the side wall you are facing and aimed three or four feet from the front corner. The ball should rebound quickly to the front wall a few inches above the tin, then die.

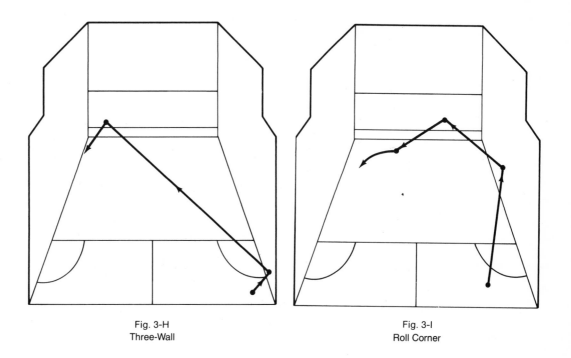

Fig. 3-H
Three-Wall

Fig. 3-I
Roll Corner

The reverse corner is hit cross-court to the far side wall. (Fig. 3-G) Aim much closer to the front wall than for a corner, and use only slight sidespin. The ball should rebound quickly to the front wall a few inches above the tin, then die.

The three-wall and the roll corner are short shots that are hit from the back court, when you are behind your opponent. Both are advanced shots that can be extremely effective when your opponent is hanging back expecting a deep drive.

The three-wall is hit with pronounced sidespin into the side wall you are facing. The ball should strike the front wall a few feet from the opposite side wall and a few inches above the tin, then, ideally, nick in the crack between side wall and floor. (Fig. 3-H) Keep your wrist firm on this shot, and use three-quarters power.

The roll corner is really a long corner shot. Aim the ball to the nearest side wall about five feet from the front corner. It should strike the front wall about six inches above the tin, then die in the front court. (Fig. 3-I) Use very little wrist snap.

Fig. 3-11 Lob Serve. 1. Server faces the side wall, rear foot in the service box.

2. As he begins his forward swing, he drops the ball and meets it knee high,

3. swinging forward and upward with a firm wrist.

SERVE While the serve in squash is not as offensive a shot as it is, for example, in tennis, it can provide the server with a significant edge and should definitely be considered more than simply the way to put the ball in play. A well-placed serve, if not an immediate winner, can at least leave your opponent seriously off balance. There are three main squash serves: the *lob,* the *hard serve,* and the *slice.* The lob is the safest and most popular; the other two, which require greater accuracy, are more likely than the lob to win you a point outright.

The lob serve is a slow, high-arcing shot that strikes high up on the front wall, drifts back slowly and grazes the side wall high near the back wall, then dies along the back wall. (Fig. 3-J) This serve has several advantages: of the three serves, it is the easiest to execute and the least

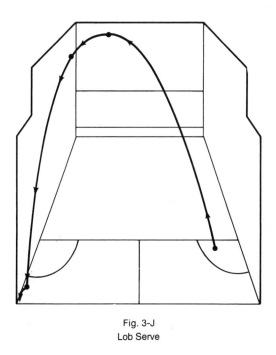

Fig. 3-J
Lob Serve

4. He follows through high above his left shoulder.

taxing on your energy; in addition, you finish it well balanced and with ample time to move to the T.

To serve a lob from the right-hand court, assume an open stance facing the right front corner. Place your back foot in the right service box, pointing toward the right side wall, with your forward foot pointing toward the front wall. From the left-hand court, maintain a closed stance—feet, again, at right angles but your body facing the right side wall. On either side, your feet should be about shoulder-width apart, your knees bent, and your weight mainly on your back foot.

Begin the serve with your racquet already back, holding it at waist level and pointing toward the right rear corner. Your elbow is in close to your body and your wrist lower than your racquet head and cocked. Hold the ball at waist level, in the fingers of your left hand. As you begin swinging

Fig. 3-12 Hard Serve. 1. Player has tossed the ball above and slightly in front of his right shoulder, taken his racquet back, and cocked his wrist.

forward, drop the ball and meet it when it is about knee high, using no wrist snap so that you maintain maximum control. Keep your racquet face open and swing upward smoothly in order to send the ball high up on the front wall and also to put topspin on it, which will make it travel back in a higher arc—the higher the better for a more vertical drop in the back court. Remain low as you swing, and shift your weight forward. Follow through high above your left shoulder. (Fig. 3-11)

Aim your lob serve near the top of the front wall, just to the left of center from the right-hand court, just to the right of center from the left-hand court.

The hard serve, which is hit with an overhead motion for maximum speed, is the one most likely to win you an immediate point. It is an especially effective serve if you are playing on a warm court, where the ball's speed will be accentuated; it can also be devastating against a tired

 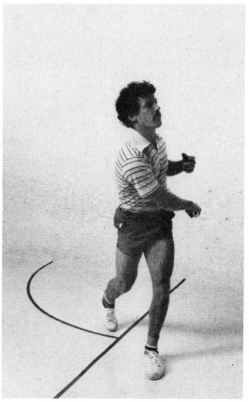

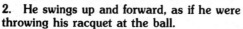

2. He swings up and forward, as if he were throwing his racquet at the ball.

3. His follow-through is across his body and down to the left.

opponent. However, it requires great accuracy of execution and, used often over the course of a match is itself a rather tiring serve to hit. It has the further disadvantage that you finish the serve off balance, allowing an opponent who can volley the return to capitalize on your vulnerable position. Therefore use this serve sparingly—as an occasional surprise—both to conserve energy and to prevent your opponent from getting used to it.

From either side of the court, assume a closed stance—facing the right side wall. To disguise your intention, take the same backswing initially as for the lob serve. Toss the ball up above and slightly in front of your right shoulder, high enough so that your arm and body will be fully extended on impact. At the same time, take your racquet back over your right shoulder into the backscratching position, with your wrist cocked back. When the ball has reached the peak of the toss, swing up and forward, as if you were throwing your racquet at it. Snap your wrist sharply on

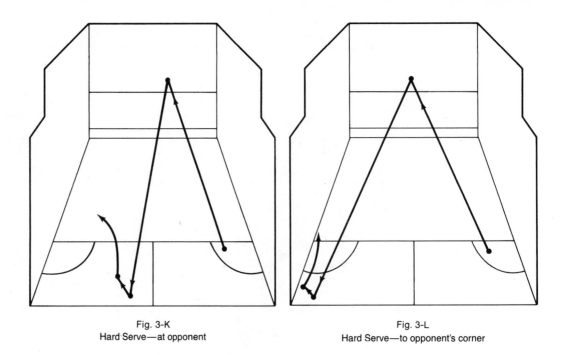

Fig. 3-K
Hard Serve—at opponent

Fig. 3-L
Hard Serve—to opponent's corner

contact, and let your swing carry your weight forward. Follow through by continuing your swing across your body and down to the left. (Fig. 3-12)

This serve can be aimed at various spots on the front wall, depending on where you want the ball to land. Three good targets are right at your opponent, into his back corner, or to the T.

To send the ball right at your opponent, aim slightly to *your* side of the center of the front wall, just high enough to make the ball reach the back wall on the fly. If you hit it higher, you will sacrifice speed unnecessarily; naturally, the taller and stronger you are, the lower you can aim. The ball should shoot back quickly and hit the back wall very near the floor. (Fig. 3-K)

To send the ball to your opponent's back corner, aim your hard serve slightly *beyond* the center, again, high enough to hit the back wall on the fly, near the floor and far side wall. (Fig. 3-L)

To make your hard serve go through the T, aim about a foot from your opponent's side wall and lower than for the others—just above the service line—so that the ball hits the floor before reaching the back wall. It should richochet quickly to the side wall, picking up sidespin, fly in front of the receiver and bounce in his service court near the T, then scoot to the back wall in your service court. (Fig. 3-M) The combination of its high speed and unusual angle makes this a particularly difficult serve to return.

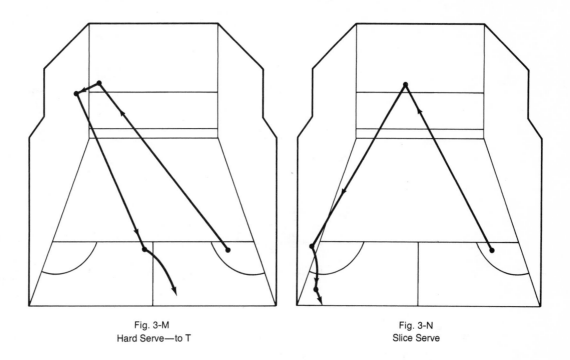

Fig. 3-M
Hard Serve—to T

Fig. 3-N
Slice Serve

For the slice serve, the ball is hit at shoulder height with sidespin and backspin. It strikes the front wall just above the service line, hits low on the side wall in the receiver's court, then takes a low bounce near the back wall and dies. (Fig. 3-N) This serve requires less accuracy to execute than the hard serve (but more than the lob), and many players have difficulty handling its pronounced spin. It's a good alternative if you find that your opponent is having no trouble with your lob serve, or if the ceiling is too low to permit an effective lob. Use it sparingly, though, so that it remains a surprise.

Once again, to hide your intention, take the same stance and initial backswing as for the other serves. Toss the ball up slightly in front of your right shoulder and just above your head—lower than for a hard serve—as you take your racquet back to the side at about shoulder level. Your wrist should be cocked back, and your elbow should be away from your body. When the ball comes down to shoulder height, swing your open-faced racquet sideways from right to left, contacting the ball in its lower right side as you snap your wrist sharply. Follow through across your body; your racquet will finish by pointing toward the left side wall.

Aim this serve just above the service line, slightly beyond the center of the front wall.

Fig. 3-13 Player on the left awaits her opponent's serve, facing the side wall in a low, crouched position with her racquet already back.

RETURN OF SERVE

The receiver is at a distinct disadvantage in squash. The server controls the center of the court, and his serve will probably force the receiver deeper into the back court to return the ball. Since he is on the defensive, his return should be a safe shot, aimed well above the tin and hit for *length* in order to force the server into the back court, allowing the receiver to replace him on the T. All but the poorest of serves should be volleyed; a well-volleyed return can offset some of the server's advantage by rushing him. In general, the most effective return is a deep alley. This shot will not only force the server to give up the T but, if it is kept close to the side wall, also make him worry about hitting that wall with his racquet.

Ready position for returning serve is somewhat different from any other position in squash. Standing about four feet from the back wall, face the side wall of the court being served to, with your heels on the center line; this means that you will have to watch the server over your shoulder. Take the usual low, crouched stance, but wait with your racquet already back. (Fig. 3-13)

If your opponent serves a lob, straighten up out of your crouch and raise your racquet higher, until your cocked wrist is level with your shoulder; your racquet should point toward the top of the back wall. Move in quickly to the side wall so that you are ready to volley the ball when it is still a foot or two above your head and well in front of you. As it drops

Fig. 3-14 Player has just returned his opponent's serve down the side wall to a length.

down from the side wall, swing upward, straightening your arm and snapping your wrist on impact. Though you will be more erect than for most squash shots, and therefore won't be able to manage as pronounced a weight shift, lean your body into the shot as much as you can. (Fig. 3-14) Follow through, with your racquet pointing toward the top of the front wall at the end of the stroke.

If your opponent has hit his lob serve too hard and it looks as if the ball will reach the back wall before hitting the floor, let it bounce; then move in for a put-away drive from center-court, aiming just above the tin.

Intercept a hard serve before it reaches the back wall. You won't need to use much power; the speed of the serve itself will provide all the velocity you need. Step into the ball and volley it with a slightly open racquet face, keeping your wrist firm for maximum control. Your racquet face should remain open as you follow through toward the front wall.

Volley a slice serve before it reaches either the side wall or the floor. Quickly move to the side wall and bend low, so that you are directly behind the ball as it heads back. Then "throw" your open-faced racquet forward, meeting the ball well in front of you and snapping your wrist sharply. Follow through low, with your racquet pointing toward the front wall.

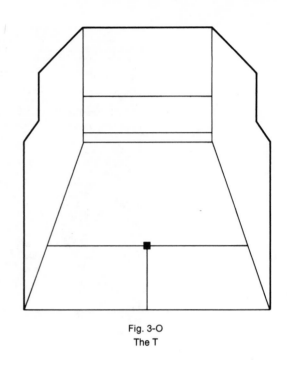

Fig. 3-O
The T

TACTICS The basic tactic in squash is to take control of the center-court area, known as the T, where the center line bisects the service line. (Fig. 3-0) Like the player at the net in tennis, the player who controls the T in squash controls the rally. From the T he has the best chance of reaching any of his opponent's shots, and of forcing his opponent to chase the ball all over the court and to hit weak, inaccurate shots from off-balance positions. Therefore two of the most important tactics of the game are to move back to the T immediately after every shot you hit, and to aim your shots away from the center to keep your opponent out of that command position; remember that you are obligated to give him a fair opportunity to reach and/or hit the ball. Send the ball into the corners and near the walls instead. If you are unable to reach the T before your opponent hits his shot, stop where you are, because you are better off being slightly out of position than being caught moving the wrong way.

Use the lob serve most of the time, as it is the safest and easiest to execute. Save the hard serve and the slice for variety and surprise. Try to volley the return of serve; in general, keep the ball deep to force the server back, so that you can take the T. Play this shot safe; use mainly deep alleys, with an occasional deep cross-court for variety. Try for a winner only if the serve is very poor.

When you are playing in the back court, and your opponent has control of the T, the situation is much the same as when you are returning serve. It is practically impossible to hit a low, fast put-away drive; most likely your shot would either hit the tin or your opponent would put the ball away from midcourt. Instead, try to make him abandon the T with a deep shot—usually a deep alley, which will force him not only to retreat into the back court but also to worry about hitting the side wall with his racquet as he makes his return. Be careful not to hit your drives too low when you are trying to dislodge your opponent from the T; the ball should come back to bounce near the service line. Use the lower-percentage deep cross-court drive for the sake of surprise when your opponent is moving or leaning toward the side wall in expectation of your deep alley. Cross-court drives must be hit more accurately than alleys when your opponent is stationed on the T; make sure that the ball rebounds off the front wall at an angle wide enough to prevent him from cutting it off at midcourt.

If you find that your opponent on the T is intercepting and volleying your drives, use cross-court and alley lobs to dislodge him instead. Make sure that your lob doesn't hit the side wall and that it bounces near the service line. As previously mentioned, always send your lob down the alley when you are on the defensive, struggling to reach your opponent's deep put-away drive.

A useful rule of thumb for beginning players is always to hit the ball directly to the front wall when in the back court. Unless they are executed with great control and finesse, shots hit to a side wall first tend to come out to the center of the court, giving your opponent an easy set-up. For more advanced players, three-walls and roll corners can be extremely effective from the back court if your opponent is moving back expecting a deep drive or a lob.

Look for opportunities when you're in the back court to seize the offensive. If your opponent hits a weak shot, move in and cut it off with a volley or half-volley. If he hits the ball too hard or too high, so that it comes well out from the back or side wall, try to put it away with a low, hard drive.

When you are stationed on the T, your choice of shots is much wider, giving you a better opportunity to run your opponent, keep him off balance, force him further and further out of position, and put the ball away. Alleys and cross-court drives hit from the T can safely be aimed closer to the tin than drives from the back court, and it is easier to make the short shots die off the front wall. Use a variety of shots when you're in control of the T, choosing according to your opponent's position and expectations. Because a squash court is longer than it is wide, usually the most logical pattern of play is to alternate deep shots with short shots, which will keep your opponent running up and back. When you get him out of position in the front court, hit an offensive drive; when he is out of position in the back court, use one of the short shots. You don't want to be too predictable, though, or he'll know where to run for your next shot. Once you have established a pattern, alter it unexpectedly by hitting two in a row to the same area of the court to catch him moving or leaning the wrong way. Disguising your shots, as well as changing the pace and the degree of spin you use, will prevent him from setting up properly for his shot.

When retrieving your opponent's attempted short put-away takes you into the front court in a mad dash from the back court, you are on the defensive and your alternatives are quite clear-cut. If your opponent stays back, hit a defensive, wristy drop shot; if he moves up, hit a lob, a deep cross-court, or an alley. When his short attempted winner is poor and you have more time, hold your shot until the last moment to keep him from anticipating it, then go for a winner yourself: hit a low, fast cross-court or alley if he is moving in, a drop or other short shot if he hangs back. Then, as always, get back to the T to prepare for a possible return.

SQUASH CHECKLIST

1. Keep your eyes on the ball.
2. Move back to the T after every shot.
3. Stay low. In general the best shots in squash are contacted about knee high.
4. Direct your shots away from your opponent to force him to run.
5. Aim drives a few feet higher above the tin when hitting to force your opponent off the T than when hitting for a winner.
6. Vary and, if possible, disguise your shots to prevent your opponent from anticipating.
7. Until you have developed enough control and finesse to keep your side-wall-first shots from coming out to the center of the court, direct your shots to the front wall first.
8. Rely mainly on the lob serve.
9. Try to return serve with a volley.

Fig. 4-1

RACQUETBALL

ABOUT RACQUETBALL Racquetball was invented in 1949 at the Greenwich, Connecticut, YMCA, where a former tennis and squash instructor named Joe Sobek took up paddleball and decided that it might be a livelier and more exciting game if it were played with strung racquets. Sobek designed an implement the same size as a paddle but strung loosely with nylon, and the game he called "paddle rackets" was born. It caught on quickly, despite his initial difficulty in having a suitable ball manufactured.

Sobek found the ideal ball—an A. G. Spalding red and blue rubber children's ball—in a five-and-ten-cent store. When the paddle rackets pioneers had depleted the existing stock, they discovered that the firm had stopped making that particular ball before World War II. The people at Spalding said they'd be happy to produce another batch—but only with a minimum order of eighteen hundred. Sobek decided to go ahead. But he quickly found that the new ball was too lively. Like fine steak, the original supply had benefited, at least for Sobek's purposes, from the aging process, which had caused the balls to deflate just the right amount. Sobek was stuck with eighteen hundred very lively rubber balls and continued his search all over the country, until the Seamless Rubber Company (Seamco) in nearby New Haven, Connecticut, produced a satisfactory substitute.

When paddle rackets players moved to other parts of the country, they took the game with them. By the mid-1960s, there were several versions of paddle rackets being played, and the Midwest had become the center of the action. In 1968, at a combined tournament and conference held at the Jewish Community Center in Milwaukee, players consolidated forces, standardized the rules and equipment, and coined a catchier name for their sport: racquetball was officially on its way. The International Racquetball Association was formed in 1969 to govern the game. It was headed by Robert Kendler, who had also founded the United States Handball Association. Kendler subsequently resigned from the IRA over a dispute with its directors and formed the rival United States Racquetball Association, which is now much the stronger organization, directing affiliate racquetball associations in all fifty states. State affiliates conduct their own amateur tournaments, for which the USRA provides some financial support.

The USRA's professional wing, the National Racquetball Club (NRC) oversees the game's pro athletes. The pro tour, which makes stops in more than a dozen major cities, always commands an enthusiastic gallery. The spectators devour the action as the pros collide, crash into walls, dive to the floor to retrieve low shots, and, as often as not, argue vociferously with each other and with the tournament officials over calls. The reverential hush that traditionally prevails at tennis tournaments is conspicuously absent from racquetball contests.

Racquetball is currently in the middle of a tremendous boom in the United States that is the envy of all the related sports. "We'll move over tennis in five years," predicts Kendler. "We are going to make racquetball the number one sport in America, and soon."

GOVERNING BODIES

United States Racquetball Association
4101 Dempster Street
Skokie, IL 60076

Official magazine: *National Racquetball*

American Amateur Racquetball Association
5545 Murray Road
Memphis, TN 38117

Official magazine: *Racquetball Magazine*

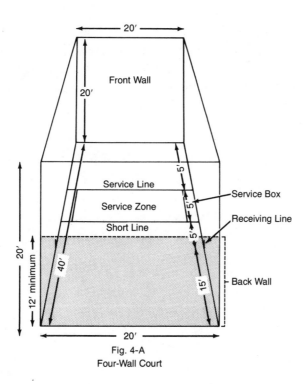

Fig. 4-A
Four-Wall Court

COURT The official racquetball court, 40 feet long and 20 feet wide, has front and side walls that are 20 feet high and a back wall that is at least 12 feet high. These are also standard four-wall handball/paddleball court dimensions.

All lines on the court are 1½ inches wide. The short line is midway between and parallel to the front and back walls, dividing the court into equal front and back courts. The service line is parallel to and 5 feet in front of the short line. The space between the outer edges of the short and service lines is the service zone. A service box is marked off at each end of the service zone by lines 18 inches from and parallel to each side wall; these only come into play in doubles. Five feet behind the short line, 3-inch vertical lines are marked on each side wall; these are the receiving lines. (Fig. 4-A)

The four-wall court is painted white, with red lines. The walls are usually made of concrete, plaster, or plastic, although both prefabricated walls—which make construction easier—and glass walls—for spectators—are becoming increasingly popular. High-quality hardwood is generally used for the floor.

Racquetball is also played, informally, on one- and three-wall handball/paddleball courts. The one-wall court is 20 feet wide and 34 feet

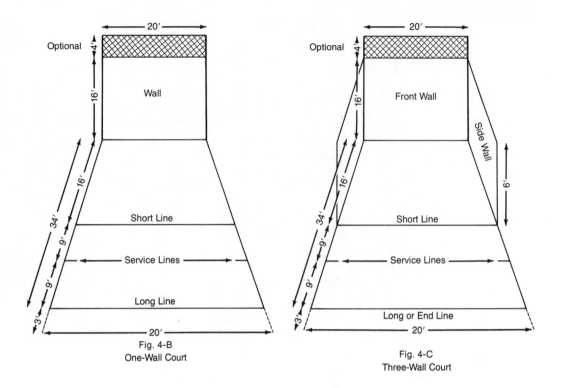

Fig. 4-B
One-Wall Court

Fig. 4-C
Three-Wall Court

long from the wall to the back edge of the long line. The wall, which is 16 feet high, is sometimes topped by a 4-foot high wire fence to catch errant balls. The short line is 16 feet from the wall. Extending in from the side lines, parallel to and midway between the long and short lines, are lines at least 6 inches long called the service markers. The imaginary extension and joining of these lines indicates the service line. The service zone is the area bounded by the short, service, and side lines. The receiving zone is the area bounded by the short, long, and side lines. (Fig. 4-B)

The three-wall court has the same dimensions and lines, with the addition of side walls that extend from the top of the front wall back, slanting downward to a height of 6 feet at the short line, at which point they stop. (Fig. 4-C)

RACQUET A racquetball racquet has a strung oval or near-oval head and a short handle. It is approximately 18 inches long and 9 inches wide at the widest part of the head. The frame may be made of any material; the strings may be of nylon, gut, or metal. (Under International Racquetball Association rules, metal strings are permitted only if they do not mark or deface the ball.) Attached to the handle of the racquet is a thong, which must be

Fig. 4-2

securely wrapped around your wrist during play as a safety precaution.

Although you can spend well over a hundred dollars for a racquet, $20 or $30 will buy you one that is perfectly adequate. Racquets are made of wood, aluminum, or fiberglass. Avoid the wood models; while they are the least expensive and the most durable, they have thick, unwieldy frames and a smaller "sweet spot"—the portion in the center where the ball comes off most accurately—than the others. Like wood, aluminum is extremely durable, but it is also rather stiff. For the hard-hitting player, an aluminum racquet offers greater power, but because of its stiffness it will give less control than a racquet made of fiberglass. Fiberglass is a more flexible material, and a racquet made of it will be easier to control. However it is also very fragile; the first time you hit a wall with a fiberglass racquet, it is likely to break. Thus, while most expert players prefer fiberglass for the control it offers, beginners are better off with aluminum. Some of the newer aluminum models are designed with an I-beam construction, which is said to offer improved flexibility. An aluminum racquet's control can also be increased somewhat by having it strung more loosely.

Racquets come with various head shapes, including modified rectangular, owl's head, teardrop, and oval; head shape, however, makes little discernible difference and is strictly a matter of individual preference.

Racquets range in weight from about 8½ to 10 ounces; the lighter ones, usually preferred by women, are easier to swing; the heavier ones, which men generally choose, give more power. They also come in standard and "extra" lengths. The additional inch in the handle affords greater leverage and reach but less control; because control is considered more important, the longer-length racquets are not widely used.

Most racquet models are available in only a few grip sizes: small (4⅛), medium ($4^5/_{16}$), and large (4½). The relatively small grip (which can easily be built up with tape) is to permit the wrist flexibility that is a key element of most racquetball strokes. However, if your racquet has *too* small a grip, it will twist in your hand. When you select a racquet, see that when you grip it your third and fourth fingers are just touching the pad below your thumb. (For junior players, there are lighter, shorter racquets with smaller grips.)

Handles are covered with either leather or rubber. Leather, which is slightly more expensive, is less slippery when wet; rubber will last longer. Your choice.

Racquetball racquets are almost always strung with nylon, even those the pros use. In general, the more expensive racquets are strung with better-grade, longer-lasting nylon. Nylon is more durable and less costly than gut, and its low string tension—26–34 pounds—makes the racquet easier to control and is resilient enough to provide excellent "touch."

BALL The ball is made of hollow, pressurized rubber. It is 2¼ inches in diameter and weighs approximately 1.4 ounces. From a 100-inch drop it should bounce 68–72 inches at 76°F (24°C) to meet USRA standards; by IRA standards it should bounce 68–72 inches from a 100-inch drop at 70°–74°F (21°-23°C).

Balls usually come two to a can; cans cost about $3 each. Even within the same can, liveliness and durability may vary. Most manufacturers will refund the price of the ball if it breaks while the logo is still visible, however, to the relief of players and manufacturers alike, ball breakage is not as much of a problem as it used to be.

DRESS AND ACCESSORIES Clothing worn in tournaments can be white or any color that contrasts with the dark ball, which makes good sense for social racquetball, too. While a tennis outfit or any similar comfortable and easily laundered active sportswear is perfectly acceptable, typical racquetball attire was until recently a pair of gym shorts and a T-shirt. However, to the delight of manufacturers of more stylish sportswear, it's no longer considered quite so "in" to look like a full-time jock on the court. As racquetball becomes more fashionable, players are beginning to wear clothing designed expressly for the game by some of the big names in active sportswear.

Whatever you put on your body, wear good-quality sports shoes, as racquetball is a sport that places great demands on your feet. Most players wear tennis shoes, although some prefer high-top basketball shoes because they provide better support and traction in this game of quick starts and frequent changes of direction. Always wear socks. A thick pair over a thin pair will give greater absorbency.

Racquetball is a strenuous game; be prepared to perspire. To keep their playing hand dry, many players wear a thin leather glove. The glove, which should be of thin, tacky, washable leather, will also help prevent blisters. Gloves come in full and half-fingered models; you may find that the half-fingered type gives you better "feel." A supply of head and wrist sweatbands will also help keep perspiration under control. Expect to go through a few of each during the course of a match.

The serious injury most likely to occur on a racquetball court is one to the eye; the best means of protecting your eyes is with an eyeguard. These are made of either aluminum tubing or plastic and come in various shapes. Try on several different models to find the one that affords you the best peripheral vision.

If you play with eyeglasses, make sure they have plastic shatterproof lenses, and attach a safety strap to them.

METHOD OF PLAY   Some of the differences between singles and doubles are noted in what follows, but see Rules (pp. 229–238) for a complete explanation.

A racquetball game is won by the first player (or side) to score 21 points; you don't need to win by a two-point margin as in tennis and some of the other racquet sports. Each rally is worth one point, and only the serving side can score points. A match is won by the first player (or side) to win two games. In USRA and NRC tournaments, if the score is tied at one game, the third, tiebreaking game is 11 points; in IRA tournaments it is 15 points.

The player (or side) winning the coin toss serves first in the first game. The opposing player (or side) serves first in the second game. The player or side scoring more points in games one and two combined serves first in the tiebreaker. When the server loses the exchange, the receiver becomes the server. This transfer is called a handout.

In doubles, at the beginning of each game, only the first server on the side serving first serves; when he is out, the side is out and the other side serves. During the rest of the game, both players on each side serve in turn until a handout occurs. The teams must keep the same order of service throughout the game. The server need not alternate serves to his opponents.

The server may put the ball in play from anywhere inside the service zone, which includes its boundary lines, and he must remain in the zone until the served ball has passed the short line on its way back from the front wall. To serve, he bounces the ball on the floor within the service zone and strikes it on the first bounce, hitting it directly to the front wall. On the rebound, it must land on the floor behind the short line, either with or without first touching one of the side walls.

In doubles, the server's partner must remain in the service box, with his back to the side wall, until the served ball has passed the short line on its way back from the front wall.

There are three types of defective serves—*dead-ball, fault,* and *out.* A dead-ball serve is an otherwise legal serve passing so close to the server or his partner that the receiver's view is obstructed (screen serve), or a serve hitting any part of the court that under local rules is out of play, such as a crack in the wall. There is no penalty for a dead-ball serve; the server gets another try, but any preceding defective serve still stands.

Faults include balls that go out of court on the serve; foot faults (the server leaves the service zone, or his partner leaves the service box, before the served ball has passed the short line); serves that hit the floor before crossing the short line on the rebound from the front wall (short serve); and serves that hit two side walls, the back wall, or the ceiling before bouncing on the floor. Two consecutive faults result in a handout.

Outs include striking at and missing the ball completely; the server or his partner being hit by the serve; if the serve touches the server on the rebound; if it hits the floor, ceiling, or side wall before reaching the front wall; or if it simultaneously hits the front wall and the floor (crotch serve). An out serve results in an immediate handout.

The receiver(s) must stand at least five feet behind the short line until the ball is served and cannot return the ball until it has passed the short line. The return of serve may be hit on the fly after it has traveled at least five feet past the short line. All subsequent shots may be hit either on the fly or after one bounce.

Opposing sides alternate hitting the ball, which may be returned either directly to the front wall or via any combination of side walls, back wall, and ceiling, as long as the returned ball doesn't touch the floor before reaching the front wall. If the ball nicks in the juncture of the front wall and the floor, it is not a good return.

Switching hands to hit a ball is an out, but the racquet may be held with both hands.

The ball may only be struck once on each return. If a player swings at but misses the ball, he may keep trying to return it until it bounces twice and is out of play. In doubles, if one player swings at but misses the ball, both he and his partner may keep trying to return it until it goes out of play.

Because racquetball is played in close quarters, the potential for injury on the court is considerable; therefore there are detailed and stringent rules concerning obstruction. In essence, players are entitled to a direct path to the ball, a clear view of it, and enough room to swing at it. There are two kinds of interference—*dead-ball hinders* and *avoidable hinders.* Play stops immediately following a hinder call of either type.

Dead-ball hinders, which are of an unintentional and unavoidable nature, result in the replaying of the point. A dead-ball hinder is when the ball hits any part of the court that under local rules is out of play, such as a lighting fixture or a crack in the wall; when a returned ball hits an opponent on the fly before it reaches the front wall; when there is unintentional body contact with an opponent that interferes with his seeing or returning the ball; when the ball passes between a player's legs or so close to him that it interferes with his opponent's ability to see or return it; or when there is any other unintentional interference that prevents the striker from seeing or returning the ball. It is also a dead-ball hinder if the striker hits his opponent with his racquet on the backswing.

Avoidable hinders result in a point or loss of serve, depending on whether the offender was receiving or serving. Avoidable hinders include not moving sufficiently to allow an opponent his shot; moving into an opponent's way and blocking him; moving into the way and being struck by the ball an opponent has just played; and deliberately pushing or shoving an opponent during play.

In doubles, both members of a team are entitled to the same unobstructed opportunity to play the ball, even if it would naturally be one partner's shot.

GRIP You should adjust your grip for different strokes in racquetball. Use the forehand grip for most of your shots—serves, lobs, and volleys, as well as forehand drives. To find it, hold your racquet at the throat with your free hand, with the face perpendicular to the floor, and "shake hands" with the handle. Extend your index finger forward slightly for greater control. The V

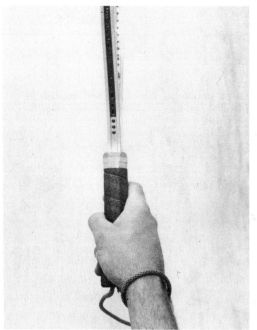

Fig. 4-3 The Forehand Grip

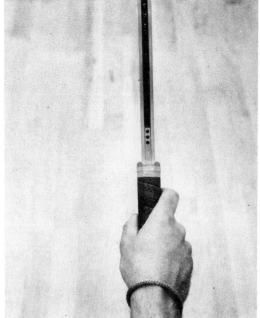

Fig. 4-4 The Backhand Grip

formed by your thumb and index finger should be directly on top of the handle, and the butt of the handle should rest in the fleshy part of your palm. (Fig. 4-3)

Use the backhand grip for backhand drives, ceiling balls, and overheads. Find it by assuming the forehand grip and rotating your hand about one-eighth turn to the left, so that the V formed by your thumb and index finger is on the top left bevel of the handle. Make sure that your thumb is wrapped around the handle, not resting along the back of it. Again, extend your index finger slightly. (Fig. 4-4)

Save your strength by relaxing your grip between shots; hold the racquet tightly only when you are actually stroking the ball.

READY POSITION The position to take while waiting for your opponent to hit the ball is much the same as in squash: face the front wall, with your feet about shoulder-width apart, knees flexed, and weight forward on the balls of your feet. Lean well forward. Hold the racquet in front of you, waist high and head up, ready for a quick backswing. Stay alert, and, of course, always keep your eyes riveted on the ball. However, for your own safety, never face your opponent directly while he is making his shot. Instead,

Fig. 4-5 Player awaits her opponent's serve in ready position—weight forward, knees flexed, racquet poised in front of her, and above all, *alert*.

Fig. 4-6 The nonhitting players watch the striker by looking over their shoulders; they don't turn their bodies. When your opponent or your partner is hitting behind you, this is a safety precaution as well as a more efficient method of watching him.

turn your head toward him just enough so that you can watch him out of the corner of your eye. It's also a good idea to shield your face with your racquet head or with your arm, especially if you're not wearing an eyeguard.

The area of the court to which you should try to return after every shot is *center court*—a step or two behind the short line. This position will enable you to hit and to return the widest variety of shots. (See "Singles Tactics.") For court positions in doubles, *see* "Doubles Tactics," p. 126.

STROKES   *Forehand.* The moment you see that your opponent has hit to your forehand, move quickly behind the ball and turn your body parallel to its line of flight. At the same time, take your racquet back about head high, with your wrist cocked and your elbow bent. Your hips and shoulders should be rotated back slightly, and your weight mainly on your rear foot. As the ball approaches, take a long stride toward it with your front foot, bending at the knees and waist to get down with it. Swing smoothly downward, leading the stroke with your elbow and letting your hips and shoulders rotate into it. Just before impact, whip your forearm through and begin to uncock your wrist sharply. This is important; it is the wrist snap

Fig. 4-7 1. Forehand Drive: As the ball approaches, player is sideways to its flight with his racquet back and his weight on his back foot.

2. He steps into his shot and swings downward, contacting the ball low.

3. He stays down for the follow-through, which is above his left shoulder.

that will give your shot pace. Meet the ball when it is about knee high and even with your front foot, as you shift your weight forward. After contact, stay low for the follow-through, finishing with your racquet above your left shoulder and fairly close to your body; there is no need (and it would be dangerous) to take a big, roundhouse follow-through. It's also unnecessary to blast the ball with all your might; for most shots you should use about 80 percent power. (Figs. 4-7–9)

Backhand. The backhand is essentially the reverse of the forehand, but there are a few differences.

As soon as you see that the ball is coming to your backhand side, adjust your grip, move quickly into position behind the ball and turn your body parallel to its line of flight. Take your racquet up and back across your body at about head height, cocking your wrist. Your elbow should be bent, your hips and shoulders rotated back, and your weight mainly on your rear foot. As the ball approaches, take a step toward it with your front foot—a shorter step than for a forehand—and bend at the knees and waist. Swinging your racquet forward and down, meet the ball just ahead of your front knee—slightly further in front of you than for a forehand. Straighten your arm as you swing, and begin to snap your wrist just before impact for more power. Stay low for the follow-through, finishing with the racquet about head high. (Figs. 4-10–12)

Fig. 4-8 Backhand Drive: Player is sideways to the ball's flight. His racquet and his weight are both back.

2. He meets the ball knee high and out in front of him, his arm straight. Ideally, he should have taken a shorter step toward the ball.

3. His knees remain bent for the follow-through.

OFFENSIVE SHOTS

Pass shots. Pass shots, or drives, are hard-hit shots that come off the front wall and travel past your opponent. A well-hit pass shot will force an opponent stationed in center court to retreat into the back court; such a shot may be an outright winner if he is near the front wall or moving forward.

Use the basic forehand or backhand stroke to hit a pass shot, meeting the ball between knee- and waist-high (the lower the better). Hit it hard enough so that your opponent is unable to cut off your shot at midcourt, but not so hard that the ball sets up off the back wall for an easy return.

You can aim your pass shot either down the wall or cross-court. (Fig. 4-D) A down-the-wall pass should strike the front wall about three feet up from the floor, and one to three feet from the side wall. Ideally, on its way back it will cling close to the side wall but not touch it. Down-the-wall passes are most often hit along the left side wall, to send the ball to your (right-handed) opponent's backhand.

The cross-court pass, or V ball, is easier to hit than the down-the-wall version and can be used to return almost any shot in the game. Aim is about three feet up from the floor, and a foot or so beyond the center of the front wall. The ball should die in the back corner. V balls are usually played from the right side of the court, to send the ball to your opponent's backhand.

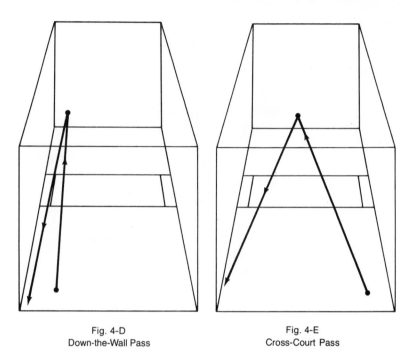

Fig. 4-D
Down-the-Wall Pass

Fig. 4-E
Cross-Court Pass

Kill shots. The kill is a hard-hit shot that strikes the front wall so low to the floor that the ball is either very difficult or else completely impossible to return. It is the ultimate offensive shot in racquetball. A perfect kill shot, called a *flat rollout,* hits the front wall so low that it doesn't come off the floor at all; it is absolutely irretrievable. However, it is also very difficult to execute; if you hit the ball *too* low, it will graze the floor before reaching the wall; this is called a skip ball and means that you've lost the point.

Kill shots are generally played from the front half of the court, when your opponent is behind you; the closer you are to the front wall, the easier it is to kill, or "shoot" the ball. Hitting a kill shot from the back court—usually done when an opponent's too-hard shot "sets up" off the back wall—is more difficult, but among good players it is a favorite point winner.

Kill shots can be played three different ways: directly to the front wall, angled off either side wall to the front wall, or angled off the front wall to either side wall. For all three types, it is important to let the ball drop as low as possible before striking it.

The straight kill, hit directly to the front wall, is the easiest to execute and the most commonly used. Contact the ball when it is no more than a foot off the floor, bending low to get down with it. Hit the ball hard, aiming three to six inches up from the floor. (Fig. 4-F)

Fig. 4-9   A Straight Kill

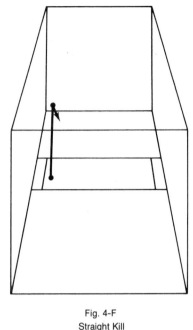

Fig. 4-F
Straight Kill

The side-wall–front-wall kill, or pinch shot, is hit into a side wall within three feet of the front corner, so that the ball rebounds off the front wall toward the opposite side wall. (Fig. 4-G) This shot should usually be hit fairly hard, though an occasional soft pinch shot is a good change of pace.

The front-wall–side-wall kill is seldom used because its last angle is toward the middle of the court; try it only when your opponent is seriously out of position or very deep in the back court. Send the ball cross-court low to the front wall, close to and angled toward the corner, so that it richochets low to the side wall and dies. (Fig. 4-H)

Ball off the back wall. Any time your opponent hits a shot too hard or so high that it rebounds off the back wall (a frequent occurrence in beginning and intermediate play), he has given you one of the game's ideal set-ups: the opportunity to end the rally with a pass shot or even a kill off a ball whose momentum is already forward. While the shot itself is not difficult, learning to gauge the ball's rebound off the back wall and to position yourself correctly requires practice.

Turn sideways and take your racquet back as usual, then move back toward the back wall, using a sideways slide step. Make sure you move back far enough; you want to be behind the ball after it caroms off the back wall, and the more slowly it is traveling, the less it will come out. On the other hand, you don't want the ball to crowd you, so avoid getting too

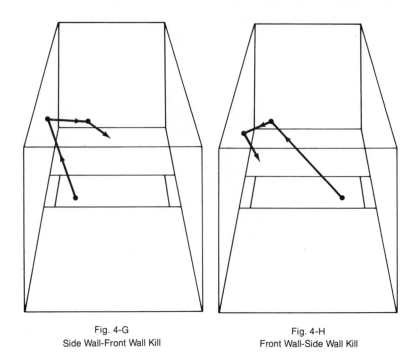

Fig. 4-G
Side Wall-Front Wall Kill

Fig. 4-H
Front Wall-Side Wall Kill

close to the back wall. When the ball comes off the wall, let it go by you. Shift your weight forward as you wait for it to drop to knee-height or lower; then meet it off your lead foot as usual. Drive or kill the ball straight to the front wall. Remember to follow through completely. (Fig. 4-14)

Volley. Use the volley to cut off your opponent's passes and other deep shots, to catch him out of position, or to quicken the pace of the game.

The stroke is the same one used for forehand or backhand ground strokes, but because taking the ball before it bounces gives you less time, the volley is a more difficult shot. Try to meet the ball when it is well in front of you and between knee- and waist-high. Make sure to tighten your grip on impact, because the ball will be traveling with greater force on the fly and you don't want the racquet to twist in your hand. Hit the most offensive shot possible, preferably a pass or a kill.

Drop shot. The drop shot is a difficult shot, one that requires great control and a light touch, especially with today's livelier ball. It is most often used to "dig out" your opponent's attempted kill shot, but it can be employed to good effect whenever you are near the front wall, and your opponent is deep in the back court.

The drop shot is always hit as a forehand. Drop your racquet low, take a long step toward the ball, and gently but firmly "dump" it low into one

Fig. 4-10 Player has plenty of time to wind up for an offensive forehand drive off the back wall.

Fig. 4-11 Player's drop shot will die off the front wall.

of the front corners, using either an underhand or a sidearm stroke. Keep your wrist firm, and take very little swing. (Fig. 4-15) The ball should die before your opponent can reach it.

Offensive overheads. Overhead drives and *overhead kills* can be extremely effective attacking shots, but because they are difficult to place accurately, most players use them very rarely, to surprise an opponent with a sudden change of pace. Both types of offensive overhead—the drive and the kill—are used when the ball is about to pass over your head. Both use the same overhead stroke as the more common overhead shot known as the ceiling ball, described in the next section.

The stroke is like an overhead throw or an abbreviated tennis serve. Take your racquet up and back behind your head, with your elbow bent and your wrist cocked, until the racquet head points almost straight down. As the ball approaches, swing up and forward, meeting it when it is above your head and a foot or so in front of you. Angle your racquet face downward to send the ball low. Follow through across your body to the left.

An overhead drive can be hit either cross-court or down the wall. Aim the ball about three feet up from the floor, and hit it hard enough to make it travel into the back court but softly enough to keep it from rebounding off the back wall, which would give your opponent an easy return.

An overhead kill is a more difficult shot, because there's less leeway for error. The ball must be aimed as low on the wall as possible; if it is even slightly mis-hit, it can easily strike the floor before the wall. Well hit, however, it can be an effective surprise during a ceiling ball rally. It is simple to disguise, because the strokes for both shots are the same, yet the overhead kill ends up in the front court instead of landing deep. Aim most overhead kills cross-court for a greater margin of safety, and into a side wall first to slow the ball's momentum.

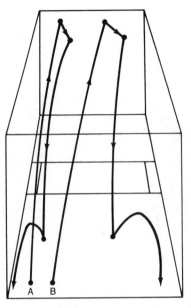

Fig. 4-I
Ceiling Ball—
Down-the-Wall and Cross-Court
A   B

**Fig. 4-12 Forehand Ceiling Ball:
1. Player waits for the ball with her
racquet back behind her head. Her
wrist is cocked and her elbow bent.**

**DEFENSIVE
SHOTS** Play one of the defensive shots—*ceiling ball, Z ball, around-the-wall ball,*
or *lob*—when you are out of position or off balance and thus prevented
from hitting an offensive shot. Any one of these slow, controlled shots will
enable you to gain time and a better court position; at the same time it
will force your opponent into the back court, where he will have to hit
defensively in return.

Ceiling ball. The ceiling ball, which first hits the ceiling a few feet from
the front wall, rebounds off the front wall, takes a high bounce around
midcourt, and then dies near the back corner, is racquetball's
bread-and-butter defensive shot. (Fig. 4-I) It can and should be used
whenever the ball is traveling over your head and you are unable to let it
drop low enough to drive it. Ceiling balls are almost always played from
the back court, and usually to your opponent's weaker, backhand side.
Your opponent will be presented with a ball that is at least shoulder high
in deep back court, which he will be forced to return defensively—
probably with another ceiling ball. In fact, long ceiling ball rallies,
with each player waiting for the other to make an error, by hitting, for
instance, a shallow ceiling ball or one that sets up off the side or back
wall, are very common in racquetball.

The forehand ceiling ball is hit like the offensive overheads. Take your

2. She makes contact above and in front of her. Her racquet face is open to send the ball up to the ceiling.

3. She follows through over her left shoulder.

racquet back behind your head, wrist cocked and elbow bent, and swing upward to meet the ball when it is above and in front of your body. To direct the ball to the ceiling, keep the racquet face open. Snap your wrist for extra power. Hit the ball hard enough to send it deep into the court, but not so hard that it pops off the back wall. Follow through down and across your body to the left. (Figs. 4-16–18)

If the ball is head high or lower, use more of a sidearm stroke, directing the ball to the ceiling by opening your racquet face and swinging upward.

Ceiling balls can be hit either down the wall or cross-court. The down-the-wall shot is more effective—almost impossible to cut off—but it is also more difficult to execute. Ideally, the ball hugs the side wall but never touches it—a "wallpaper ball." The cross-court ceiling ball is safer and easier. Aim it near the center, again, a few feet from the front wall.

The backhand ceiling ball is by far the more common shot, as players usually direct their ceiling balls to each other's backhands. To hit a backhand ceiling ball, you use the basic backhand stroke, but open the face of your racquet and take it back higher. Swing at an upward angle, and make contact with the ball when it is between waist- and head-high. Keep your wrist firm when hitting the ball above head level. (Fig. 4-19)

115

Fig. 4-13 The stroke for a backhand ceiling ball is essentially a high backhand.

Z-ball. For intermediate players, both the Z-ball and the around-the-wall ball can be useful occasional alternatives to the ceiling ball. In top-class racquetball, however, these shots are seldom played, because advanced players can generally return them offensively.

The Z-ball is hit cross-court to the front wall near the far corner and the ceiling. It rebounds quickly to the side wall, travels cross-court in a high arc to the rear of the opposite side wall, then, due to its reverse spin, travels almost parallel to the back wall—a back wall "wallpaper ball." (Fig. 4-J) It is usually played from around midcourt. The closer you are to one of the side walls, the easier it is to execute the shot. Use the same forehand or backhand stroke described in the section on pass shots, but meet the ball about waist high. Hit it hard to the front wall, aiming about three feet down from the ceiling and three feet from the far side wall. It should usually be played to your opponent's backhand.

Around-the-wall ball. Like the Z-ball, the around-the-wall ball (AWB) is hit high and hard cross-court, but in this case the ball is sent to the far side wall, near the corner and close to the ceiling. It then bounces off the front wall, goes cross-court to hit the other side wall at about midcourt, drops sharply to the floor at around three-quarters court with an eccentric spin, then dies against the back wall. (Fig. 4-K) Using the same stroke as for a Z-ball, aim about three feet down from the ceiling and three feet

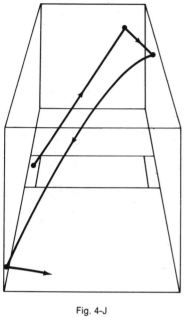

Fig. 4-J
Z-Ball

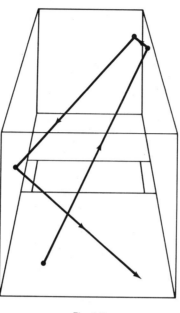

Fig. 4-K
Around-the-Wall Ball

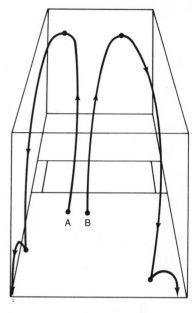

Fig. 4-L
Lob-Down-the-Wall and Cross-Court
A   B

from the front corner. Follow through high. The AWB is a somewhat easier shot to execute than the Z-ball, and it can be played from a deeper position on the court. Like the Z-ball, it is usually played to the opponent's backhand.

Lob. The lob, which is hit high and softly to the front wall, takes a high bounce around midcourt and then dies near the back wall. (Fig. 4-L) It used to be the most common defensive shot in racquetball. Even now, if it is hit well, it is an extremely effective shot—one that gives you ample time to regain a stronger position while forcing your opponent out of the center. But with today's livelier ball, it has become difficult to avoid overhitting the lob, and the shot has been largely replaced by the ceiling ball. Now it is used mainly in desperate situations—for instance, when you are forced way back in the court and have to struggle just to stay in the point—and as an occasional return of serve.

Use the basic forehand or backhand stroke to lob. Swing gently but firmly, opening your racquet face slightly to send the ball high; aim about three-quarters of the way up on the front wall. Lean your weight into your shot, then follow through in the direction of the ball's flight.

You can aim you lob either cross-court or down the wall. In either case, it is important that the ball not even so much as graze the side wall, at least not until it has reached the rear of the court, so that you don't give your opponent an easy shot.

Fig. 4-14 Garbage Serve:
1. Facing the right side wall with her racquet back, player drops the ball in front of her.

2. She makes contact about waist-high . . .

3. . . . and follows through above her left shoulder. *Note: The same motion is used for the high* Z *serve.*

Ball into the back wall. This is a desperation shot to be played only when your opponent's shot has gone past you without enough momentum to rebound off the back wall, giving you no other alternative. In this situation, your only option is to slam the ball into the back wall in the hope that it will reach the front wall on the fly. Swing upward, aiming about five feet up from the floor, then get out of the way so that the ball doesn't hit you or your racquet when it caroms off the back wall. This shot won't win you any points, and it may give your opponent a midcourt set-up that he can kill on the fly, but there will be times when it is your only hope for keeping the rally alive.

SERVE Even though an ace is something of a rarity in racquetball, the serve is the most important offensive shot in the game. The server, of course, is the only one who can score points, and he controls not only the shot itself but also the all-important center-court position. Moreover, through his choice of one of the five basic serves, the server can dictate the tempo of play. If he chooses, say, a drive or a low Z serve, both of which are hit low and hard, he will probably be setting the stage for a short, fast rally; if on the other hand he hits a "garbage," a high Z, or a lob serve, which are all

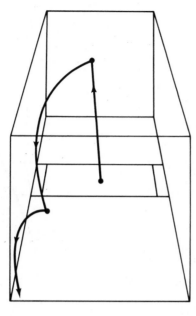

Fig. 4-M
Garbage Serve

high and soft, he will most likely be initiating a ceiling ball rally.

A good server knows the value of variety. Mix up your serves—not only the type but the pace and placement as well—so that the receiver can't plan his return. Direct most of your serves deep to his backhand—his weaker stroke—serving to his forehand occasionally only for the sake of surprise.

To begin any serve, face the right side wall, racquet back, feet comfortably spaced. You should almost always serve from the center of the service zone, give or take a few steps. This will keep the receiver guessing and also automatically put you in control of center court.

The "garbage," or half-lob, serve is one of the most popular, because it is easy to execute and extremely effective. It is a soft serve that *looks* simple to put away, but in fact it isn't at all; that's what makes it so effective. To hit it, drop the ball so that it rebounds between waist- and chest-high, then meet is softly at the peak of the bounce, keeping your wrist firm. (Fig. 4-20) Aim about halfway up on the front wall, a foot or so past the center. The ball should come off the front wall softly, hit the floor a few feet behind the short line, then take a shoulder-high bounce—forcing your opponent to play a ceiling ball or some other

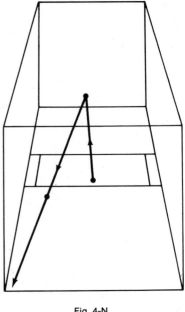

Fig. 4-N
Drive Serve

defensive return—before dying at the base of the back wall near a corner. (Fig. 4-M) Just make sure the ball doesn't touch the side wall, at least not until it has reached the rear of the court; otherwise it could pop out and give the receiver an easy setup.

The drive serve is hit low and hard to the front wall and lands deep in the back court. (Fig. 4-N) It requires more precision than the garbage serve, but when it is well hit, it is the most effective serve of all; it can even be an ace, especially against a receiver who is slow on his feet or tired. For the drive serve, stand toward the rear of the service zone so that you can step into the ball as you swing. Drop the ball softly in front of you, bending low to get down with it, and contact it off your lead foot when it is knee high or lower. (Fig 4-21) Hit with about 80 percent power. Aim no more than three feet up from the floor, and about a foot past the center. The ball should bounce just beyond the short line, then shoot low into the back corner.

Both the low and high Z serves hit the front wall near a corner, rebound off the side wall and travel cross-court before bouncing on the floor and hitting the opposite side wall. When directed to your opponent's backhand they are known as reverse Z serves and are particularly effective.

Fig. 4-15 Drive Serve: 1. Facing the side wall, player drops the ball in front of him and begins to wind up.

2. Bending his knees to get down with the ball, he leads the stroke with his elbow.

3. Impact is low and in front of him.

4. He stays low for the follow-through, letting his weight continue to come forward. *Note: The same motion is used for the low* Z *serve.*

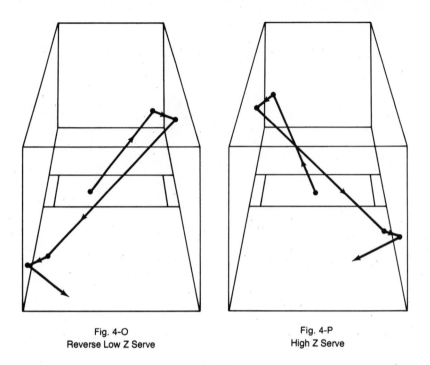

Fig. 4-O
Reverse Low Z Serve

Fig. 4-P
High Z Serve

Although the low Z can be executed from the center of the service zone, it is easier if you stand slightly off center. Drop the ball gently in front of you, as for a drive serve, and hit it with the same stroke when it is knee high or lower. Aim about three feet up from the floor and a foot from the far side wall. The ball should carom quickly off the front wall, ricochet into the side wall, come back cross-court (move out of its way!), hit the floor about five feet beyond the short line, rebound off the other side wall one to four feet from the back wall, then spin crazily toward the receiver's backhand. (Fig. 4-O) (Never hit the low Z serve to his forehand, because he could probably return it offensively with his stronger stroke.)

The high Z serve is both safer and easier. It can be played to the receiver's forehand almost as effectively as to his backhand because on either side, it will force a defensive return. Stand in the center of the service zone to hit it. Drop the ball so that it comes up between waist- and chest-high, and use about half your power, aiming approximately six feet up from the floor and one foot from the far side wall. The ball will take the same path as the low Z, but higher in the air. (Fig. 4-P)

The lob serve is hit high to the front wall, brushes against the side wall, bounces deep in the back court, then dies near the back wall. (Fig. 4-Q) It

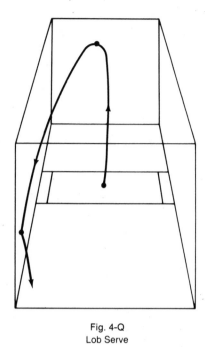

Fig. 4-Q
Lob Serve

is used less often than the others because, like the lob itself, it is difficult to hit accurately. When well hit, however, it is an effective serve, because it presents the receiver with a very deep ball that is practically impossible to return offensively. To execute a lob serve, drop the ball so that it rebounds to about chest height, and hit it softly, using the same stiff-wristed action as for the garbage serve. Swing upward, keeping the face of your racquet open. Aim about three-quarters of the way up on the front wall and one to two feet beyond the center. The ball should arc back slowly, graze the rear side wall high up, then drop into the back corner. Make sure you aim off center and high enough for the ball to graze the side wall on its way back; otherwise it will bounce off the back wall and give your opponent an easy setup. Almost always direct your lob serves to his backhand side.

RETURN OF SERVE As the receiver, you are definitely on the defensive, positioned in deep back court, with the server occupying the center. Unless his serve is very poor and allows you to drive or kill it, your main objectives when returning serve are to keep the ball in play and to draw the server out of center court so that you can assume control of that vital position. This means that most of the time your return should be one of the defensive shots.

Wait for the serve facing the front wall in good ready position, about an arm and racquet's length from the back wall and slightly left of center, because the server will probably direct most of his serves to your backhand. Don't hug the left side wall; that would just be inviting him to send a low, hard drive serve down the right side wall for a probable ace.

Whenever possible, volley the return of serve. This will give the server less time to prepare for his next shot, and keep you from being crowded against the side or back wall.

The safest and most commonly used return is the ceiling ball. In effect, this shot will neutralize the server's advantage by forcing him to retreat and make a defensive reply from the back court, while giving you the opportunity to reach center court. Direct most of your ceiling ball returns to the server's backhand corner to draw a weaker response.

You can use the around-the-wall ball, the lob, and the Z-ball as occasional alternatives to the ceiling ball return when your opponent's serve is soft. Since these are lower-percentage shots than the ceiling ball, use them sparingly, just often enough to keep the server guessing.

Use the more offensive pass or kill shot return whenever your opponent gives you the opportunity, for example when his serve comes off the side wall around midcourt, or off the back wall with enough force for you to set up and take a full swing. You can hit your pass return either down the wall or cross-court; the down-the-wall shot is easier and less risky. Hit the kill return hard and directly to the front wall, near the nearest front corner.

SINGLES TACTICS The command position in racquetball—the best place to hit winning shots—is the middle of the court, a few steps behind the short line. (Fig. 4-R) In center-court position, not only do you have the greatest choice of shots, but you are also almost equidistant from all corners of the court and thus least vulnerable to being beaten by your opponent's shot.

Try, therefore, to move back to the center after every shot, so that you are in control of the rally. Equally as important as returning to the center is *not* hitting the ball *through* it. Keep your shots in the corners and near the walls of the court; otherwise, in addition to giving your opponent a setup, you will be forced to relinquish the center, because if you interfere with your opponent's ability to see or play the ball, he may call a hinder.

The simplest way to gain control of center court is by winning the previous rally, which will earn you the right to serve and, thus, start the

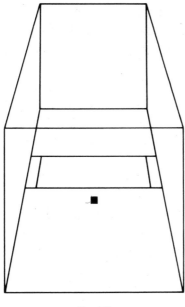

Fig. 4-R
Center-Court

point in the center. Being the server also has the advantage of allowing you to play more aggressively and take more risks than the receiver, because only the server can score points.

Immediately after serving, move back a few steps to the center-court position behind the short line, which will put you in the best spot to cover your opponent's return.

Always hit the most offensive shot of which you are capable. Generally speaking, the better the player, the farther back in the court from which he can score; top players, for instance, are able to hit kill shots from almost anywhere on the court.

A good thumb rule for average players, however, is to play a defensive game from the back court—try to force your opponent out of the center, or simply prevent him from scoring, primarily by hitting ceiling balls and other defensive shots. Attempting to end the point with a floor-skimming kill shot when your opponent is in possession of the center is a low-percentage proposition that can easily backfire by setting up the ball for him to rekill. Instead, play a patient, steady game when you are deep in the court; wait for your opponent to make the errors.

With good front or center-court position, you can and should play offensively. Try to win the point outright with a pass or kill shot, or create a setup for your next shot. Play aggressively: move in to cut off your opponent's pass shots, and rekill his kill shot attempts; put the ball out of his reach; hit where he isn't.

Variety is a key tactic in racquetball, as in all the racquet sports. While you should concentrate mainly on your opponent's weaker side, hit to both sides of the court and mix up your shots in order to keep him guessing and on the run and to force him to hit from awkward, off-balance positions.

Conversely, try not to let your opponent fool you. Watch for telltale habits that enable you to predict when he is about to make a certain shot—nearly every player has them. Also try to get a sense of what shot he is likely to call upon in a given situation. The better your anticipation, the less often you'll be caught off balance.

DOUBLES TACTICS

Racquetball doubles is a wonderful game for older and less athletic players who don't have the stamina necessary for singles—but it's also popular with a good many excellent younger players who appreciate its more subtle logistics. (Of course, it's also a hit at clubs that don't have enough courts to go around, and with players who prefer to divide up court costs four ways!) What doubles players quickly discover is that while the format requires less physical exertion than singles, it demands considerably more mental effort. In addition, with four enthusiastic, determined racquet wielders charging around in a confined space, doubles is potentially chaotic and even hazardous. To play safe, enjoyable doubles you need to develop a sixth sense for when to duck or get out of the way; you should also become familiar with certain court-coverage techniques and tactics that are unique to the doubles game.

There are two basic formations in doubles: side-by-side and front-and-back. Side-by-side is the simplest and most widely used, by both novices and advanced players. In this arrangement, one player covers the left half of the court and the other covers the right. (Fig. 4-S) If you and your partner are both right-handed, the player whose backhand is stronger should play the left side and also take the shots that go down the middle; thus, the player on the right rarely has to hit backhands. When the team consists of a right-handed and a left-handed player, the left-handed player should play the left side, so that both side walls, which are the main "passing lanes," are covered by the players' forehands; the partner with the better backhand should take the shots that go down the middle.

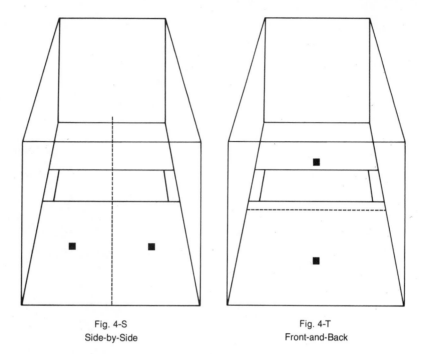

Fig. 4-S
Side-by-Side

Fig. 4-T
Front-and-Back

In front-and-back, or the I formation, one player covers the court in front of the short line and his partner covers the back court. (Fig. 4-T) This arrangement is most suitable when the two partners have certain complementary assets: the player in the back court should be particularly adept at hitting ceiling balls and kill shots from deep court, and the front court player should be especially quick and aggressive, and a good kill shot retriever. Incidentally, it should be pointed out that in both formations, these "divisions of labor" are not meant to be rigid. If the ball comes to your partner's territory and he is out of position, naturally you should take the shot if you possibly can.

As you are not obligated to alternate serves between your opponents in doubles, it makes sense to direct most of your serves to the weaker of the two. All of the serves described for the singles game are fine for doubles as well, with one exception: avoid hitting low drive serves into the back corner behind your partner, because there's a strong possibility that he'd be hit by the receiver's most logical return—a down-the-wall pass.

As the receiver, volley the return if possible, just as in singles, so that your team is not forced way out of position, and also to give your opponents less time to get set for their next shot. Volleying the return is more easily done in doubles, with each receiver covering only half the court.

Fig. 4-16

As in singles, holding center-court position is the key to control. In order to keep the game safe and orderly, many experienced players abide by the tacit rule of center-court exchange, which states that the team that has just hit the ball is entitled to occupy the center. Throughout the rally, then, the two teams are constantly exchanging positions.

Also as in singles, you should direct most shots to your opponents' backhands. If both opposing players are right-handed, an extremely effective shot is a cross-court pass from the right, which the left-side player will be forced to take with his backhand. Against a lefty-righty team, shots hit down the middle will be to the backhands of both players, and also just might cause confusion between them as to who should take the shot.

When you're playing to win, it makes sense to hit mainly to the weaker opponent. Not only will you elicit weak returns, but the hapless fellow's partner will be forced to look on uselessly while his wearying teammate keeps making errors. Eventually the better player may get so fed up that he begins to poach in his teammate's territory, leaving his own area unprotected. And when you finally do hit an occasional shot his way, chances are he will be "cold." It's worth noting, however, that in social doubles, isolating the weaker partner is not likely to make for the most amiable atmosphere.

The crowded court makes good communication between partners essential. You and your teammate should decide in advance, of course, which formation you're going to use to cover the court, as well as who will be taking confusing shots, such as those down the middle. A call system during the game is useful for the inevitable ambiguous situations. Be brief and precise: "Yours!" "Mine!" "Switch!"—and try not to wait until the last moment to make your call.

Always be aware of your partner's position, and be prepared to cover for him if necessary—by switching places temporarily, by retrieving balls that he swings at and misses (perfectly legal), and by hitting a ceiling ball or a lob to give him time to retreat if he is caught near the front wall.

Finally, give your partner plenty of encouragement. Keeping up the morale and confidence of your team can be difficult sometimes, especially when you're losing, but it will definitely add to your enjoyment of the game, and probably to the quality of your play as well.

RACQUETBALL CHECKLIST

1. Keep your eyes on the ball at all times, but never face your opponent directly—you could get hurt.
2. Move back to the center of the court after every shot.
3. Stay on the balls of your feet between shots so that you can get a quick start.
4. Take your racquet back as soon as you know to which side your opponent is hitting.
5. Always try to be parallel to the ball's line of flight when you make your shot.
6. Keep your knees bent so that you can meet the ball when it has dropped low—knee high to hit pass shots, ankle high to hit kills.
7. Direct most shots to your opponent's backhand, usually the weaker stroke.
8. Develop enough accuracy to keep your shots from setting up off the back or side wall.

Fig. 5-1

PADDLE TENNIS

ABOUT PADDLE TENNIS In 1898, fifteen-year-old Frank Peer Beal of Albion, Michigan, barred from the tennis courts at Albion College where his older brother played, decided to create a substitute game in his own backyard. He halved the dimensions of a tennis court to 39 feet by 18 feet, fashioned a net from some leftover chicken wire, and devised a game played with short-handled, homemade wooden paddles, a sponge rubber ball, and tennis rules. It was a kind of miniature tennis.

When young Beal grew up he became associate minister of the Judson Memorial Church in Greenwich Village in New York City. He remembered his game and laid out some paddle tennis courts in the church gymnasium for the neighborhood youngsters. In 1921, when he was also recreation chairman of the Community Councils of New York, he persuaded the Department of Parks and Recreation to build a number of courts around the fountain in nearby Washington Square. The kids took to the game quickly, and the first citywide tournament was held there the following year. In 1923 the American Paddle Tennis Association was formed—the name was changed to United States Paddle Tennis Association in 1926—with Beal as its first president, an office he held until his death in 1965.

Ironically, it was during the Depression that the fortunes of paddle tennis received their greatest boost, when thousands of public playgrounds were built in the nation's cities as part of Franklin Delano Roosevelt's Works Progress Administration. Paddle tennis courts were often included in these playgrounds, particularly in New York City and Los Angeles. The game was chosen partly because of the court's small size: four could fit in the space that would have been required, for example, for just one tennis court. About eight thousand courts were built during the late 1920s and early 1930s, and there were about a million players nationwide. New York City alone had more than a thousand courts, not only in playgrounds but also painted on streets and on the cement bottoms of the city's immense municipal swimming pools, for use during the fall and winter.

The sport was generally viewed as a children's game, a steppingstone to tennis. In fact Bobby Riggs, tennis star of the late 1930s and early 1940s, was boy's paddle tennis champion of Los Angeles in 1930–32. Tennis greats Richard "Pancho" Gonzales and Althea Gibson also got started with paddle tennis—Gibson was New York City women's champion in 1939 at the age of twelve.

For a time there were two different versions of paddle tennis: one played by children on the original court and another (the brainchild of one man, Murray Geller) played by adults on a larger court with revised rules. Eventually the smaller courts were abandoned. There are currently two other slightly different versions of the game, one played in New York and the other in California. Both are played on the same size court—20 feet by 50 feet—but with slightly different court lines and rules. The two are similar enough to enable players from the East to participate in West Coast tournaments and vice versa.

GOVERNING BODIES United States Paddle Tennis Association
189 Seeley Street
Brooklyn, NY 11218

Official magazine: *Paddle World*

American Paddle Tennis League
259 McCarty Drive
Beverly Hills, CA 90212

Quarterly newsletter

COURT The 20-by-50-foot paddle tennis court is set up much like a tennis court (see diagram), except that there are no doubles alleys; the same size court is used for both singles and doubles. The net is 31 inches high when supported by a steel cable; if there is no cable, one inch of sag is allowed

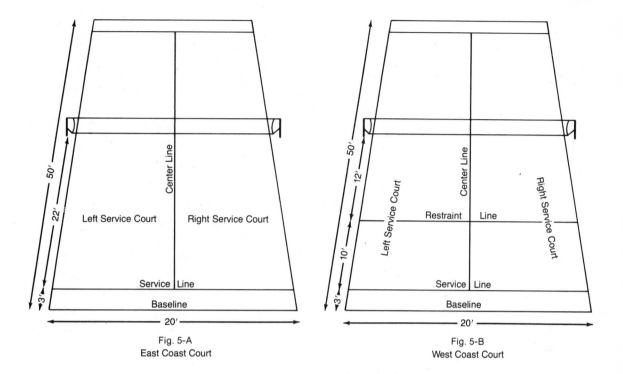

Fig. 5-A
East Coast Court

Fig. 5-B
West Coast Court

at the center. There should be at least 15 feet of unobstructed backspace behind each baseline and 10 feet of sidespace outside each sideline. (Fig. 5-A)

On the West Coast, only 10 feet of backspace and 7½ feet of sidespace are required. California courts also have bucket, or restraint, lines, parallel to the net, 12 feet from it on either side (see p. 136 for the bucket rule). (Fig. 5-B)

Courts may be built of any material suitable for tennis courts. Because paddle tennis is largely an outdoor, all-weather sport, low-maintenance surfaces, such as cement and asphalt, are the most appropriate in areas with cold winters.

PADDLE A paddle tennis paddle has a short handle and an oval face. Under United States Paddle Tennis Association regulations, it may be no more than 17½ inches long and 8½ inches wide and may have either a perforated or a solid face. No extraneous materials may be applied to the face, and no strung racquets are permitted.

American Paddle Tennis League rules call for a paddle of the same

Fig. 5-2

dimensions, with the additional requirement that it weigh no more than 18 ounces. It may be textured.

Paddle specifications are almost identical to those for platform tennis, and the same paddles can be used for both sports. There are also paddles made specifically for paddle tennis; these are slightly lighter and more flexible.

Paddles are available in aluminum and fiberglass as well as in wood, and perforations are optional, but most experienced players prefer the "bite" and "hit" of perforated wood paddles.

BALL The rules call for a "deadened" tennis ball. Before play, a USTA-approved, pressurized ball is punctured with a hypodermic needle (which requires a prescription) or a safety pin to reduce its internal pressure so that when it is dropped from a height of 6 feet onto the court

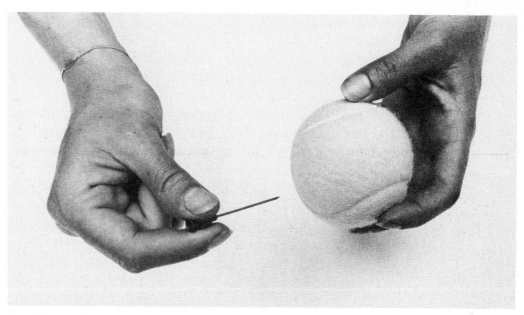

Fig. 5-3 Paddle tennis is played with a punctured tennis ball that should bounce six to eight inches lower than a regular tennis ball.

surface it bounces between 31 and 33 inches (6–8 inches lower than a regular tennis ball).

Only one ball is used per set. Most players prefer heavy-duty balls, because they stand up better on the hard courts. A ball generally lasts a set for good players, somewhat longer for beginners.

DRESS Though players usually wear tennis clothes in tournaments, there are no requirements regarding attire, and for casual play dress is typically more informal than for tennis. In cold weather, a warm-up suit, a sweat suit, or a sweater and slacks that keep you warm but leave you unencumbered are advisable. Good tennis shoes are a must, as most courts have hard surfaces.

METHOD OF PLAY Paddle tennis rules are essentially the same as tennis rules. The exceptions, and the differences between the East and West Coast versions, will be noted below. When Easterners play in West Coast tournaments, they play with West Coast rules, and vice versa. (See pp. 239–240 for complete rules.)

Scoring is as in tennis: both players start with a score of 0, called "love." The first point is 15, the second is 30, the third is 40, and the fourth is game. If the score reaches 40 all it is called "deuce," and then one player is called "advantage." The team that wins six games by a margin of two games wins the set. A 12-point tiebreaker is played when the score reaches six games all. Tournament matches are usually two out of three sets, although sometimes three out of five are played in the finals.

Only one serve is allowed for each point, and it must be delivered with an underhand stroke. (Otherwise the server's advantage would be enormous on the small court.) If the serve is a fault, the server loses the point. Lets are replayed, as in tennis.

Before beginning to serve, the server must stand with both feet at rest behind the baseline and within imaginary extensions of the center and side lines. He may take one step with either foot, and also begin a follow-through step before contacting the ball. However, he may not complete his follow-through step, nor may he step on or inside the baseline, until he has struck the ball. As in tennis, he serves for the first point from behind the baseline on the right-hand (deuce) side into the service court diagonally opposite, and for the second point from the left-hand (ad) side, alternating for each point until the game ends.

There are two acceptable methods of serving. The server may either bounce the ball on the court and hit it on the rebound, or he may project it into the air and hit it on the fly. Whichever technique he chooses, he must contact the ball when it is no higher than 31 inches above the court surface. He must use the same method for an entire set; if he wishes he may switch to the other at the start of a new set.

The receiver must let the ball bounce in the correct service court before hitting it back over the net. The point continues until one player hits the ball into the net or out of bounds, or fails to hit it at all before it has bounced twice and is out of play.

In West Coast *doubles* only, the return of serve is governed by the bucket rule, designed to limit the serving team's advantage: both feet of all four players must remain behind the restraint line, which is 12 feet from the net, until the receiver's paddle has contacted the ball—although the receiver himself may cross the restraint line to return a shallow serve. A violation of the bucket rule results in the loss of a point. If both sides bucket, the point is replayed.

In both the East and West Coast versions of *singles,* the shot following the return of serve is governed by the one-bounce rule, devised to keep the server from rushing the net following his serve. The server, like the receiver, must let the ball bounce once on his side of the net before he may volley. In other words, he may not volley his opponent's return of serve.

There is one association of players in southern California—the American Paddle Tennis League—that plays with slightly different rules. Under APTL regulations, only the one-bounce serve is allowed and the served ball may rise no higher than ten feet above the court surface.

SHOTS AND TACTICS Paddle tennis calls for the same strokes, shots, and tactics as tennis, but because of the small court, there is a greater emphasis on net play. The strokes and shots mentioned in the following discussion of doubles and singles tactics are covered more fully in the tennis chapter, pp. 37–63.

DOUBLES As doubles is by far the more popular form of the game, it will be considered first.

Serve. In doubles, the serving team has the decided offensive advantage, and winning the serve is crucial. In fact, in advanced play, one service break normally decides the set.

The regulation underhand serve may be hit with either a sidearm stroke or a true underhand stroke, as long as the ball is met no higher than 31 inches above the court surface. The sidearm stroke is like a tennis forehand: face the right sideline and contact the ball slightly in front of your body. (Fig. 5-4) The underhand stroke is the same except that you begin with the paddle head pointing downward. Most players put slice on their serves. This is done by contacting the ball on its lower outside edge, in order to make it curve away from the receiver's body on his forehand side, or into his body on the backhand side.

To keep the receiver back, aim your serve as deep in the service court as possible; as the service line is only three feet from the baseline, this can be very deep indeed. In general, your serve should force your opponent to hit the return he likes least, which for most players is a backhand. You can also send your serve deep down the middle once in a while for the sake of surprise. Though a shallow serve will often lose you the point almost immediately, occasionally a *very* shallow serve—just dinked over the net—can be extremely effective against an unsuspecting, slow, or tired receiver.

Fig. 5-4 The serve in paddle tennis is hit with an underhand stroke. Note the paddle face, angled for slice.

Fig. 5-5 The basic tactic of paddle tennis is to get to the net and hit a volley . . .

Return of serve. In the East Coast version of paddle tennis, both the receiver and his partner should begin the point standing behind the baseline. On the West Coast, the bucket rule makes it more effective for the receiver's partner to take a position just behind the bucket line, in order to give his team a better chance of taking command of the net.

The receiver's main objective is to keep the ball in play. Generally direct the return of serve away from the net player by driving it at the incoming server; but vary it occasionally by aiming your drive right at the net player, if he is not expecting a return sent his way, or by lobbing it over his head.

General doubles tactics. Paddle tennis doubles is characterized by long exchanges that include many lobs and overheads, with plenty of opportunities to run down balls whose angles take them as much as fifteen or twenty feet off the court. As in tennis, the basic tactic is to get to the net as quickly as possible. The team at the net tries to end the point with volleys (shots taken on the fly) and overheads (shots hit when the ball is above the head). The opposing team, back on the baseline, drives (forehand and backhand groundstrokes) and loles (shots hit softly and high over an opponent's head). (Fig. 5-5)

If you are an advanced or even an intermediate player, you should

Fig. 5-6 . . . or an overhead.

Fig. 5-7 Taking the net: Here the defensive team has rushed the net, forcing their opponents back to the midcourt area.

always follow your serve to the net in doubles, joining your partner, who begins the point there. Beginners and older, slowed-down players might prefer to play one up at the net and one back on the baseline to cover the lobs. But even if you use this formation, the player who is back should come in at the earliest opportunity—usually when an opponent hits a short shot.

The team on the offensive at the net should direct its volleys either deep up the middle or right at an opponent's feet, and its overheads either to an opponent's backhand or up the middle. Overheads should always be taken on the fly in doubles, because letting an opponent's lob bounce first would give the opposing team time to come in and take control of the point. (Fig. 5-7)

The team on the baseline is on the defensive and should concentrate on playing a steady game, because the longer the point continues, the more the odds shift in their favor. From the back court, the objective is to force the serving team to retreat to the baseline. This is accomplished mainly by hitting deep lobs over their heads. Because the paddle tennis court is only twenty feet wide, and there are two players to spread out and cover it, it is much harder for the team in the back court to pass the team at the net with drives than it is in tennis.

But also because of the small court, overheads are much easier to return

Fig. 5-8 Poaching: Player moves across
suddenly to cut off a ball hit to his partner. A
surprise offensive maneuver.

than in tennis, and there are often five or six lob-overhead exchanges in
one point. These points usually end when the team at the net either puts
the ball away, misses an overhead completely, or hits a weak one that can
be directed at the hitter's feet before he gets back to the net. If he is able
to return this shot at all, he will probably pop it up in the air, allowing his
opponent to volley it away.

SINGLES In singles, the one-bounce rule, which requires the server to stay back and
return his opponent's return of serve with a groundstroke, gives the
receiver the offensive advantage, because he is permitted to come to the
net following his return. In fact, in advanced play, where the server is
almost always "broken"—loses his serve—holding serve is considered a
break and can be the decisive factor in the set. Even at the intermediate
level it is not nearly as difficult to break your opponent's serve as it is, for
example, in tennis.

As in doubles, slice your serve if possible, aim it deep in your
opponent's service court, and serve mainly to his weakness—probably his
backhand—varying this with an occasional surprise serve down the middle.

In advanced play, the receiver should try to hit a return that allows him to
follow his shot to the net, unless the serve is hit so hard and deep that it
forces him to stay back. The two most effective returns are drives hit deep

Fig. 5-9 A classic paddle tennis situation:
The team in the back court, on the defensive,
lobs; their opponents at the net are prepared
to volley or hit an overhead.

to the server's backhand—generally his weaker stroke—and drives up the middle, which will prevent the server from hitting his next shot at enough of an angle to pass the incoming receiver.

In intermediate play, the receiver may prefer to stay back on his return. Then both players hit groundstrokes from the baseline, each waiting for the other to hit a short ball which can be returned to the opponent's weakness and followed to the net. From there the next shot can be volleyed away.

The player who is on the defensive on the baseline should try to pass the net player with either passing shots or lobs. Lobbing is a more risky tactic in singles than in doubles, because if the lob isn't high enough, the resulting overhead smash will be extremely difficult to return without a partner to help cover the court.

PADDLE TENNIS CHECKLIST

1. Always keep your eyes on the ball.
2. Whenever possible, seize the offensive by coming to the net.
3. Aim your serve as deep in the service court as possible.
4. Vary your serves, returns, and other shots to keep your opponent(s) guessing.
5. Be prepared to run. Good players are able to return a high percentage of their opponents' shots.

Fig. 6-1

PLATFORM TENNIS

ABOUT PLATFORM TENNIS

It was the late fall of 1928 in Scarsdale, N.Y. The tennis season was drawing to a close, and Fessenden S. Blanchard and James K. Cogswell—friends, neighbors, and avid tennis players—were trying to think of an active outdoor sport that would see them through the winter. They decided to build an elevated court on a rocky corner of Cogswell's estate, figuring they'd use it for badminton, deck tennis, and volleyball. But it was the game of paddle tennis, at that time primarily a New York City children's playground game, that proved to be best-suited for Cogswell's court.

The only problem was the necessity of chasing after the ball every time it bounced or rolled off the elevated court. The two men's solution was to enclose the area with an eight-foot-high chicken wire fence—which set the stage for the creation of a completely new game. As the story has it, one day during a doubles match a hard-hit ball bounced on Blanchard's side of the court and lodged in the back wires. In a moment of inspired improvisation, he raced out of the court and around to the back of the fence crying "It's still in play!" whereupon he gave a mighty swat that sent the stuck ball sailing back over the net. While his partner fended off the opposition, Blanchard scrambled back into the court, and the rally continued. No one seems to remember who won that historic point, but Blanchard's high-spirited competitiveness gave platform tennis its most distinctive feature—the use of the screens as a playing surface—though nowadays they have smaller openings so that the ball can't get stuck in them.

The new sport (which was then called paddle tennis, even though the screens made it quite a different game from its namesake) caught on rapidly in the Scarsdale area. The Fox Meadow Tennis Club, the oldest tennis club in Westchester County, put up a court and hosted the first formal tournament; the national championships are still held there every March. Soon neighboring country clubs were also putting up courts, attracted in those harsh economic times by the game's ability to bring in revenue during the winter.

The American Paddle Tennis Association was founded in 1934 to oversee the new game's development. In 1950 the organization changed its name to the American Platform Tennis Association in an attempt to clear up the confusion that existed between the newer game and its predecessor.

The first national championships, in 1935, included singles, doubles, and mixed doubles events. Singles was dropped after three years because the players felt that it wasn't a viable form; whoever got to the net invariably had an overwhelming advantage. Singles has always been played in California, however, and recently the A.P.T.L. officially approved the form.

GOVERNING BODY American Platform Tennis Association
52 Upper Montclair Plaza
Upper Montclair, NJ 07043

Official magazine: *Platform Tennis*

COURT A platform tennis court is a rectangle 44 feet long and 20 feet wide, within a playing area of 60 feet by 30 feet. It is laid out like a miniature tennis court. The net which divides it across the middle is 34 inches high at the center and 37 inches high at the ends.

The 12-foot-high screens completely surrounding the court are made of taut, one-inch hexagonal galvanized steel wire mesh—chicken wire—supported by a wooden or metal superstructure. The back screens are 8 feet behind the baselines; the side screens are 5 feet out from the sidelines. The space between the court lines and the screens are part of the playing area, but they are not part of the court itself. (Fig. 6-A)

The traditional court is elevated on concrete piers, and the deck is roughened with chemicals or an abrasive material such as sand, steel

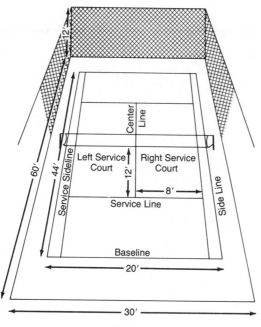

Fig. 6-A
Platform Tennis Court

aggregate, or crushed walnut shells to provide extra traction. Hinged flaps running around the perimeter of the court, just above the deck, are usually installed for easy maintenance; they are called snow boards in the North and leaf gates in the South. In the North the deck is often heated to melt snow and ice.

Where snow and/or rough terrain are not problems, courts are usually laid at ground level, like tennis courts, with concrete or asphalt surfaces and, of course, the standard platform tennis superstructure and screening.

An all-wood court is the least expensive elevated court to build—currently about $13,000; however, a good deal of annual maintenance is necessary—replacing rotted, cracked, and warped boards and repainting and resurfacing the deck. All-aluminum courts, a fairly recent development, have a higher initial cost (currently a hefty $20–23,000) but require much less maintenance and will last longer than wood. There are also courts that combine an aluminum deck and a wooden superstructure—not quite as expensive as all aluminum but needing somewhat more maintenance. The APTA furnishes a list of approved court contractors and, for do-it-yourselfers, complete plans ($100).

Fig. 6-2

PADDLE A platform tennis paddle is no more than 17 inches long with an oval, perforated face—up to 87 perforations are permitted—to reduce air resistance and "grab" the ball. The paddle's surface must have a flat, smooth finish.

Paddles cost between $16 and $50. They are traditionally made of hardwood—rock maple is considered the best—with aluminum or plastic bindings around the rim. Recently paddles made of aluminum, fiberglass, and plastic have come on the market; often open at the throat and having fewer perforations, these are designed to absorb some of the ball's impact.

Paddles range in weight from 14 to over 18 ounces. Lightweight paddles make it easier to control the ball; heavy paddles give your shots more power. Make sure you choose one that is light enough to swing comfortably and provide adequate control.

There is a limited choice of grip sizes, but grips can be built up or shaved down. Some paddles come with a cowhide strap attached to the handle; as few players use it, it is best to buy one with a detachable strap.

Paddles are similar to those used for paddleball, so when you purchase one, look for the words "Approved by the APTA" to avoid ending up with a paddleball paddle by mistake. Platform tennis paddles are perforated over the entire face, while paddleball paddles usually have solid portions in the center.

BALL   The ball is made of solid sponge rubber covered with fuzzy nylon flocking in either orange or the more popular optic yellow. It is about 2½ inches in diameter and weighs between 70 and 75 grams. When dropped from 90 inches onto a concrete slab at 70°F (13°C) it should rebound 43–48 inches. Within this range are high- and low-bounce balls, low-bounce for warm weather and high-bounce for colder weather (which has a deadening effect).

Balls come three to a box for $3–$4. They wear out quickly because of the gritty deck surface, usually lasting a set or two for serious players, somewhat longer for duffers. Only one ball is used per set. In wet weather it is necessary to change balls more often because they absorb water rapidly.

DRESS   There is no dress code for platform tennis; in fact, until very recently tennis whites or a "real" warm-up suit were likely to mark you as a greenhorn in this game, which has always had a kind of reverse snobbery—the shabbier a player's attire, the better-heeled he was likely to be. Typical attire is still casual and comfortable—jeans or old corduroy slacks with a cotton knit turtleneck shirt under a couple of sweaters. In cold weather, wear layers rather than one heavy garment so that you can "peel" as you warm up. If it's extremely cold you may want to wear a hat, thermal underwear, perhaps thin leather gloves. There is also a kind of mitten available with openings at both ends; it allows you to grip the paddle directly with your hand and still keep warm.

If you play platform tennis in warm weather, a pair of tennis shorts or a tennis skirt is fine, but you may prefer wearing slacks; otherwise a fall on the abrasive deck surface could be a most unpleasant experience.

Wear athletic shoes that provide good support, with well-cushioned inner soles and uppers in a material that breathes, such as canvas. Most players wear tennis shoes. Since the rough deck surface is very hard on them, be prepared to go through several pair per season, or to have them resoled (about $15). The Royal Edge by Pro-Keds is one brand of shoe designed specifically for platform tennis; it has a durable, polyurethane sole and a reinforced toe section, which is the part that usually wears out first.

Socks should be thick and absorbant. In freezing temperatures, you may want to wear thermal socks.

METHOD OF PLAY
Until recently doubles was the only form of platform tennis played in APTA-sanctioned tournaments. In June 1979, the Association approved on a one-year, trial basis, a singles game which utilizes the standard singles court, all four screens, and a single serve.

The rules for platform tennis are almost identical with those for tennis; the main difference will be noted in the following discussion. See pp. 241-248 for complete rules.

Platform tennis is scored in points, games, sets, and match. Both sides start each game with a score of 0, called "love." The first point is called 15, the second 30, the third 40, and the fourth game. If the score reaches 40 all, it is called "deuce." At deuce, one side must win two consecutive points to win the game. One point above deuce is called advantage for the side winning it. The first side to win six games by a margin of two wins the set, unless a 12-point tiebreaker is played. The first side to win two out of three sets wins the match, except in the late rounds of some tournaments, when the best three out of five sets are played.

Sides alternate serving games. The side that correctly calls the toss of the paddle wins the right to serve first, or to choose from which side of the court to begin play. Sides change ends after the first, third, and every subsequent odd-numbered game of each set.

In doubles, partners decide who will serve and receive serve first for the team. They must keep the same order for an entire set.

The server delivers the serve from behind the baseline, between imaginary extensions of the center mark and the sideline. His feet may not touch the baseline or the court inside it until he has made contact with the ball. He serves for the first point from behind the right-hand (deuce) court, and for the second point from behind the left-hand (ad) court, alternating in this way until the game is over.

To serve, he projects the ball into the air and strikes it with his paddle before it touches the ground, sending it diagonally over the net into the opposing team's service court. The serve may be delivered with an overhand, underhand, or sidearm stroke.

To limit the server's offensive advantage, only one serve is permitted for each point. If the serve is a fault, the server loses the point. Faults include footfaulting, missing the ball completely, and failing to serve the ball into the proper service court.

Lets are replayed, as in tennis. Lets include the served ball touching the net, band, or center strap before landing in the proper service court, the server serving before the receiving team is ready, and the served ball hitting an overhanging obstruction such as a tree limb or a crossbeam. The first call of a footfault against each server in an unofficiated match (in which case faults are called by the receiving team) is considered a let, or "grace fault."

The receivers alternate returning the serve. After the ball passes over the net and bounces in the proper service court, the receiver returns it back over the net, and the point continues until one player fails to make a good return, either by hitting the ball into the net or out of bounds, or by failing to hit it at all before it has bounced twice and is out of play. A ball that touches the net, post, cord, band, or center strap, or a ball that is returned outside the post, either above or below the level of the net, is still in play, so long as it then hits the deck within the proper court.

If a player touches the net, post, cord, band, or center strap, or steps inside the opponent's court while the ball is in play, he loses the point, even if the opponent's shot is going out.

A ball that first bounces on the deck within the play lines and then into the back and/or side screens, top rails, or snow boards is still in play and may be returned over the net. Please note, however, that the ball must be hit directly over the net, as in tennis; it may not be returned by being hit into the screens first.

A side loses the point if its shot bounces over the screens (until 1974, this was a let and was replayed), if it hits the ball through the open space between the net and the post, or if the ball touches a player or his clothing.

Only one player may strike the ball on each return. Partners' paddles may clash, but if both players hit the ball, either simultaneously or consecutively, the return is illegal.

GRIP As in tennis, you adjust your grip for various strokes. For ground strokes, most players use the Eastern forehand and backhand grips, because they are the most comfortable and allow the most versatility in shot-making.

To assume the Eastern forehand grip, hold your paddle with the face perpendicular to the deck and "shake hands" with the handle. The V between your thumb and index finger should be just to the right of the handle's flat, top plane. Separate your index finger slightly from the others for greater control. (Fig. 6-3)

To find the Eastern backhand grip, start with the forehand grip and give your hand a one-quarter turn to the left, which will put the V between your thumb and index finger on the left side of the handle. (Fig. 7-A)

For serving and volleying, use the Continental grip, which is midway between the other two. Find it by holding the paddle with the Eastern forehand grip and then turning your hand slightly to the left, so that the V between your thumb and index finger is on top of the handle. (Fig. 9-A)

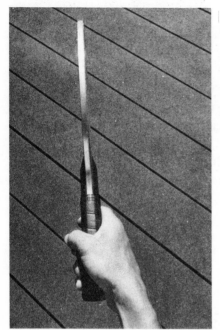

Fig. 6-3 Eastern Forehand Grip

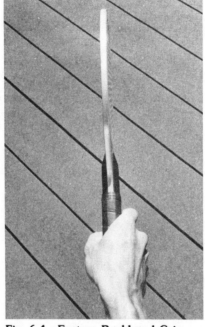

Fig. 6-4 Eastern Backhand Grip

Fig. 6-5 Continental Grip

With all three grips, squeeze the handle firmly when you are hitting the ball and relax your grip between shots so that your hand and arm don't get tired.

READY POSITION Maintain a good ready position between shots so that you can get a quick start. Face the net with your feet about shoulder-width apart, your knees flexed, and your weight forward on the balls of your feet. Hold your paddle directly in front of you with the forehand grip, supporting it with your free hand. You should be relaxed and alert, watching the ball intently and ready to move quickly in any direction as soon as it leaves your opponent's paddle. (Fig. 6-6)

COURT POSITION When you're playing in the back court, wait for your opponents' shots a few inches behind the baseline, near the center of your half of the court. When you're playing net, you should be about three or four feet away from it, again, approximately in the center of the side you are covering. (Fig. 6-B)

Fig. 6-6 A good ready position between shots will allow you to move quickly in any direction.

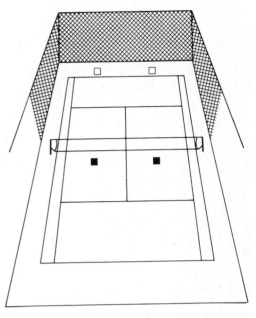

Fig. 6-B
Court Positions—On the Baseline and At the Net

Fig. 6-B Court Positions. Teammates usually stay back together and come to the net together in platform tennis.

STROKES *Forehand drive.* The forehand drive is the most frequently hit stroke in the game. It is similar to a tennis forehand but abbreviated. Due to the smaller size of both court and paddle, you don't need as long and sweeping a motion.

Watch the ball from a solid, aggressive ready position, and get set for your shot as early as possible. As soon as you see that your opponent has hit to your forehand, pivot to the right so that you are side-on to the net. As you pivot, begin your backswing, taking your paddle straight back at waist level. By the time the ball bounces, your paddle should point toward the back screen and your feet should be planted at about a 45-degree angle to the net—in an open stance—with your weight on your back foot.

Time your stroke so that you contact the ball when it is about waist high and slightly in front of you. As you swing forward, keep your knees bent and your wrist firm, step into the ball—shifting your weight from your back foot to your front foot—and let your shoulders and hips rotate forward. As in tennis, your power comes not from your arm and wrist but from your weight shift and the forward rotation of your torso. Follow through forward and upward in the direction of the ball, finishing with your paddle about head high. (Fig. 6-7)

Backhand drive. The backhand is also an abbreviated version of its counterpart in tennis. It requires more preparation time than the forehand, so it is especially important to get set for your shot as quickly as you can.

Fig. 6-7 Forehand. 1. Player turns sideways and takes his racquet back quickly.

2. He steps forward to meet the ball when it is slightly in front of his body, leaning his weight into the shot.

3. He follows through smoothly forward and upward.

The moment you see that the ball is coming to your backhand, pivot out of ready position to the left so that you are sideways to the net. Your feet should be almost parallel to it, in a more closed stance than for a forehand. At the same time, adjust your grip and begin to take your paddle back across your body at waist level, guiding it back with your left hand. At the peak of your backswing, your paddle should point toward the back screen and your weight should be on your back foot.

Meet the ball when it is waist high and slightly in front of you. Keep your knees bent, your grip and wrist firm, and your elbow in close to your body. As you swing, shift your weight from back foot to front foot and let your upper body rotate forward. Follow through forward and upward in the direction of the ball, letting your paddle finish at about shoulder height. (Fig. 6-8)

Spin. Spin is extremely useful in platform tennis. To hit the ball hard and still keep it within the boundaries of that small court takes a good deal of control—and spin adds control. As a rule, players hit their forehands with topspin and their backhands with backspin, although in fact either spin can be used with either stroke.

Topspin accentuates the ball's forward rotation, causing it to travel in a lower, shorter arc and enabling you to safely hit harder than you could

Fig. 6-8 Backhand. 1. Player is turned sideways to the net, her racquet is back, her knees are bent, and she is behind the ball.

2. She meets it waist-high in front of her, shifting her weight forward . . .

3. . . . and following through in the direction of her shot.

with a flat shot. Apply topspin by taking a lower backswing than you normally would and swinging upward through the ball. Follow through higher than for a flat shot; essentially, you're exaggerating the low-to-high motion of the basic swing.

Backspin makes the ball rotate backward as it travels forward, causing it to float higher in flight and then take a low, vertical bounce. This will force your opponent to hit upward—a defensive shot—to get the ball over the net. For backspin, you swing from high to low. Take your paddle back higher than the ball, keeping your paddle face open, then on impact brush under the ball by rolling your wrist under. Follow through low. (Fig. 6-C)

Lob. The lob, high and slow, is a versatile shot that is used a great deal in platform tennis. Mainly employed defensively, it's the shot players generally use to return the ball off the screens. Lobbing is also a good way to keep the ball in play when you are out of position, or to slow down the pace of a fast game. It's a smart tactic to lob when an opponent has a weak overhead, or when your opponents have the sun in their eyes. It can also be an extremely effective offensive shot when the opposition is camping too close to the net: a quick, unexpected lob will force a hasty retreat.

The shot is hit with the basic forehand or backhand stroke, but in order

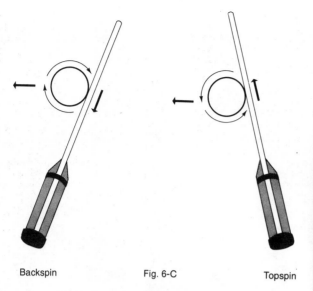

Backspin   Fig. 6-C   Topspin

Fig. 6-C Spin. Swing upward to hit the ball with topspin. Swinging slightly downward, open the face of your paddle and brush under the ball to impart backspin.

Fig. 6-9 A Backhand Lob: Player bends deeply to get his open-faced paddle under the ball.

to give the ball height, take your paddle back lower than usual—about knee high—open the face to a 45-degree angle to the deck, and make contact *underneath* the ball. Swing up and forward with a firm wrist, and follow through higher than for a drive, in the direction of the ball's flight. (Fig. 6-9)

Send your lobs deep—within three or four feet of the baseline—either over an opponent's backhand side to force an awkward, rushed overhead, or else deep down the middle to cause confusion as to which of your opponents should return the shot. When the sun is overhead, take advantage of it by directing your lob to the player who seems most bothered by it.

An offensive lob, which is meant to force your opponents to retreat from the net, has more speed and a lower trajectory than a defensive lob. Don't open the face of your paddle until the last moment, so that your opponents expect a drive, then hit up so that the ball sails just above their outstretched paddles and lands fairly deep—between the service line and the baseline. If you succeed in prying your opponents away from the net, you and your partner should come in quickly before they have a chance to regain the offensive.

Volley. The majority of the points in platform tennis are won at the net,

Fig. 6-10   A Forehand Volley: Player meets the ball well out in front of her, keeping her paddle face slightly open to impart backspin.

Fig. 6-11   A Backhand Volley: To volley a wide shot, player crosses over with her outside foot.

making the volley one of the most important shots in the game.   Good reflexes are essential because the ball moves much faster on the fly than after it has bounced, and time between volleys can be very short.

The standard volleying position in platform tennis is three or four feet away from the net—closer to it than in tennis. It is safe to play in so close because both the small court and the presence of the screens limit your opponents' ability to lob successfully over your head. Wait for the ball in a low, forward-leaning position. Keep your elbows in front of your body and make sure that the head of your paddle is higher than your wrist and above net level, to enable you to attack the ball as early as possible. Use the Continental grip for both forehand and backhand volleys, but wait with your paddle at a 45-degree angle to the net, prepared for a backhand volley; chances are that more than half the volleys you'll hit will be backhands.

Take almost no backswing when you volley; the stroke is essentially a compact, forward punch, with your paddle face opened slightly to impart backspin. Keep your wrist locked and grip your paddle tightly to prepare for the ball's impact. Meet the ball out in front of you; hit it crisply and lean your weight into your shot. (Fig. 6-10) Take a short follow-through, then return quickly to return position.

Fig. 6-12 A half-volley is hit with an open paddle face, so that the ball will clear the net.

Use the backhand volley not only for balls that come to your left but also for shots aimed directly at you, because usually you won't be able to get out of the ball's way in time to hit a forehand. In fact, many players even volley balls that come slightly to their right with their backhand stroke, finding it a less cramped shot when time is short. (Fig. 6-11)

Ideally, the ball will be between waist- and shoulder-high when you hit it. For lower volleys, get down with the ball by bending more at the knees; otherwise it's liable to end up in the net. As for high volleys, a hard-hit ball that is traveling higher than your shoulders is probably on its way out. Let it go; you can always retrieve it off the screens if you have misjudged it.

Since your goal at the net is to force your opponents to stay deep in their back court, off balance and on the defensive, keep your volleys low and aim them deep, generally to a back corner. Try aiming your volley down the middle occasionally to try to cause confusion about who should take the shot.

Drop volley. The drop volley falls just over the net and then dies. It is a "touch" shot which when used unexpectedly can be an outright winner in club platform tennis; top players rarely use it though, because their level of anticipation is so high that the player who hits it is likely to get the ball driven right back at him at point-blank range.

You have to be practically on top of the net to hit a good drop volley. Disguise your shot by beginning as for a regular volley; then just at the moment of impact open the face of your paddle to impart backspin, and barely touch the ball with it. Rather than following through forward, pull your paddle back toward you; the ball should bounce no more than a few inches beyond the net. Depending on your opponents' positions, you can either angle it sharply or drop it right over the net in front of you.

Half-volley. The half-volley is a defensive stroke hit immediately after the ball has bounced, when it is still very low to the deck. It is a reflex shot that is learned mainly through experience, and one that is best avoided when possible: having to hit a half-volley usually means that you were caught out of position, near the service line, by a ball aimed at your feet that you could neither volley nor drive. Whenever possible, you should let a hard-hit shot that bounces at your feet come off the screens instead of half-volleying it; you'll be able to do much more with it.

When you are forced to hit a half-volley, take your paddle back quickly and bend very low. Try to catch the ball when it is still rising from the deck, and keep your paddle face open slightly so that your shot clears the net. Take a short, smooth follow-through. (Fig. 6-12)

Lob volley. The lob volley is an advanced shot that is generally used only when all four players are at the net with the intention of driving the opposition back. It must be disguised, so that your opponents think you're about to hit the ball low and hard. Therefore, begin the lob volley as a normal volley, but at the last moment open your paddle face and hit up on the ball. Be sure to aim high enough and deep enough to sail the ball over your opponents' outstretched paddles. If your lob volley is too low, you'd better duck or turn your back to the net, conceding the point; otherwise you'll most likely end up eating your opponent's point-blank overhead.

Overhead. For a good net game, you need a good overhead with which to return the opposing team's lobs. Overheads are far more common in platform tennis than in tennis, simply because so many more lobs are hit. But while in tennis the overhead is usually smashed to put the ball away, in platform tennis it is generally hit with restraint, and is very often returned. An overhead that is hit too hard is likely to take a nice big rebound off the screens, giving your opponents an easy setup. It might even bounce *over* the screens, giving them the point outright.

The stroke is essentially an abbreviated serve. Timing is everything. Get set for the shot the moment you see that your opponent has lobbed. Turn sideways to the net and cock your paddle behind your right shoulder in the backscratching position. Back up, using a sideways slide step, and make sure to go back far enough; it's easier to move forward than back at the last moment. "Track" the ball by following its flight with your free

Fig. 6-13 Always try to hit an overhead before the ball bounces. If your opponent's lob is just out of range, jump up for it rather than give up your net position to retrieve it defensively off the screens.

hand. Position yourself so that it is descending slightly to your right and an arm's length in front of you, just as if you yourself had tossed it up to serve. This will enable you to position yourself properly for the ball and get your weight into your shot. When the ball is about three feet above your head, swing up and forward, fully extending your arm and body. Let your weight come forward as you swing, and follow through to the left and down. (Fig. 6-13)

Generally aim your overheads at your opponents' back corners. Ideally, the ball will bounce out of the corner into the "sweet spot," where the back and side screens meet, then come out at an unpredictable angle. Even if the ball misses the sweet spot, your opponents will have a difficult two-screen shot to return. Occasionally hit your overhead down the middle—actually just to the left of center, to the deuce (right) court player's backhand side—to draw your opponents out of their corners and possibly cause confusion between them.

Although you should hit the majority of your overheads gently, it's not a bad idea once in a while to hit one as hard as you can, like a tennis smash. Aimed directly at one of your opponents, this shot can be an outright winner if it comes unexpectedly.

SERVE You only get one serve in platform tennis; if you flub it, you lose the point. When serving, therefore, accuracy and consistency are far more important than power; platform tennis serves are typically half the speed of tennis serves, and aces are rare. A very hard-hit serve can easily backfire by "setting up" off the wires—bouncing out far enough into the court to allow the receiver to hit an offensive return.

Use the Continental grip for serving, because it will allow you to hit the ball with the most control, speed, and spin. To avoid footfaulting, stand a few inches behind the baseline, a foot or so to the right or left of the center mark. Your feet should be about shoulder-width apart, with your toes lined up toward the service court into which you're serving. Begin with most of your weight on your front foot.

The stroke is like an abbreviated, restrained tennis serve. Start with the ball and paddle together in front of you. To make the toss, extend your nonhitting arm upward and let the ball roll off your fingertips. You want to place the ball slightly to your right, an arm's length in front of you, and high enough so that you are fully extended when you hit it, but lower than a tennis toss—remember that a paddle is ten inches shorter than a tennis racquet. It should also be a bit further in front of you; a more forward toss will get you moving toward the net.

As you begin the toss, bring your paddle down and then up behind your right shoulder into the backscratching position. Keep your wrist cocked and let your weight rock back.

Time your stroke so that when you hit the ball it is at the peak of the toss; swing up and forward, with your arm and body completely extended on contact. Let your weight come forward as you swing, and snap your wrist on impact. Complete the stroke by following through across your body to the left and down. (Fig. 6-14)

To improve their control, most players develop a slice (sidespin) serve. Slice not only adds control to the serve but also throws off the receiver's timing. By causing the ball to curve to the right, either away from the receiver's body on the forehand side or into his body on the backhand side, a slice serve makes an offensive return less likely. To slice your serve, toss the ball up further to the right and strike it on its outside, upper edge.

The key to an effective serve is placement. Most important in this regard is keeping your serves deep—within a foot or two of the service line—so that the receiver is forced to stay back on the defensive. When you're serving to the receiver in the deuce court, place most of your serves deep down the center, to his backhand. By serving deep to his weaker stroke you will keep him back, giving yourself more time to get to the net, and forcing a defensive return. Of course, if you see that he can attack your serve to his backhand, or run around it, then aim wide to his forehand corner, where the side screens will restrict his angle of return. A receiver in

Fig. 6-14 Serve. 1. Player starts with the ball and paddle together in front of him.

2. He tosses the ball up to the right and slightly in front of him, as he brings his paddle into a semibackscratch position.

3. His arm and body are extended upward on impact.

4. Player's follow-through is down and to the left, and his momentum moves him toward the net.

Fig. 6-15 Starting positions: Server's partner
is at the net; both receivers are back.
Receivers stand to the left of the area each is
covering in order to "hide" their backhands.

the ad court, if he is right-handed, can more easily "hide" his
backhand—cover most of his territory with his forehand—by waiting for
the serve near his side screen. Instead of aiming for this tiny target, either
serve deep down the center to force him out of position or aim your serve
right at him to "jam" him.

RETURN OF SERVE

To win a set, you must break your opponents' serve at least once; your
best opportunity to do this is on the return of serve. Since the server only
gets one chance, he is under considerable pressure; as the receiver,
however, you do get a second chance: you can and should let very
hard-hit serves go by you and retrieve them off the screens.

Stand facing the server in ready position, on or slightly inside the
baseline. To "protect" your backhand, position yourself on the left side of
your half of the court. In other words, if you're playing the deuce court,
stand near the center mark; if you're playing the ad court, stand right near
your alley. In top-level platform tennis, the ad court player frequently waits
for the serve practically leaning against his side screen. (Fig. 6-15)

The instant the ball comes off your opponent's paddle, turn and take your backswing so that you won't have to rush your shot. Meet the ball when it is about waist high and in front of you as usual, and, ideally, when it is still on the rise from the deck. Lean your weight into your shot and follow through.

Concentrate first on keeping the ball in play, and second on placing your return effectively. The shot to use most often is a topspin forehand drive hit cross-court low and deep. Aim it at the incoming server's feet to force him to hit up defensively. Vary your returns for the sake of surprise; you can occasionally drive the ball hard directly at the net player or lob it over his head. Once in a while dink it softly and low, using underspin, either over the center of the net just beyond the net player's reach or sharply angled cross-court.

If a hard, deep serve forces you back, allow it to go into the screens. Generally return it with a lob, but if the ball comes out high enough and far enough into the court to allow you to take a full swing, by all means hit an offensive drive. Returning the ball off the screens is covered fully in the next section.

SCREEN PLAY In top-class platform tennis, it isn't at all unusual for points to go on for fifty or even a hundred shots; the momentum shifts back and forth from one team to the other due to smart defensive play. These long and exciting rallies, in which seemingly lost points are saved with desperation lobs, are made possible by the screens, the game's great equalizers. The screens neutralize many of the hard-hit shots that would otherwise be winners; they give you a second chance to stay in the point. While screen play is definitely the aspect of platform tennis that gives beginners the most difficulty, it is actually relatively easy and a lot of fun. Once you become accustomed to taking the ball "off the wires," you'll find that the screens are your greatest ally.

Beginners are often surprised by how much time they have to return the ball when they play it off the screens. Because the screens are a less rigid surface than the deck, they absorb a good deal of the ball's momentum, and it bounces off them much more slowly than it went in. Rarely is there any need to rush a screen shot, as long as you are in position for it.

The other difficulty new players commonly have with screen play is learning to gauge the angle of rebound. The ball will come out from a screen at essentially the opposite angle from which it went into it—but both the spin on the ball and the tension of the screens, which can vary from court to court, will influence the ball's path and speed. Becoming

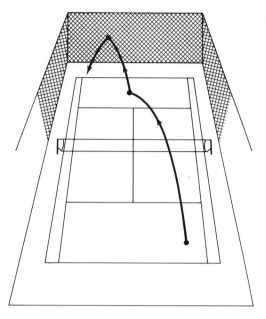

Fig. 6-D
Back Screen Shot

Fig. 6-16 A lob off the back screen. Note deep bend allowing player to get under the ball.

accustomed to a particular court, and to playing on different courts, are matters of experience and practice.

The simplest screen shot to hit is one that caroms directly off the back screen. (Fig. 6-D) Starting from a good defensive position a few inches behind the baseline in the center of your half of the court, prepare for your shot early by turning sideways to the left or right, depending on which side the ball is on, and take your paddle back as the ball goes by you on its way to the screen. Note its flight carefully and adjust your position. You want to be *behind* the ball when you make your shot; it's better to get in too close to the screen and then follow the ball out rather than have to reach behind you to hit it because you weren't close enough. Wait until the ball has ricocheted off the screen and passed in front of you, then meet it between knee- and waist-high, swinging up and out toward the net.

Screen play is usually defensive—returning hard shots that your opponents have hit through your team—and the vast majority of your screen shots will be lobs. Make the stroke as usual, getting your open-faced paddle underneath the ball and following through upward. You may have to bend very deeply at the knees and waist to get under a very low ball. (Fig. 6-16)

More difficult to judge and to time than single-screen shots are

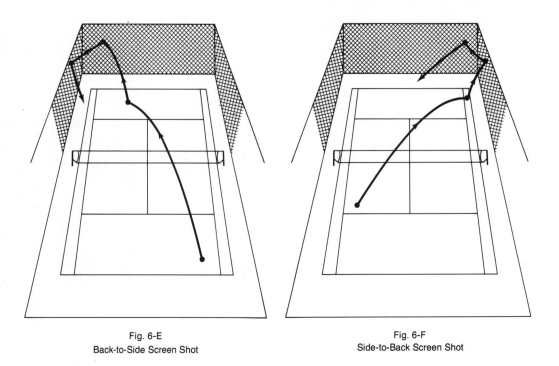

Fig. 6-E
Back-to-Side Screen Shot

Fig. 6-F
Side-to-Back Screen Shot

two-screen shots: back-to-side screen or side-to-back screen. If a ball angling toward the corner hits the back screen first, it will come off the side screen moving away from you, toward the net (assuming that you are behind the baseline). (Fig. 6-E, F) First let the ball go past you to the back screen, then move quickly to the side screen, facing it with your paddle back. After the ball has hit this screen and dropped to a comfortable height, lob it back. (Fig. 6-17)

If your opponent's shot first hits the side screen in the rear of the court, keep your distance from the corner, because the ball will be angling toward you after it caroms off the back screen and you don't want to let it crowd you. There are two ways to play this shot. You can *turn with* the ball, following its flight by facing the side screen, then the back screen, and then the opposite side screen. The advantage of using this method in the ad court is that it allows you to hit a forehand return. Alternatively, you can *back away* from the ball and return it after it has bounced out from the back screen. Right-handed players in the deuce court almost always choose to back away for a side-to-back screen shot because this method sets them up for a forehand return. It's also a simpler maneuver. Most ad court players also prefer to back away from the ball—even though it necessitates a backhand return, because backing away enables them to keep the court in view at all times, and to maintain better balance and court position.

Fig. 6-17 A lob off the side screen.

Fig. 6-18 With enough time and room to take a full swing, player is preparing to hit a drive off the back screen.

Sometimes a low or softly hit shot will hit the side screen and then slide along parallel to it, not coming out at all. Don't be afraid to scrape such a ball off the screen with your paddle. Keep your wrist loose, but try to avoid flicking your shot abruptly.

The most difficult screen shot to return is one that hits the corner where the side and back screens meet; this spot is known as the crease, or sweet spot. The ball can come out of the crease at almost any angle and head toward the middle or the side, so both you and your partner must be prepared to take the shot.

While it is true that most screen shots are defensive, occasionally a too-hard serve, drive, or overhead will carom off a side or back screen well into the court and above the height of the net. If you can get your paddle behind the ball for a full swing, you have a perfect opportunity to hit an offensive forehand drive, rather than a defensive lob. Before the ball comes off the screen, get in position with your paddle back; then hit a low, hard drive at or through your opponents. Since the ball will be moving toward the net, you should move forward with it as you swing so that you can get your weight into the shot, which will give it more velocity. (Fig. 6-18)

TACTICS In essence, the way to win in platform tennis is to *get to the net and volley.* The team at the net controls the rally; it can dictate the pace, move the opponents out of position, and set up the opportunity to put the ball away.

At the beginning of each point the serving team has a distinct advantage: the server's partner is already stationed at the net and the server's momentum is forward—while both members of the receiving team begin the point on the defensive, back on the baseline. As the server, make sure your serve is aggressive enough to *keep* the opposing team back, and *always* follow your serve in to the net—always, no matter whether you are a beginner or a tournament player. Otherwise your opponents can come in and take the offensive.

When you finish your serve, let your forward momentum plus a few quick steps bring you inside the service line for your first volley. To avoid getting caught going the wrong way, make sure you stop moving before the receiver returns the ball, and be prepared to bend—most service returns will be aimed low and at your feet. Hit your first volley deep, to the backhand corner if possible, then come in the rest of the way, joining your partner three or four feet from the net.

Poaching—intercepting cross-count returns at the net—is done quite often in platform tennis; as the court is only twenty feet wide, a decent net player should be able to cut off many of the returns hit to his incoming teammate. The team should have a system of behind-the-back hand signals for poaching—for example, a closed fist for "I'm going to poach, so get ready to switch over to my side;" an open hand for "I'm not going to poach, so stay in position." When you poach, make sure you don't leave your position too soon, or the receiver will be able to hit behind you. Wait until the moment he has committed his shot, then *move.* (Fig. 6-19)

At the net, your team will be hitting volleys and overheads. As a rule, aim your shots deep to pin your opponents back. To keep them scrambling and guessing, mix up corner shots, down-the-line shots, and shots hit down the middle. Going down the middle is an important tactic in platform tennis: it not only limits your opponents' possible angles of return but also frequently causes confusion between them as to who should return the ball.

When either you or your partner is returning serve, you both start in the back court. Playing one up, one back, as in tennis, would leave too much of the court unprotected (although recently several top tournament teams have been making platform tennis history by doing just that—using aggressive, tennis-type tactics on the platform tennis court). For the most part, in the back court you will be hitting lobs, and deep drives when given the opportunity. Play a patient, steady game while you wait for your opponents to make an error or for the chance to hit an aggressive

Fig. 6-19   A Poach: Player cuts off shot intended for his partner, who quickly switches to cover the side left open.

shot—usually an offensive lob or a hard drive hit off a short volley—that forces them to retreat and allows you to come in.

As noted, in order to limit the amount of unprotected territory, teammates move in parallel formation in platform tennis—staying back on the baseline together and coming up to the net together—with just two exceptions: when one player is serving (and his partner is playing the net), and during a *blitz*. A blitz is an attempt to go suddenly from defense to offense by rushing the net after hitting a strong return of serve or some other unexpected offensive shot. It is an aggressive, risky tactic that is usually intended to win the point outright. Blitzing is something that even top-caliber players rarely attempt more than two or three times in a match, because it is frequently an all-or-nothing proposition. But by all means try it; it's an exciting maneuver and, when it works, extremely satisfying.

When your opponent's serve or other shot is weak and you decide to blitz, move in on the ball, take a short, quick backswing, and drive or dink your return low, so that your opponent has to hit up—defensively—to clear the net. Then come in fast, and be prepared to put the ball away by aiming either between your opponents or straight at one of them. (Fig. 6-20) Meanwhile, your partner has moved over to the center of the baseline in case the opposing team's shot gets past you, which means that your blitz has failed—at which time your partner should send up a lob to give you a chance to retreat.

Fig. 6-20 A Blitz: Player in white rushes the net after hitting an offensive drive from the baseline. His partner moves to cover the back court from the center of the baseline.

TEAMWORK Even though a platform tennis doubles team has only two members, sound teamwork is every bit as essential as in any other team sport. Not infrequently, two "better" players who are more interested in displaying individual heroics than in working together will lose out to two "lesser" players who know how to function as a team—by setting up plays, compensating for each other's weaknesses, communicating, and generally cooperating with each other.

Sound tactics dictate that the stronger partner serve first; that way, in a close set he may get to serve an extra, decisive game. When the team is receiving serve, the stronger player should cover the ad court, so that he is in a position (assuming that he is right-handed) to take the shots that go down the middle, with either his forehand drive, his forehand volley, or his overhead. There is an additional advantage to putting the stronger player in the ad court: in close games, the crucial points—ad in or ad out—will fall to him.

The deuce court player's chief role is to set up his partner's forehand, mainly with deep lobs, because the proximity of his side screen will often prevent him from taking a full enough swing to hit wide-angled, offensive forehand drives. However, his screen play can—and should—be more offensive than his partner's, because most of his screen shots will be forehands whereas his partner's will more often be backhands.

You and your teammate must be aware of each other's whereabouts at all times so that one can cover when the other is out of position, which happens fairly frequently in platform tennis—for example, during a blitzing operation, or a poach, or when a lob sails over one player's head and the other goes back for the overhead.

A well-oiled team communicates often during play. Brief verbal instructions—"Yours!" "Mine!" "Switch!"—can save points by preventing mix-ups. In addition, many times the nonhitting player can help his partner out by advising "Let it bounce!" or "Hit it!" because his perspective on the ball is better. Incidentally, never yell "Yours!" when you are both at the net—there isn't enough time for your partner to react. As a rule, when an opponent hits down the middle to your team at the net, the player for whom it is a forehand volley takes it—unless the other player has hit the previous volley and is more "in" the point.

Finally, a smoothly functioning team gets along well on the court. Especially when you are losing, support and encouragement, rather than glares and criticism, will help you both stay "up" and present your opponents with a stronger front.

PLATFORM TENNIS CHECKLIST

1. Always keep your eyes on the ball.
2. Run with small steps; this will help you to maintain better balance on the small court.
3. Keep your knees bent. Bend them even more for low shots.
4. Take your paddle back quickly—for both regular shots and screen shots.
5. Always try to be turned sideways to the net when you're hitting in order to get your weight into your shots.
6. In general, you and your partner should stay back together and move up to the net together.
7. Always follow your serve to the net.
8. Use a variety of shots to keep your opponents guessing.
9. Rely on patience, steadiness, and placement, rather than power, to win points.

Fig. 7-1

PADDLEBALL

ABOUT FOUR-WALL PADDLEBALL Paddleball was invented at the University of Michigan in 1930 by a man named Earl Riskey, who got the idea from watching tennis players practice their strokes on the university's four-wall handball courts during inclement weather. An avid *paddle* tennis player, Riskey decided to experiment on a handball court with *his* favorite sport's equipment. He substituted the light, bouncy core of a tennis ball for the slow, heavy sponge rubber ball of paddle tennis and attached a rope loop to the paddle's handle to prevent it from slipping out of perspiring hands. Then, by adapting the rules of handball, he turned his creation into a sport in its own right.

Four-wall paddleball received a big boost during World War II, when it was chosen as one of the official activities of the Armed Forces Conditioning Program held at the University of Michigan. Thousands of young men from all branches of the military passed through the program and were introduced to paddleball; they took it back to their bases and later to their hometowns. Courts were built all over the country in YMCA's, Jewish Community Centers, schools, and colleges. The sport's future growth seemed assured. However, prospects just didn't pan out. Initially, its growth was hampered by the absence of any centralized organization (the National Paddleball Association wasn't founded until 1952). Since the late 1960s it has been almost completely overshadowed by the tremendous success of its buoyant offspring, racquetball, to which many paddleball players defected. The sport is still very much alive, however, in the northern Midwest, especially Michigan, Wisconsin, and Minnesota, where tournaments are held practically every week from September through March, and it is also played in southern California.

ABOUT ONE-WALL PADDLEBALL

Like four-wall paddleball, the one-wall game was descended from handball, but by a different route. Since the Middle Ages, handball has been a popular sport in Ireland. During the nineteenth century, New York City became home for wave after wave of Irish immigrants, a good many of whom took jobs with the city fire department. Between fires, the men often played handball against the side walls of their firehouses. But these brick walls didn't make particularly satisfactory handball courts, as the ball bounced off them erratically. Soon wooden-walled courts were built, and the game began to spread throughout the city.

It was during the 1930s that most of the present concrete courts were installed. Between 1934 and 1939, in the early years of Robert Moses's reign as New York City parks commissioner, hundreds of new playgrounds were constructed, almost all of them with one-wall handball courts. (Not surprisingly, a significant number of Moses's "lieutenants" were Irish.)

For many years handball was *the* sport in New York City. No one knows exactly who first had the notion of using a wooden paddle rather than the hand to hit the ball. The idea, whoever's it was, caught on: the city's two thousand graffiti-covered courts are in constant use throughout the spring, summer, and fall, with always a wait for next "winners."

GOVERNING BODIES

National Paddleball Association (Four-Wall)
411 E. 3rd St.
Flint, MI. 48503

NPA newsletter, published monthly Sept.–April

Paddleball Players Association
P.O. Box 186
Van Brunt Station
Brooklyn, NY 11215

American Paddleball Association
26 Old Brick Road
New City, NY 10956

Bi-monthly newsletter

COURTS All three versions of paddleball—four-, three-, and one-wall—are played on exactly the same courts as four-, three-, and one-wall racquetball, with the minor exception that courts built specifically for four-wall paddleball have no receiving lines. See pp. 99–100 for descriptions and diagrams.

The first outdoor one-wall paddleball courts were built with plywood walls; most of the courts constructed later were made of concrete. Some of the old wooden courts are still in existence; play off the weathered wood is uneven and noticeably slower than off the newer walls. But when *indoor* paddleball courts have wood floors—usually hardwood gym floors—the ball positively shoots off the surface, much faster than off concrete.

PADDLE Paddleball paddles have oval or squared-off faces that may be perforated or solid. For the four-wall game, NPA rules specify a wooden paddle, approximately 16 inches long, 8 inches wide, and 16 ounces in weight. The leather safety thong that is attached to the handle must be worn around the wrist at all times during play. Paddles for both the one- and four-wall games range in price from $3.95 to $30. Paddles at the high end are better made, usually of rock maple. The very cheapest paddles are not heavy or strong enough to withstand much play.

For one-wall paddleball, APA and PPA rules call for a paddle no longer than 18 inches and no wider than 9 inches. No particular material is specified, but all metal or exposed wood edges must be covered with tape. The paddle's surface may be tape-covered too, as long as the tape doesn't create a rough surface.

The perfect paddle is a particularly individual matter in one-wall paddleball. Some players use paddle or platform tennis paddles. Some wrap hockey tape around various sections of their paddle faces for extra weight and "bite" control; some drill their own holes; some even buy wood and carve their own. If you prefer your paddle store-bought, start with an inexpensive one. Most players favor laminated hardwood paddles; rock maple is considered the best. There are also magnesium, aluminum, fiberglass, and acrylic paddles marketed for the one-wall game, but veteran players tend to feel that these materials don't offer the "hit"—the response—of wood.

Paddles range in weight from 11 to 18½ ounces, though this is not always marked on the paddle. Choose one that you can swing comfortably. For men, it should probably weight between 15 and 18½ ounces, for women, between 13 and 16 ounces, and for children, between 11 and 14 ounces.

Paddles come with either solid or perforated faces. Perforations reduce

Fig. 7-2

air resistance, which permits a faster swing, but some players feel that by "giving" on impact they provide less control.

Grips range in circumferene from 4¼ inches to 4⅝ inches; again, this is not always marked. When your hand is wrapped around the correct size grip, there will be a bit of space between the tips of your fingers and your palm. If the grip is of uncovered wood, wrap a strip of nonslip material around it—tennis racquet binding, towelling, moleskin, a bicycle tire inner tube—so that it doesn't become slippery when your hand perspires.

BALL For the four-wall game, NPA rules specify the Pennsy Official National Paddleball, which is made by General Tire-Pennsylvania Athletic Products, Akron, Ohio. This ball, which is about two inches in diameter, is dark gray in color and has a tiny hole to reduce its internal air pressure and give a consistent bounce. When dropped from a height of 6 feet, it should bounce approximately 4 feet. Balls cost about a dollar and a half each, come in pressurized cans of two or three, and usually last four or five matches before going dead.

For the one-wall game, APA/PPA rules call for a rubber ball approximately 1⅞ inches in diameter and weighing about 2¼ ounces. Actually, most one-wall players use the Seamco 555 handball. These cost about a dollar apiece, come two to a can, and generally last one or two games each; then they tend to break or go dead.

DRESS Dress comfortably for paddleball, in shorts and a shirt, and a sweat suit if you play outdoors in cold weather. The NPA requires that white clothing be worn for tournaments; the APA and the PPA call for "proper attire, preferably light or white in color." Needless to say, what constitutes "proper attire" on a hot summer day in New York City is a subjective matter; just about anything goes.

Paddleball players sport a wide variety of athletic shoes—ordinary sneakers, tennis shoes, high-top basketball shoes, and handball shoes with bumpers (reinforced toes). Keeping yourself in shoes will undoubtedly be your biggest paddleball expense; the asphalt or cement surface of most outdoor courts is rough on them and an avid player can go through several pair per season.

In the continual struggle to remain reasonably dry on the court, most players find that head and wrist sweatbands are extremely useful accessories. Some players wear thin leather gloves to keep their hands dry; others dust their hands with rosin or gym chalk. Towel off as often as necessary to insure that your paddle grip stays dry; a slippery one is a hazard.

The best way to protect against being hit in the eye with the ball, which can cause a very serious injury, is with a plastic or metal eyeguard. If you wear eyeglasses, make sure the pair you use for sports have shatterproof lenses, and use a safety strap.

The most prudent players—not surprisingly, often those who have taken their knocks—wear lightweight plastic softball or hockey helmets, and/or knee pads, elbow pads, and chin straps of padded canvas or leather. These players may look more suitably equipped to tackle a Los Angeles Ram than a small black rubber ball, but they're also much less likely to be injured than their unprotected fellow players.

METHOD OF PLAY— FOUR-WALL PADDLEBALL Four-wall paddleball, which can be a game of singles, doubles, or cutthroat (three players), is played with virtually the same rules as racquetball. See pp. 249–252 for complete rules.

A paddleball game is won by the first side to score 21 points. Only the serving side can score points. A match is won by the side that wins two out of three games.

The side winning the coin toss serves first in the first game and the third, if a third is necessary. In singles, the server continues serving until he loses his serve, called a serve-out. In doubles, at the start of a game, only the first server on the side serving first serves. When he is out, the other side serves. During the rest of the game, both players on each side serve until a serve-out occurs. The service order established at the beginning of each game must be kept throughout that game. A server need not alternate serves to his opponents.

In doubles, the server's partner must stand within the service box with his back against the wall until the served ball has passed the short line.

To serve, the server must drop the ball to the floor within the service zone and strike it on the first bounce. The serve must travel directly to the front wall and then bounce on the floor behind the short line. It may touch one side wall before bouncing.

Defective serves are of two types: illegal and out. *Illegal* serves include serves that go out of the court, serves that hit the floor in front of the short line, serves that hit the back wall, ceiling, or two or more walls before hitting the floor, serves made while either the server or his partner is footfaulting, and serves that pass so close to the server's body that his opponent's view or stroke is obstructed.

A serve is *out* if the ball bounces more than twice before it is served, if it bounces against the side wall before it is served, if the server misses the ball completely, or if the ball simultaneously hits the front wall and the floor, ceiling, or side wall. One out serve results in a serve-out.

When returning serve, the receiving side must stand at least five feet behind the short line until the server has struck the ball. If the receiver returns the serve on the fly, no part of his body may cross the short line until he has made contact with the ball.

The return of serve, and all subsequent shots, may be hit either on the fly or after one bounce. The ball may hit the sidewall(s), back wall, and/or ceiling, as long as it hits the front wall before bouncing on the floor. A shot that hits the front wall and floor simultaneously is not a good return.

The paddle may be held in one or both hands, but it may not be switched from one to the other. The safety thong must be wrapped around the players' wrists at all times.

The ball may be touched only once on each return. In doubles, however, both partners may strike the ball at the same time. Also in doubles, if a player swings at the ball but misses it, he or his partner may try again to hit it, until it is out of play.

If the ball goes out of the court, the side that hit it last loses the exchange.

Obstruction. An *unintentional* hinder is called when a player unintentionally interferes with his opponent's ability to see, get to, and/or

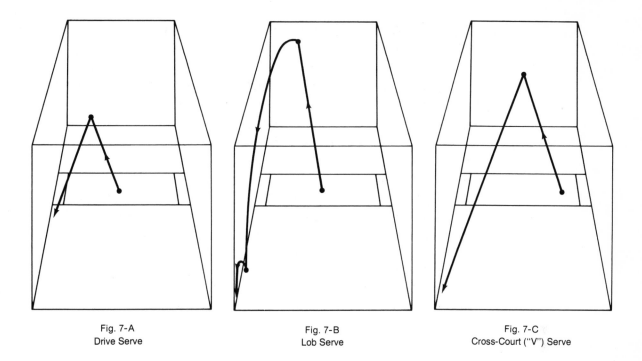

Fig. 7-A
Drive Serve

Fig. 7-B
Lob Serve

Fig. 7-C
Cross-Court ("V") Serve

strike at the ball from any part of the court or to play the ball to any wall. It is also an unintentional hinder if a player unnecessarily crowds or interferes with an opponent, even if the opponent is not actually prevented from making his shot. A player is not entitled to a hinder call unless the interference occurred before, or at the same instant as, his paddle's contact with the ball. Unintentional hinders result in a replay of the point. In doubles, it is not a hinder if a player blocks his partner.

An *intentional* hinder is called when a player fails to move enough to allow his opponent a fair shot, intentionally pushes an opponent during play, or blocks his movement by moving into his path. Intentional hinders result in a serve-out or point, depending on whether the offender was serving or receiving.

SERVE The serve is the most important shot in the game. The server, who begins the point in the offensive position in the center of the court, should hit a serve that allows him to remain there. The best way to do this is to send the serve deep, forcing the receiver to make a defensive return from the back court. There are three main serves in paddleball: the *drive*, the *lob* and the *cross-court*. Varying the height and pace of your serves, disguising them by always beginning in the same stance, probably his backhand, and serving to the receiver's weakness will help you retain the offensive when you serve.

To hit a drive serve, stand near the center of the service zone, facing the side wall. Hit the ball hard, aiming low on the front wall about seven feet from either side wall, so that the ball hits the floor just behind the short line. A low drive serve down the sidewall is one of the best serves in the game. (Fig. 7-A) An effective alternative is to aim slightly higher, which will make the ball land deep in the back court.

To hit a lob serve, you can stand near the center of the service zone or close to either side wall. Hit the ball softly and aim about three-quarters of the way up on the front wall so that the ball rebounds in a slow, high arc and bounces deep in the back court near the rear corner. (Fig. 7-B)

To hit a cross-court (V) serve, stand three to five feet from one side wall. Aim for the center of the front wall, about halfway up. The ball should carry deep to the opposite rear corner. (Fig. 7-C)

RETURN OF SERVE Wait for the serve in ready position—facing the front wall, with your knees bent, your weight forward, and the paddle held at about waist height. In singles, you should be about six feet away from the back wall and equidistant from the side walls. In doubles, both receivers should be prepared to return the serve, each standing about five feet from his side wall.

Unless the serve is poor enough to be returned with an offensive passing shot or a kill, the receiver should return it with a lob, described in the next section. This return will force the server out of the center, into the back court.

SHOTS With just a few differences, four-wall paddleball employs the same strokes, shots, and tactics as racquetball. These are summarized here, but see the racquetball chapter for complete descriptions and explanations (pp. 97–129).

The four basic shots in paddleball are *passing shots, kills, lobs,* and *drop shots.* All are hit with either the forehand or backhand stroke. For most players, the forehand is the stronger stroke. Try to be stationary and facing the side wall whenever you are hitting. Contact the ball when it is approximately even with your body and an arm's length away. For extra power, lean your weight into your shots and snap your wrist as you swing.

Passing shots should be hit hard enough to pass an opponent positioned

Fig. 7-3 Forehand: Player bends low to get down with the ball and leans his weight into the shot.

Fig. 7-4 Backhand: Player meets the ball slightly in front of his body.

in midcourt or further forward, or near either side wall, but softly enough not to carry to the back wall, which could result in a setup for the opponent. They can be hit either along a side wall or cross-court. (Fig. 7-D)

Kill shots are the most offensive shots in paddleball. They should only be attempted when you are standing in front of your opponent. Hit the ball hard and aim as low as possible on the front wall, which will make the shot either very difficult or completely impossible to return. Contact the ball no higher than knee level for kill shots. Direct the ball either straight to the front wall, to the front wall at an angle near a corner, or to a side wall at an angle near a front corner. (Figs. 7-E–G)

Lobs should be hit softly and aimed high on the front wall so that the ball sails over the head of an opponent who is in the center or further forward. The ball should land deep in the back court but not bounce off the back wall. Lobs are almost always hit down the side wall. (Fig. 7-5)

Drop shots are soft shots that require great "touch." They are used when your opponent is out of position in the back court and you are in good front court position. They are most effective when aimed near one of the front corners. (Fig. 7-I)

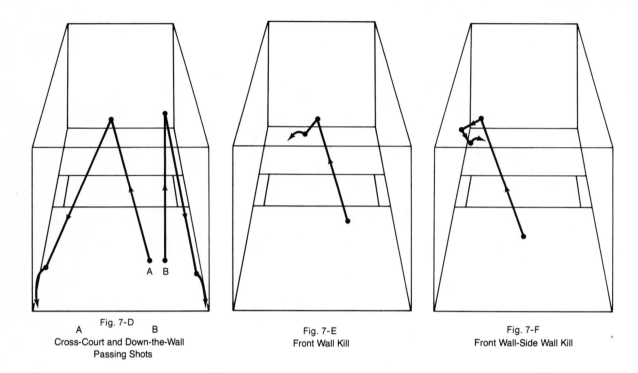

Fig. 7-D
A   B
Cross-Court and Down-the-Wall
Passing Shots

Fig. 7-E
Front Wall Kill

Fig. 7-F
Front Wall-Side Wall Kill

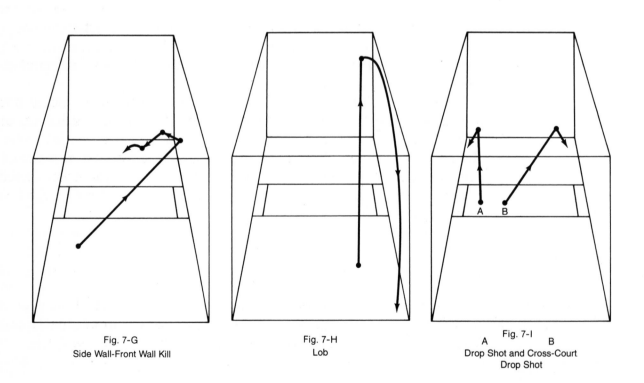

Fig. 7-G
Side Wall-Front Wall Kill

Fig. 7-H
Lob

Fig. 7-I
A   B
Drop Shot and Cross-Court
Drop Shot

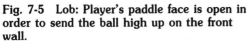

Fig. 7-5 Lob: Player's paddle face is open in order to send the ball high up on the front wall.

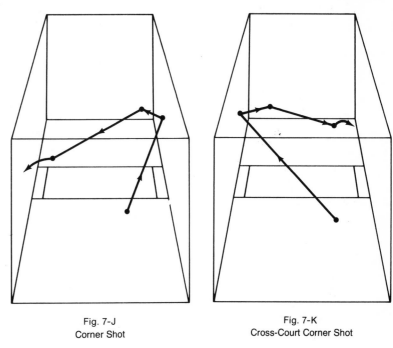

Fig. 7-J
Corner Shot

Fig. 7-K
Cross-Court Corner Shot

There are also several variations of the basic shots: *corner shots, cross-court corner shots,* and *side wall–front wall–side wall shots.* All are used mainly when your opponent is out of position in the back court.

Corner shots are hit to the nearest side wall about three feet up from the floor and three feet from the front wall. The ball should rebound to the front wall and then hit the floor. (Fig. 7-J)

Cross-court corner shots are hit to the far side wall—again, about three feet up from the floor and three feet from the front wall. The ball should rebound to the front wall and then hit the floor. (Fig. 7-K)

Side wall-front wall-side wall shots are hit from either rear corner to the near side wall at a sharp angle. The ball should travel cross-court to the front wall close to the corner, rebound to the side wall, then hit the floor. (Fig. 7-L)

GENERAL TACTICS The basic tactic of four-wall paddleball is to gain control of the center of the court, just behind the short line and equidistant from either side wall. (Fig. 7-M) This is *the* offensive position, the best spot from which to control the point. Move toward the center after every shot you hit, and hit

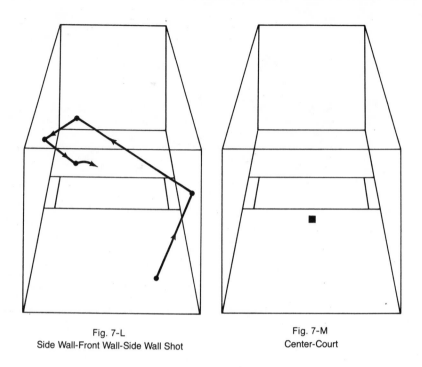

Fig. 7-L
Side Wall-Front Wall-Side Wall Shot

Fig. 7-M
Center-Court

your shots with the purpose of getting and keeping control of this all-important position. Also, try to keep your opponent out of it—remember that if your shot passes through the center, you will have to move to allow him to return it.

When you are in the offensive, center-court position, try to make your opponent run as much as possible—from side to side or up and back. If he is positioned behind you, a kill or drop shot will force him to move forward. If he is positioned in front of you, a lob or passing shot will force him to move back. You can also keep your opponent on the defensive by directing most of your shots to his weaker side—probably his backhand—and by volleying the ball—hitting it on the fly—which will rush him and prevent him from setting up properly for his next shots. Use a variety of shots and change the pace to prevent him from correctly anticipating your next move.

When you are on the defensive in the back court, with your opponent in front of you, hit lobs and passing shots to force him out of position, into the back court. Whenever you are off balance or out of position and struggling to stay in the point, lob.

Whether you are on offense or defense, keep your deep shots from bouncing off the back wall to avoid handing your opponent an easy setup shot. If *his* deep shot comes off the back wall, try to gauge its rebound

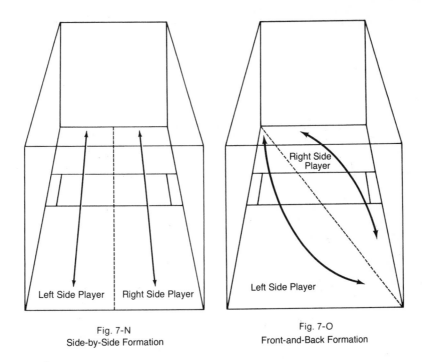

Fig. 7-N
Side-by-Side Formation

Fig. 7-O
Front-and-Back Formation

accurately so that you can move forward with the ball as you hit it; taking a position too close to the back wall is a common error.

DOUBLES FORMATIONS

There are two basic court-coverage formations in the doubles game: side-by-side and front-and-back. In side-by-side, the player with the stronger game covers the left side of the court, unless one player is left-handed, in which case he should play the left side so that both passing lanes are covered by the team's forehands. (Fig. 7-N)

In front-and-back, the player in front takes all front court shots and low shots that come out of the left front corner at an angle. The player on the left side is responsible for shots to the back court and high shots that come off the right side wall at an angle. (Fig. 7-0)

METHOD OF PLAY— ONE-WALL

For Complete Rules, see pp. 253–258. As in the four-wall version, a one-wall paddleball game is won by the first side to score 21 points by a two-point margin. The match is won by the side that wins the majority of games, usually two out of three.

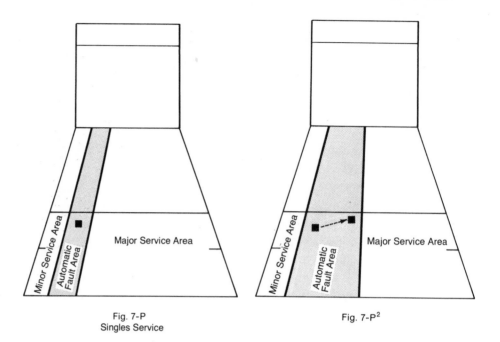

Fig. 7-P
Singles Service

Fig. 7-P²

The side winning the coin toss has the option of serving first or receiving first in the first game and the third, if there is one; the other side gets its choice in the second game. Only the serving side can score points. When the receiving side makes an out, the serving side scores one point and is also entitled to serve again for the next point. When the serving side makes an out, neither side scores. In singles, the serve then passes to the opponent. In doubles, the order of service is as follows: after the *first* out of the game, the serve passes to the other side; thereafter, *both* players on a team must lose their serves before the opposing team can serve. Either player on a team may serve first each time the team is up.

While serving, the server must remain in the service area—between the short line and the service line. To put the ball in play, he bounces it, strikes it on the first bounce, and hits it to the wall on the fly. On the rebound, it must bounce in the receiving area, between the short line and the long line.

In doubles, the server's partner must stand off the court to one side, between imaginary extensions of the short line and the service line, until the served ball has passed him on its way back from the wall.

There are two kinds of defective serves: *faults* and *outs*. Faults include foot faults by either the server or his partner, serves that land in the court in front of the short line, serves that land beyond the long line but within imaginary extensions of the sidelines, and serves that pass between the

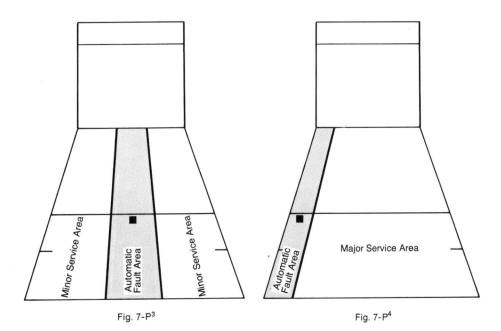

Fig. 7-P³   Fig. 7-P⁴

legs of the server or his partner. Serving two consecutive faults retires the server.

Out serves include striking at the ball and missing it, the ball hitting the floor before the wall, and the ball landing outside the sidelines. One out serve retires the server immediately.

In singles, a separate rule governs the serve and where it must be directed. In APA tournaments, the server only gets one try; any fault, therefore, results in an out. In PPA tournaments, the tournament committee determines the number of service tries.

In singles, the location of the server's feet from the start to the conclusion of his serve divides the court into three sections. Directly in front of and behind him is the *automatic fault area*. Of the two areas divided by the automatic fault area, the larger is the *major service area;* the smaller is the *minor service area*. If the server chooses to stand in the center of the service zone, the two equal sections on either side of him are both considered minor service areas. If he stands all the way to one side, there is no minor service area. The rule states that the server may serve to either the major or the minor service area, but if he chooses to serve to the latter, he must indicate this by pointing to it (See Rule 14, p. 258).

The receiving team can stand anywhere behind the service line and its extensions. The player who returns the serve must hit the ball and complete his follow-through before crossing the service line.

The return of serve, and all subsequent shots, may be hit either on the fly or after one bounce. Opposing sides alternate hitting the ball, which must reach the wall without bouncing. If it touches the floor and wall simultaneously, it is out.

Players are permitted to switch the paddle from one hand to the other in one-wall paddleball; in fact switching paddle hands, rather than hitting backhands, is the norm.

Safety. Throughout most of the game, all four paddleball players are practically on top of each other, crowding into the area around the short line and constantly jockeying for better positions. Keeping in mind that they are all swinging one-pound wooden implements, which any one of them may suddenly switch from one hand to the other, it should be easy to see that one-wall paddleball can be a rather dangerous game. In officiated matches, the referee is supposed to stop play whenever he believes a player is in danger of being struck; but there is no official during nontournament games, and the players must take responsibility for their own and each other's safety by obeying the rules.

In PPA matches, when opponents are close together, a player is obligated to give his opponent sufficient room to swing at the ball (often a matter of simply shifting his weight); otherwise he is out—he loses the serve or the point, depending on whether he had been serving or receiving. In APA matches, a player is *not* obligated to move to let his opponent see, get to, or swing at the ball, unless the opponent is moving backward in pursuit of the ball; while he may not move to block his opponent, he is entitled to stand his ground. The theory behind this rule is that a player shouldn't be penalized for making a good shot by having to give up his court position.

In both associations' rules, if the striker has a reasonable view of his opponent, and if the opponent does not move into the area of his swing, the striker is obligated to avoid hitting the opponent with his paddle. Whenever he believes there is a danger of hitting his opponent, he must call "block" and stop his swing. If the player calling "block" is in a position to have returned the ball, the point is replayed; if he isn't, he loses the point or the serve. It is also a block if an opponent unintentionally gets in the way of the striker's backswing.

If a player swings when there is an obvious potential for injury, or if his opponent forces contact by moving into the striker's swinging area, the offender may be penalized at the referee's discretion; penalties range from warnings to removal from the tournament. If the striker hits his opponent in the course of a normal follow-through, the referee may allow play to continue unless one or both players has reacted significantly to the contact; then he may stop play and/or invoke penalties.

Nonhazardous interference. When the team that has just hit the ball moves in a way that causes no danger but interferes with the striker's ability to move or play the ball, the striker may request a block by calling "block"; but he continues to play the ball. (If the opponent's movement places his own team at a disadvantage, the striker may refrain from calling a block.) The referee then confirms the striker's call by stopping play, or denies it by remaining silent. To be granted a block, a player must be in a position to have returned the ball.

It is also a block if a player's movement interferes with his opponent's view of the ball, if a player unintentionally interferes with an opponent's backward movement to the ball, or if he accidentally bumps into his opponent, preventing him from playing his shot. However, in the last case, if the ball is out the player is out (loses the point or the serve).

If a player intentionally moves alongside or in front of an opponent about to strike the ball or, in doubles, moves alongside or in front of the striker's partner, he is out. He also loses the exchange if he interferes with his opponent's backward movement to the ball, intentionally uses his body or paddle to prevent the ball from reaching the wall, or intentionally moves to block part of the wall. Pushing an opponent—intentionally or not—also results in an out for the offender.

If the player who is about to strike the ball suddenly moves backward, bumping into an opponent behind him, forcing the opponent out of the play, or creating the possibility of hitting the opponent on the backswing, he is out.

In general, if the ball hits an opponent on its way to the wall, a block is called if the ball would have been fair; if not, the side that hit it loses the rally. A team hit by a ball it has just played loses the rally, even if a block has been called. For exceptions and other situations, see p. 256, Rule 8n, o.

ONE-WALL SKILLS

Ready position. The stance to take whenever your opponent is playing the ball is the same as in most of the other racquet and paddle sports: face the wall, feet about shoulder-width apart, knees flexed, and weight forward on the balls of your feet. Grip the paddle in your playing hand, with your other hand holding it lightly or poised very nearby, ready to take it in a quick switch (more on this later). It is extremely important, of course, to keep your eyes riveted on the ball at all times.

Grip. You have a choice among three basic grips in paddleball: the choke, the Eastern forehand, and the power grip. You may want to experiment with all three to see which feels most comfortable. Some

Fig. 7-6 Teammates in back are both ready to return the shot, and all three nonhitting players are focusing intently on the wall.

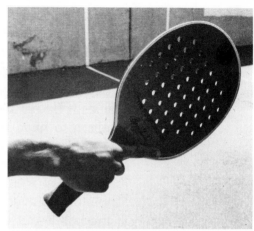

Fig. 7-7 Choke Grip—best for beginners and for "touch" shots.

players like to change their grip for different strokes; others prefer using the same grip throughout.

The choke grip gives the most control, and for this reason it is the best one for beginners, though many experienced players use it too, especially for touch shots. Its one drawback is that it permits your wrist little freedom of movement. While a firm wrist provides better control, it also limits the amount of power you can transmit to the ball. To find the choke grip, position your paddle with the face perpendicular to the ground, then grasp it so that the neck sits in the V between your thumb and forefinger. Your forefinger should rest against the base of the paddle, and your thumb should be touching your middle finger. (Fig. 7-7)

The Eastern forehand grip gives you more reach but slightly less control than the choke. By allowing you to cock and uncock your wrist, it also gives you greater power. Find it by holding your paddle at the throat with your free hand, with the face perpendicular to the floor, and "shaking hands" with the handle. Extend your index finger forward slightly for greater control. The V formed by your thumb and index finger should be on top of the handle, and the butt should rest in the fleshy part of your palm. (Fig. 7-8)

As its name implies, the power grip offers the greatest power, but, in the familiar trade-off, the least control. It is the most effective grip for hitting overhead serves and smashes, but only young, strong hitters who rely more on strength than finesse to make their points should use it for other shots. To find it, position the paddle with the face *parallel* to the ground; then close your hand around it near the end of the handle, as if you were making a fist. (Fig. 7-9)

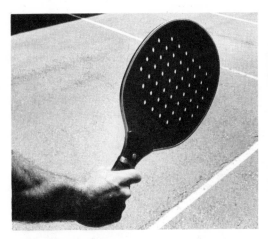
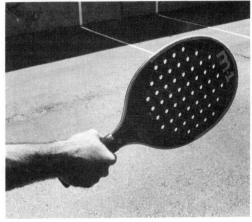

Fig. 7-8 Eastern forehand grip lets you snap your wrist for greater power.

Fig. 7-9 Power Grip—used primarily for overhead serves and smashes.

Your grip doesn't change for the backhand in paddleball. If you use the choke or the Eastern forehand grip, you simply turn your wrist and hit the ball with the other side of the paddle. You use the same side of the paddle with the power grip—but the stroke is somewhat awkward and more difficult to make.

STROKES   *Forehand.* The forehand is *the* basic stroke in one-wall paddleball. Instead of hitting backhands, players switch the paddle from one hand to the other whenever time permits, so that they can hit forehands on both sides; the backhand is generally used only when there isn't enough time to switch paddle hands. In addition to being a more powerful, more controlled stroke than the backhand, the forehand provides greater reach, so that you can return more shots without having to sacrifice good court position.

As soon as the ball comes off the wall, take a short backswing at waist level; keep your elbow bent, rotate your hips back slightly, and shift your weight back. Because of the game's fast pace, most of your strokes will have to be abbreviated, and you will have to hit most of them facing the wall—in an open stance—rather than turning to face the right or left sideline. This is especially true in the front court, where you have less time between shots and turning your body might leave you out of position. In the back court, however, sometimes you will have enough time to assume a closed stance—with your feet angled toward the right sideline—and to take a fuller backswing and swing.

Fig. 7-10 Forehand. 1. Here player has enough time to turn sideways to the wall as he begins to take his paddle back.

2. He takes a short backswing . . .

Meet the ball when it is slightly in front of you, preferably at hip level or lower, letting your weight come forward as you swing. Follow through in the direction of your shot. (Fig. 7-10)

If you're using the choke grip, your wrist should remain locked throughout the stroke. With the Eastern forehand or the power grip, you can cock your wrist on the backswing and snap it on impact for more power.

Adjust the angle of your paddle face for the type of shot you want to hit. For a *killer,* aim as low as possible so that the ball skims low to the wall and dies before your opponent can reach it; for a *drive,* aim about halfway up on the wall, to make the ball carry into the back court. (Fig. 7-Q, R)

Switching hands. Switching the paddle from one hand to the other allows you to hit forehands on both sides—and consequently to be more aggressive on your weaker side than if you were hitting backhands. It also gives you more reach, allowing you to cover the court more effectively. The practice has its roots in handball, in which players may strike the ball with either hand.

It is a straightforward operation, but you will have to practice before you can switch hands quickly and smoothly; you will probably also need some

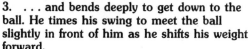

3. . . . and bends deeply to get down to the ball. He times his swing to meet the ball slightly in front of him as he shifts his weight forward.

4. His follow-through is in the direction of his shot.

practice hitting the ball with your "opposite" hand. (Fig. 7-11) A good way to get started is to go out on the court by yourself with two paddles, playing one hand against the other. Begin at the short line, and move in closer to the wall as you become more proficient. When you find that you can work easily with two paddles, try your hands with one.

When you're playing in the front half of the court, where you have less time to make your shots, you may want to keep both hands on the paddle between shots, gripping more firmly with your normal playing hand; it's easier just to let go with one hand than to switch hands, especially when you're rushed. This cannot be done, however, with the power grip.

Backhand. When play is too fast to permit switching paddle hands, you use the backhand, as in the other racquet and paddle sports. It is essentially a forehand in reverse.

If you have enough time, step back with your left foot toward the left sideline. Simultaneously take your paddle back across your body, with your elbow slightly bent and your wrist cocked; let your hips pivot back. Leading the stroke with your elbow, meet the ball just ahead of your body, uncocking your wrist and straightening your arm on impact. Follow through in the direction of your shot. (Fig. 7-12) For additional power on

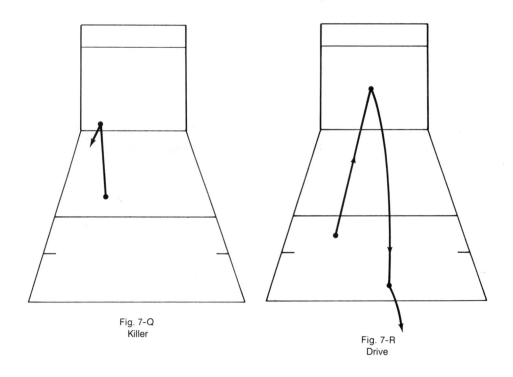

Fig. 7-Q
Killer

Fig. 7-R
Drive

Fig. 7-11 Switching: Because it lets you hit forehands on both sides, switching allows you to play much more aggressively.

shots away from your body you can place your free hand flat against the back of the paddle and push forward with it as you swing.

Volley. Take the ball on the fly whenever possible. Volleying is a more aggressive tactic than allowing the ball to bounce first, because it gives your opponent less time to get set for his next shot; often you can catch him off balance or out of position with your volley.

You too have less time in which to react when you volley, so it's important to maintain an alert, aggressive ready position between shots—weight forward, paddle up, knees flexed. The moment the ball comes off the wall, get your paddle back. If you're in the front court, save time by taking a very short backswing; in the back court, take your paddle back as usual. The stroke itself is the standard forehand, backhand, or opposite-hand forehand, with the paddle face angled appropriately to direct the ball high or low, left or right. (Fig. 7-13)

Perhaps the most difficult volley to make is when the ball comes shooting off the wall straight at you. If you have time, turn sideways to the wall and volley it as usual. If you're rushed, remain facing the wall; just hold your open-faced paddle in front of you and block the ball with your backhand, taking no backswing or follow-through. This "lift shot" isn't likely to score any points for you, but at least it will keep the ball in play.

Fig. 7-12 Backhand. 1. Player turns sideways and takes his paddle back as he moves into position.

2. He gets behind the ball and meets it just in front of him.

3. His follow-through is in the direction of his shot.

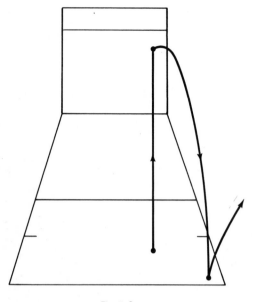

Fig. 7-S
Lob

Fig. 7-13　A Forehand Volley: Note player's forward-leaning, aggressive stance as he meets the ball well out in front of him.

Lob. The lob, which floats over your opponent's head and out of his reach, is an extremely versatile shot. By slowing down the pace of the rally, it can give a weary player new life or allow an out-of-position player time to get back into the point. As it is a difficult shot to return offensively, a good lob can also minimize the advantages of a physically stronger opponent. Hit when your opponent has the offensive "inside" position (in front of you), a lob will force him to retreat; it can even be an outright winner if he is moving forward anticipating a killer or a drop shot.

Use either the choke or the Eastern forehand grip to lob. The stroke itself is the basic forehand, backhand, or opposite-hand forehand, but in order to direct the ball upward, open the face of your paddle and follow through higher than usual. (Fig. 7-14) The harder you swing and the higher you aim, the deeper your lob will travel. When you are in the back court, with your opponent positioned in front of you, hit a *defensive* lob, aiming about three-quarters of the way up on the wall so that the ball lands just inside the long line. When you are both in the front court, use a

Fig. 7-14   A high, slow lob gives everyone a momentary rest. It is hit with an open paddle face to send the ball high up on the wall.

shorter *offensive* lob, aiming about halfway up on the wall and hitting in an upward trajectory so that the ball is still rising as it rebounds. This shot will come off the wall hard and fast and sail over your opponent's head before he has had a chance to react. It is especially *effective* when hit off the short hop and disguised until the last moment; your opponent is almost certain to be moving forward expecting a killer.

Half-volley. Taking the ball on the short hop—a half-volley—can be an offensive shot in paddleball. Any time you hit the ball when it is low to the ground you have the opportunity to hit a killer, a shot aimed so low on the wall that it is practically impossible to return. Even if you don't manage to end the point with your half-volley, you will still be rushing your opponent, just as with a volley, preventing him from setting up properly for his next shot.

To hit a half-volley, you must lean your weight forward and get very low by bending more at the knees and waist. Drop your arm straight down to place your paddle in the path of the ball, and meet it just as it

Fig. 7-15 Half-Volley: Note player's deeply bent knees, allowing him to get down with the ball.

Fig. 7-16 A Drop Shot: Player comes over the top of the ball to make it die off the wall.

comes off the ground. Keep your swing low and angle your paddle face according to the type of shot you want to make—parallel to the wall for a killer, up for a lob or high drive. Follow through along a path more or less parallel to the ground. (Fig. 7-15)

Drop shot. The drop shot, which dies off the front wall, is an advanced "touch" shot in what is essentially a power game. Only use it when your opponent will have to race in for it, because if he has time to set up properly he can probably kill it or slam it hard directly at you. The shot works best, in fact, if you can force him to run around your partner to retrieve it. It's also a good shot in singles—an almost certain winner if directed to the corner from which your opponent is furthest.

Generally play the drop shot when you're in the front position, around the short line. For complete control use the choke grip. Take a slightly lower backswing than usual, but for the purpose of disguise try to use more or less the same stroke as for a forehand drive; note, however, that your elbow should remain bent, almost locked, for this shot. Meet the ball waist high or higher, coming over the top of it with your wrist at the last second; the topspin this creates is what will make it die. Aim low, no higher than one foot up from the ground. The follow-through is high, and you should finish with the face of your paddle facing down. (Fig. 7-16)

Overhead. There are actually four different types of overheads in one-wall paddleball—overhead lobs, drives, drop shots, and smashes. All four are used to return lobs and other high-bouncing shots, and all except the overhead smash are hit with essentially the same stroke; the main differences among them are the angle of the paddle face and the direction of the follow-through.

When your opponent lobs, the first thing you must do is resist the natural impulse just to reach up over your head with your paddle, without first taking a backswing or shifting your weight back; that sort of haphazard approach will give your shot little power or accuracy. Instead, as soon as you determine that your opponent's shot will be a high one, take a step back with your right foot, which will turn your body toward the right front corner of the court and also serve to transfer your weight back. At the same time, take your paddle back by bringing it up behind your right shoulder; your elbow should be slightly bent. Meanwhile, track the flight of the ball with your free hand in order to position yourself properly. When it is either directly above or slightly behind your head, meet it with an upward, forward swing.

The overhead lob can be either an offensive or a defensive shot, like the lob itself. The swing is soft and slow. Your paddle face should be tilted back on impact and during the follow-through so that the ball strikes the wall three-quarters of the way up and comes back to bounce near the long line. A difficult variation of this shot, known as a lob on a lob, makes it possible to hit an offensive shot on a defensive play: your opponent lobs and takes the "inside" position—moves in front of you; then you lob the shot back from the long line, catching him out of position near the wall.

The overhead drive is an offensive shot that is more likely to draw a weak return or win the point outright because your opponent has less time to retrieve it. It is usually hit from just behind the short line, harder and faster than the overhead lob and aimed lower on the wall—six to nine feet up from the floor. It can be aimed directly at an opponent, to a corner, or between your opponents. Keep your paddle face parallel to the wall on contact and during the follow-through.

The overhead drop is a very difficult, low-percentage "finesse" shot that is rarely used. It must be hit softly, from around the short line, and aimed low on the wall—no higher than two feet up—so that the ball takes almost no bounce. If it is hit too hard or too high, it will hang in the air, allowing your opponent plenty of time to reach it. Swing softly, and at the point of contact angle your paddle downward by bending your elbow and turning your wrist downward slightly. Follow through toward the base of the wall.

The overhead smash is always hit from a position close to the wall—no more than four feet away—using a motion like a tennis overhead; it is

Fig. 7-17 A left-hander's Overhead Drive. 1. Paddle up and back, weight back, eyes riveted on the ball.

2. When it is overhead, he swings up and forward.

Fig. 7-18 Overhead Smash: Sometimes you must leave the ground entirely to hit this offensive shot.

3. His arm is fully extended on impact.

4. He follows through down and across his body.

meant to end the point outright. Use the power grip. Turning quickly to face the right front corner, take your paddle back behind your right shoulder into the backscratching position, cock your wrist, and let your weight shift onto your back foot. With your free hand, track the ball. When it is above and in front of your head, swing up and forward, fully extending your arm. Snap your wrist on impact and lean your weight into the shot for more power. Follow through forward and down to the left or right, depending on the direction of your shot. (Fig. 7-18) In general, aim very low on the wall, to make the ball take a short, high bounce. This shot is especially effective when aimed so that it comes off the wall directly at an opponent.

SERVE *Overhead serve.* This is the most effective and most common serve. It makes the ball travel hard and fast, yet doesn't require great strength to execute. The server can effectively disguise the ball's direction, keeping the receiver in the dark until the last moment. This serve also allows the server to remain deep in the court, strategically the best position from which to cover his opponent's return.

Fig. 7-19 Overhead Serve: 1. Player bounces the ball so that it rebounds above his head and slightly to his right.

2. At the same time, he takes his paddle into the backscratching position and gets his weight back.

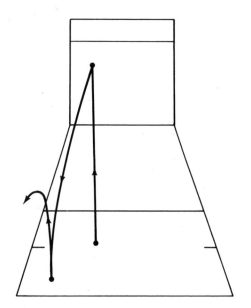

Fig. 7-T
Overhead Serve

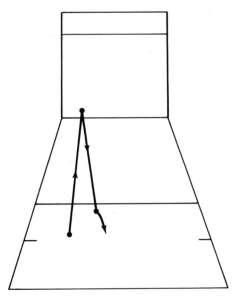

Fig. 7-U
Underhand Serve

200

3. He meets the ball with his arm and body fully extended.

4. His weight comes forward as he follows through down and across his body.

The overhead serve is hit much like an overhead smash. Use the power grip. Standing deep in the service area, face the right front corner. Bounce the ball so that it rebounds above your head and slightly to your right. At the same time, take your paddle back into the backscratching position, cocking your wrist and letting your weight rock back. When the ball reaches the peak of its bounce, swing hard, up and forward, meeting it with your arm fully extended and your paddle face parallel to the wall on impact. Shift your weight forward as you swing, and follow through forward and down. (Fig. 7-19)

Aim about three-quarters of the way up on the wall, so that the ball bounces high and lands deep in the back court near the long line, forcing the receivers back and virtually insuring a defensive return.

Underhand serve. The underhand serve, which must be hit very low and hard, is a much lower-percentage serve than the overhead. When hit with power and accuracy, it can often be an ace; when it is *not* well hit, a good opponent can return it offensively with a volley. It is generally more useful in singles than in doubles.

Fig. 7-20 Underhand Serve. 1. Server drops the ball in front of him . . .

2. . . . as he takes his paddle back and cocks his wrist.

Use any of the three grips. Facing the right sideline, toss the ball lightly in front of you so that it takes a low bounce as you point your paddle downward and bring it back with a straight elbow and a cocked wrist. Bending low at the knees and waist, meet the ball in front of you at calf level or lower. Snap your wrist sharply on impact for additional power and let your weight come forward. Follow through in an upward arc, finishing above your left shoulder. (Fig. 7-20)

The most effective but also the most difficult way to hit this serve is to aim it low—no higher than thirty inches above the floor—so that it bounces just past the short line—a receiver standing too deep may not even reach it.

The underhand serve can also be hit at an angle so that it shoots off the court to the left or right. It is, therefore, quite an advantage in singles, because the receiver cannot know what to anticipate. He has to stand on the long line prepared to come in quickly if the serve is sent to the short line, but he also has to be ready to move laterally in either direction in case you angle the serve off the court.

3. He meets the ball low, snapping his wrist on impact . . .

4. . . . and stays low for the follow-through, which is upward toward his left shoulder.

You may want to take two or three approach steps into your underhand serve in order to give it more power. Be aware, though, that those extra steps will reduce your control; over the course of an entire match, they will also cut down on your stamina.

RETURN OF SERVE   Wait for your opponent's serve in good ready position, near or on the long line. When returning a serve, your main objective is to hit a shot that will prevent the serving team from responding offensively. Try to return the serve on the fly, which is easier to do off an underhand than off an overhead serve.

The most effective return off either an overhead or an underhand serve is a high, deep lob. This is a safe shot that will force the serving team out of the front court, as long as you aim it high enough on the wall so that it lands deep, bouncing at around three-quarters court.

Varying your return is one reliable way to neutralize your opponent's serve. A good finesse return—used only to return an overhead serve—is the slice. As you swing forward, make contact with the ball on its outer edge to give it sidespin, which will slow it down and cause it to land in front of the short line and hook to the right after bouncing. Aim this return high on the wall, like a lob.

Off a weak serve—too short, too soft—hit a powerful drive designed to shoot off the wall right at your opponent.

Off a *really* poor serve, try a killer, or a low drive angled off the court, which will take the server way out of position and should allow you to move in and jump on his next shot.

TACTICS *Doubles.* As doubles is the predominant form of one-wall paddleball, it will be considered first.

You and your partner should decide in advance how you are going to divide up responsibility for the court. If you are both right-handed, the better player should take the left side, allowing him to cover the middle, where most shots are hit, with his forehand. If one player is a lefty, he should take the right side, so that both strong hands are covering the middle. Most of the top teams, incidentally, are righty-lefty combinations. Whatever the handedness of the players, the stronger, more aggressive of the two should be responsible for playing the "in" (front court) game; his partner should stay back to set up plays and cover lobs. Teammates don't go in and back together, as in many of the other racquet and paddle sports. Instead, each player jockeys for his own best position by trying to outmaneuver the opponent on his side of the court.

The serve should be an offensive shot, hit either overhead or underhand. As already noted, for most players the overhead serve is a better choice. Hit it hard so that the ball goes deep to the back court, and generally aim it either to a corner or to an opponent's weaker side; hit down the middle occasionally if this causes confusion between your opponents. The lower, harder-hit, riskier underhand serve is more likely to be an ace or, at the very least, to draw a weak return that you can put away. But your underhand serve had better be first-rate; otherwise a good receiver will be able to drive or kill it. Hit the underhand serve very hard and aim it low, so that it bounces around the short line.

When your team is receiving serve, both you and your partner should be prepared to take the shot, each covering as much of your respective territory as possible with your stronger hand. See the previous section for a discussion of the various returns and when to use each of them.

After the return of serve, all four players generally take up positions in the area between the short line and the service markers, with one partner playing "in" (nearer the wall, where most of the points are made) and the other playing back.

Teamwork—compatibility on the court, complementary styles, and total cooperation—is enormously important. A team is like a marriage; in fact when one splits up, players refer to it as a divorce. It takes a great many hours of practice for two players to "gel" into a real team—ever when the chemistry is there to begin with. A good team is a pleasure to watch: each player seems to know precisely what the other is going to do at all times, and where to be to back him up or cover the return. But since so much of one-wall paddleball consists of pickup games, players need to develop techniques individually that enable them to click together quickly. Here are some general principles of good teamwork:

There will inevitably be times when you or your partner will have to call shots and communicate information during play. Use brief, one- or two-word instructions. For example, if you're both within range of the ball and you feel that you've got the better shot, avoid both the possibility of a collision and of allowing the ball to go between you by yelling "Mine!" or "Got it!" If you can't get to the ball, or if your partner seems to have the better shot, call "Yours!" to let him know that you're not going for it. If you move over to cover a shot in his territory, shout "Switch!" so that he moves over to cover the area you've left open; at the first good opportunity—usually a lob—yell "Switch!" again, and return to your accustomed positions. If you see that the ball is on its way out, call "Out!" to warn your partner not to hit it; he may not have as good a perspective on it as you do.

APA rules do not require moving to allow an opponent his shot, so if you play by those rules you can use your partner's body to block your opponent out of the play. For instance, if your teammate is inside (directly in front of an opponent), place your shot low, directly in front of him; if he is behind his opponent, lob over them. Conversely, if it's your partner who is being blocked, free him by forcing his opponent to move for the ball.

You can also use your own body to block your opponent. When you are in the inside position, hit the ball softly to the wall right in front of yourself, forcing your opponent to go around you to return it.

Note that PPA rules do require that you yield to allow your opponent to swing. In essence, the idea is to hit either where your opponents aren't, or where they don't expect you to hit, or both. If one opponent is up front, for example, or leaning forward anticipating a killer; fake the kill, then pass him with a drive, or sail a lob over his head. If he is deep in the court, an overhead drop (a difficult shot to make) can be particularly effective because it can be disguised until the last instant.

Smart players often do the unexpected. Instead of always hitting to open court, try sending the ball right *at* an opponent occasionally. If your shot is chest high, or if it lands right at his feet, there is little he will be able to do with it.

Look for and play to the other team's vulnerabilities. One opponent is undoubtedly weaker than the other, and both probably have their shortcomings. Test out their overheads, their backhands, their ability to handle a sudden change of pace. How well do they cover the court? Do they leave the middle open? What about the corners? Remember, even terrific teams do some things better than others.

Any time you extract a soft, weak return, seize the opportunity to go on the offensive by moving forward. If the ball is low, get down with it and hit a killer; if it's high, hit either a hard drive close to your body or, on occasion, an overhead smash.

Whenever you're in trouble—out of breath, overpowered, legally blocked out of a strong position, unable for any reason to make an offensive return—*lob*.

Singles. If you're quick, possess extra stamina and excellent anticipation—or simply want to hone those aspects of your doubles games—try singles. It's strenuous, it's fast, and it requires a great deal of running. There's no partner with whom to share responsibility for covering the court, and as often as not, the outcome of a tough match will hinge upon which player has more stamina. Even the best strokes are useless if you are tired. As a matter of fact, when some players are comfortably in the lead early in a match and have an opportunity to put the ball away, they will keep it in play instead, just to make their hapless opponent chase it down and expend more energy.

Precisely because the most difficult aspect of singles is covering the court, the basic tactic of the game is to run your opponent around as much as possible, to keep him out of breath, off balance, and unable to play the shot he'd like. Even when he succeeds in getting the ball back, if you can keep him on the run, most of his shots will be weak and you'll be in control of the rally.

Strategically, the best spot on the court in singles is the center, because standing there you are equidistant from all corners. In reality, you will be constantly moving—from side to side, up and back, diagonally—but after each shot, at least move *toward* the center; this will greatly improve your chances of reaching the next one.

The absence of a partner makes it extremely important to be able to switch hands well in singles. By extending your reach, switching will allow you to cover the court with fewer steps, leaving you more energy late in the match.

Fig. 7-21 Singles—guaranteed to do wonders for your endurance.

When you serve in singles, your main objective, again, is to force the receiver to move. Because your location determines the boundaries of the area to which you must serve (*see* Method of Play), he will have to cover more ground if you stand all the way to one side or the other. A right-handed server should stand on the left side, so that he is covering most of the court with his forehand. A left-handed server should stand as far over to the right sideline as possible. Two of the most effective serves are the underhand hit low and hard and the overhead angled to the corner. The latter will force the receiver off the court to retrieve it—opening the entire area for your next shot, which should be hit to the opposite side from which the return was made. Even if the receiver gets to *that* one, he'll be well on his way to weariness and frustration.

Mix up the placement of your serves in order to keep your opponent guessing. Some other service placements that give many receivers difficulty are deep to his weaker side, down the sideline, and low to the receiver's feet. No matter which serve you use, be ready to move for your opponent's return as soon as you've put the ball in play.

When you are receiving, it's best to assume that the serve will be deep and to position yourself accordingly behind the long line; it's easier to move and to hit while moving forward than backward—but be ready to come in quickly, in case the serve is low and hard. Take a position to the left of the area being served to so that you're covering most of it with your stronger hand. Try to anticipate the serve by noting the angle of the server's paddle face and any telltale movements of his feet and body. If at all possible, make the server run. In general, drive your return down one of the sidelines or into a corner. If you can't hit a strong return, lob to his weaker side.

During the rally, the idea, once again, is to keep your opponent running as much as possible to tire him out and prevent him from setting up for an offensive shot. You can alternate deep shots with short, or deep drives to the left with some to the right. Once you've set up a pattern, you can hit two shots in a row to the same place, which will almost certainly catch your opponent going the wrong way.

Work your opponent's weaker side in order to draw defensive returns. By forcing him to move toward his weaker side you will also open up the other side of the court for a putaway shot.

A major element of singles strategy is knowing how to pace yourself. Near the beginning of the match, when the score is, say, three all, you probably feel like a powerhouse, able to go all day if necessary. But the road to 21 points, or two games out of three, can be a long and tiring one, and whatever energy you save early you'll be grateful for later. So unless you're playing just for the exercise (and who ever is, entirely?), or unless the game is within a few points of ending and you're losing, don't waste precious energy by running down shots that are virtually impossible to retrieve.

PADDLEBALL CHECKLIST

1. Always watch the ball.
2. Keep your knees bent so that you can contact the ball at the lowest possible point and send it along a low path to the front wall.
3. Get your paddle back quickly.
4. Lean your weight into your shots.
5. Hit where your opponent isn't.
6. Concentrate on hitting to your opponent's weaker side.
7. Screen your shots from your opponent's view with your own or your partner's body.
8. *One-Wall only:* Whenever possible, switch paddle hands to hit forehands off your weaker side instead of using your backhand.

APPENDIX

OFFICIAL RULES AND REGULATIONS

In the cases of sports with two governing bodies using similar but slightly different rules, the more widely followed version appears in the text and the variations are provided in footnotes.

TENNIS   Source: *Official USTA Tennis Yearbook, 1979*

THE SINGLES GAME

RULE 1

Dimensions and Equipment

The court shall be a rectangle 78 feet (23.77 m) long and 27 feet (8.23 m) wide. It shall be divided across the middle by a net suspended from a cord or metal cable of a maximum diameter of one-third of an inch (0.8 cm), the ends of which shall be attached to, or pass over, the tops of two posts, 3 feet 6 inches (1.07 m) high, and not more than 6 inches (15 cm) in diameter, the centers of which shall be 3 feet (0.91 m) outside the court on each side. The net shall be extended fully so that it fills completely the space between the two posts and shall be of sufficiently small mesh to prevent the ball's passing through. The height of the net shall be 3 feet (0.914 m) at the center, where it shall be held down taut by a strap not more than 2 inches (5 cm) wide and white in color. There shall be a band covering the cord or metal cable and the top of the net for not less than 2 inches (5 cm) or more than 2½ inches (6.3 cm) in depth on each side and white in color. There shall be no advertisement on the net, strap, band, or singles sticks. The lines bounding the ends and sides of the court shall respectively be called the baselines and the sidelines. On each side of the net, at a distance of 21 feet (6.40 m) from it and parallel with it, shall be drawn the service lines. The space on each side of the net between the service line and the sidelines shall be divided into two equal parts, called the service courts, by the center service line, which must be 2 inches (5 cm) in width, drawn halfway between, and parallel with, the sidelines. Each baseline shall be bisected by an imaginary continuation of the center service line to a line 4 inches (10 cm) in length and 2 inches (5 cm) in width called the center mark, drawn inside the court at right angles to and in contact with such baselines. All other lines shall be not less than 1 inch (2.5 cm) nor more than 2 inches (5 cm) in width, except the baseline, which may be 4 inches (10 cm) in width, and all measurements shall be made to the outside of the lines.

Note: In the case of the International Tennis Championship (Davis Cup) or other official championships of the International Federation, there shall be a space behind each baseline of not less than 21 feet (6.4 m), and at the sides of not less than 12 feet (3.66 m).
The center of the posts in doubles should be 3 feet outside the doubles court.
The net should be 33 feet (10.058 m) in the clear for a singles court, and 42 feet (12.802 m) wide for a doubles court. The net should touch the ground along its entire length and come flush to the posts at all points.
It is important to have a stick 3 feet, 6 inches (106.68 cm) long, with a notch cut in at the 3-foot mark for the purpose of measuring the height of the net at the posts and in the center. These measurements always should be made before starting to play a match. When a singles match is to be played with a doubles net in place, a singles stick should be placed 36 inches (91.44 cm) outside each sideline to make the net 42 inches (106.68 cm) high at those points.

RULE 2

Permanent Fixtures

The permanent fixtures of the court shall include not only the net, posts, cord or metal cable strap, and band, but also, where there are any such, the back and side stops, the stands, fixed or movable seats and chairs around the court, and their occupants, all other fixtures around and above the court, and the chair umpire, net umpire, line umpires, and ball boys when in their respective places.

RULE 3

Ball—Size, Weight, and Bound

The ball shall have a uniform outer surface and shall be white or yellow in color. If there are any seams they shall be stitchless. The ball shall be more than two and a half inches (6.35 cm) and less than two and five-eighths inches (6.67 cm) in diameter, and more than 2 ounces (56.7 g) and less than two and one-sixteenth ounces (58.5 g) in weight. The ball shall have a bound of more than 53 inches (135 cm) and less than 58 inches (147 cm) when dropped 100 inches (254 cm) upon a concrete base. The ball shall have a forward deformation of more than .220 of an inch (.56 cm) and less than .290 of an inch (.74 cm) and a return deformation of more than .350 of an inch (.89 cm) and less than .425 of an inch (1.08 cm) at 18 lbs. (8.165 kg) load. The two deformation figures shall be the averages of three individual readings along three axes of the ball and no two individual readings shall differ by more than .030 of an inch (.08 cm) in each case. Regulations for conducting tests for bound, size, and deformation of balls may be found in the Appendix hereto.

Note: At the annual general meeting of the ITF held on July 12, 1967, it was agreed that for the time being nonpressurized balls and low-pressure balls may not be used in the International Tennis Championship (Davis Cup), unless mutually agreed by the two nations taking part in any particular event.
How often may the player have new balls?
The ball-change pattern is specified by the referee before the match is started. According to tournament regulations the chair umpire may call for a ball change at other than the prescribed time when in his opinion abnormal conditions warrant so doing. In a nonofficiated match the players should agree beforehand on this matter.

RULE 4

The Racquet

The racquet shall consist of a frame and a stringing. The frame may be of any material, weight, size, or shape.
The strings must be alternately interlaced or bounded where they cross, and each string must be connected to the frame. If there are attachments, they must be used only to prevent wear and tear and must not alter the flight of the ball. The density in the center must be at least equal to the average density of the stringing. The stringing must be made so that the move between the strings will not exceed that which is possible, for instance, with eighteen mains and eighteen crosses uniformly spaced and interlaced in a stringing area of 75 square inches.

Note: The spirit of this rule is to prevent undue spin on the ball that would result in a change in the character of the game.

RULE 5

Server and Receiver

The players shall stand on opposite sides of the net; the player who first delivers the ball shall be called the server, and the other the receiver.

Case 1. Does a player, attempting a stroke, lose the point if he crosses an imaginary line in the extension of the net, (a) before striking the ball or (b) after striking the ball?

Decision. He does not lose the point in either case by crossing the imaginary line provided he does not enter the lines bounding his opponent's court. (Rule 20) In regard to hindrance, his opponent may ask for the decision of the umpire under Rules 21 and 25.

Case 2. The server claims that the receiver must stand within the lines bounding his court. Is this necessary?

Decision. No. The receiver may stand wherever he pleases on his own side of the net.

RULE 6

Choice of Ends and Service

The choice of ends and the right to be server or receiver in the first game shall be decided by toss. The player winning the toss may choose, or require his opponent to choose

a) The right to be server or receiver, in which case the other player shall choose the end; or

b) The end, in which case the other player shall choose the right to be server or receiver.

NOTE: These choices should be made promptly, and are irrevocable.

RULE 7

Delivery of Service

The service shall be delivered in the following manner. Immediately before commencing to serve, the server shall stand with both feet at rest behind (i.e., farther from the net than) the baseline, and within the imaginary continuations of the center mark and sideline. The server shall then project the ball by hand into the air in any direction and before it hits the ground strike it with his racquet, and the delivery shall be deemed to have been completed at the moment of the impact of the racquet and the ball. A player with the use of only one arm may utilize his racquet for the projection.

Case 1. May the server in a singles game take his stand behind the portion of the baseline between the sidelines of the singles court and the doubles court?

Decision. No.

Case 2. If a player, when serving, throws up two or more balls instead of one, does he lose that service?

Decision. No. A let should be called, but if the umpire regards the action as deliberate he may take action under Rule 21.

Case 3. May a player serve underhand?

Decision. Yes. There is no restriction regarding the kind of service that may be used; that is, the player may use an underhand or overhand service at his discretion.

RULE 8

Foot Fault

The server shall throughout the delivery of the service

(a) Not change his position by walking or running.

(b) Not touch, with either foot, any area other than that behind the baseline within the imaginary extension of the center mark and sideline.

Note: The following interpretation of Rule 8 was approved by the International Federation on July 9, 1958:

(a) The server shall not, by slight movements of the feet which do not materially affect the location originally taken up by him be deemed "to change his position by walking or running."

(b) The word "foot" means the extremity of the leg below the ankle.

Comment: This rule covers the most decisive stroke in the game, and there is no justification for its not being obeyed by players and enforced by officials. No tournament official has the right to request or attempt to instruct any umpires to disregard violations of it.

RULE 9

From Alternate Courts

(a) In delivering the service, the server shall stand alternately behind the right and left courts, beginning from the right in every game. If service from a wrong half of the court occurs and is undetected, all play resulting from such wrong service or services shall stand, but the inaccuracy of the station shall be corrected immediately it is discovered.

(b) The ball served shall pass over the net and hit the ground within the service court which is diagonally opposite, or upon any line bounding such court, before the receiver returns it.

Comment: The receiver is not allowed to volley a served ball, i.e., he must allow it to strike in his court first. (See Rule 18a)

Note: In matches played without umpires, it is customary for the receiver to determine whether the service is good or a fault; indeed each player makes the calls for all balls hit to his side of the net. (In doubles, the receiver's partner makes the calls with respect to the service line.) It is the prerogative of the receiver, or his partner, to call a foot fault or faults, but only after all efforts (appeal to the server, requests for monitoring help, etc.) have failed, and the foot faulting is so flagrant as to be clearly perceptible from the receiver's side.

RULE 10

Faults

The service is a fault

(a) If the server commit any breach of Rules 7, 8, or 9.

(b) If he miss the ball in attempting to strike it.

(c) If the ball served touch a permanent fixture (other than the net, strap, or band) before it hits the ground.

Case 1. After throwing a ball up preparatory to serving, the server decides not to strike at it and catches it instead. Is it a fault?

Decision. No.

Case 2. In serving in a singles game played on a doubles court with doubles and singles net posts, the ball hits a singles post and then hits the ground within the lines of the correct service court. Is this a fault or a let?

Decision. In serving it is a fault, because the singles post, the doubles post, and that portion of the net, strap, or band between them are permanent fixtures. (Rules 2 and 10, and note to Rule 24) Explanation: The significant point governing Case 2 is that the part of the net and band "outside" the singles sticks is not part of the net over which this singles match is being played. Thus such a serve is a fault under the provisions of article (c) above . . . By the same token, this would be a fault also if it were a singles game played with permanent posts in the singles position (See Case 1 under Rule 24 for difference between "service" and "good return" with respect to a ball's hitting a net post.) Comment: In doubles, if the server's delivery hits his partner, the serve is a fault (not necessarily loss of point). (See Rule 40.)

RULE 11

Service After a Fault

After a fault (if it be the first fault) the server shall serve again from behind the same half of the court from which he served that fault, unless the service was from the wrong half, when, in accordance with Rule 9, the server shall be entitled to one service only from behind the other half. A fault may not be claimed after the next service has been delivered.

Case 1. A player serves from a wrong court. He loses the point and then claims it was a fault because of his wrong station.

Decision. The point stands as played and the next service should be from the correct station according to the score.

Case 2. The point score being 15 all, the server, by mistakes, serves from the left-hand court. He wins the point. He then serves again from the right-hand court, delivering a fault. The mistake in station is then discovered. Is he entitled to the previous point? From which court should he next serve?

Decision. The previous point stands. The next service should be from the left-hand court, the score being 30–15, and the server has served one fault.

Note: When a first service is belatedly determined by the officials to have been a fault—either during the ensuing rally or after the point has been played out—the chair umpire is authorized to grant a full "let" (i.e., first service to come) on the ground of the nature and extent of the delay. Of course, if such belated call were on a second service the server would lose the point.

RULE 12

Receiver Must Be Ready

The server shall not serve until the receiver is ready. If the latter attempt to return the service, he shall be deemed ready. If, however, the receiver signify that he is not ready, he may not claim a fault because the ball does not hit the ground within the limits fixed for the service.

Note: The server must wait until the receiver is ready for the second service as well as the first, and if the receiver claims to be not ready and does not make any effort to return a service, the server may not claim the point, even though the service was good.

RULE 13

A Let

Note: A service that touches the net in passing yet falls into the proper court (or touches the receiver) is a let. This word is used also when, because of an interruption while the ball is in play, or for any other reason, a point is to be replayed.

In all cases where a let has to be called under the rules, or to provide for an interruption to play, it shall have the following interpretations:

(a) When called solely in respect of a service, that one service only shall be replayed.

(b) When called under any other circumstance, the point shall be replayed.

Note: A spectator's outcry (of "out," "fault," or other) is not a valid basis for replay of a point, but action should be taken to prevent a recurrence.

Case 1. A service is interrupted by some cause outside those defined in Rule 14. Should the service only be replayed?

Decision. No, the whole point must be replayed. Explanation: The phrase "in respect of a service" in (a) means a let because a served ball has touched the net before landing in the proper court, or because the receiver was not ready. Case 1 refers to a second serve, and the decision means that if the interruption occurs during delivery of the second service, the server gets two serves.

Example: On a second service a linesman calls "fault" and immediately corrects it (the receiver meanwhile having let the ball go by). The server is entitled to two serves, on this ground: The corrected call means that the server had put the ball into play with a good service, and once the ball is in play and a let is called, the point must be replayed. Note, however, that if the serve were an unmistakable ace—that is, the umpire was sure the erroneous call had no part in the receiver's inability to play the ball—the point should be declared for the server.

Case 2. If a ball in play becomes broken, should a let be called?

Decision. Yes.

Note: A ball shall be regarded as having become "broken" if, in the opinion of the chair umpire, it is found to have lost compression to the point of being unfit for further play, or unfit for any reason, and it is clear the defective ball was the one in play.

RULE 14

The Service Is a Let

The service is a let

(a) If the ball served touch the net, strap, or band, and is otherwise good, or, after touching the net, strap, or band, touch the receiver or anything which he wears or carries before hitting the ground. In case of such a let, that particular service does not count, and the server shall serve again; but a service let does not annul a previous fault.

Comment: Also, a let called for the reason the receiver had indicated he is not ready, on second service, does not annul a fault on first serve.

(b) If a service or a fault be delivered when the receiver is not ready. (See Rule 12.)

RULE 15

When Receiver Becomes Server

At the end of the first game, the receiver shall become the server, and the server receiver; and so on alternately in all the subsequent games of a match. If a player serve out of turn, the player who ought to have served shall serve as soon as the mistake is discovered, but all points scored before such discovery shall be reckoned. If a game shall have been completed before such discovery, the order of service remains as altered. A fault served before such discovery shall not be reckoned.

Note: If an error in serving sequence occurs and is discovered during a tiebreaker game, the serving sequence should be adjusted immediately so as to bring the number of points served by each player into the fairest possible balance. All completed points shall count.

RULE 16

When Players Change Ends

The players shall change ends at the end of the first, third, and every subsequent alternate game of each set, and at the end of each set unless the total number of games in such set be even, in which case the change is not made until the end of the first game of the next set.

If a mistake is made and the correct sequence is not followed, the players must take up their correct station as soon as the discovery is made and follow their original sequence.

Explanation: If the mistake is discovered during a game, the change in ends will be made at once, with all points that have been played counting, and the rest of that game, even if it be only one point, counting as a game. If the mistake is discovered at the end of a game, action that involves the smallest number of changes to get back to the original sequence of court occupancy, with an equitable division of games-per-end-per-player, should be taken.

RULE 17

Ball in Play Till Point Decided

A ball is in play from the moment at which it is delivered in service. Unless a fault or let be called, it remains in play until the point is decided.

Comment: A point is not "decided" simply when, or because, a good shot has clearly passed a player, nor when an apparently bad shot passes over a baseline or sideline. An outgoing ball is still definitely "in play" until it actually strikes the ground, backstop or a permanent fixture, or a player. The same applies to a good ball bouncing after it has landed in the proper court. A ball that becomes imbedded in the net is out of play.

Case 1. A ball is played into the net; the player on the other side, thinking that the ball is coming over, strikes at it and hits the net. Who loses the point?

Decision. If the player touched the net while the ball was still in play, he loses the point.

RULE 18

Server Wins Point

This server wins the point
(a) If the ball served, not being a let under Rule 14, touch the receiver or anything that he wears or carries, before it hits the ground.
(b) If the receiver otherwise loses the point as provided by Rule 20.

RULE 19

Receiver Wins Point

The receiver wins the point
(a) If the server serve two consecutive faults.
(b) If the server otherwise lose the point as provided by Rule 20.

RULE 20
(Formerly Rule 18)

Player Loses Point

A player loses the point if
(a) He fail, before the ball in play has hit the ground twice consecutively, to return it directly over the net (except as provided in Rule 24a or c).
(b) He return the ball in play so that it hits the ground, a permanent fixture, or other object, outside any of the lines which bound his opponent's court (except as provided in Rule 24a and c).
(c) He volley the ball and fail to make a good return even when standing outside the Court.
(d) He touch or strike the ball in play with his racquet more than once in making a stroke.

Explanation: A player may be demeed to have touched the ball more than once if the ball takes an obvious second trajectory as it comes off the racquet, or comes off the racquet in such a way that the effect is that of a "sling" or "throw" rather than that of a "hit." Such strokes are informally referred to as "double hits" or "carries." Experienced umpires give the player the benefit of the doubt unless they see such a second trajectory or a definite "second push."

(e) He or his racquet (in his hand or otherwise) or anything that he wears or carries touch the net, post (singles stick, if they are in use), cord, or metal cable, strap, or band, or the ground within his opponent's court at any time while the ball is in play (touching a pipe support running across the court at the bottom of the net is interpreted as touching the net).
(f) He volley the ball before it has passed the net.
(g) The ball in play touch him or anything that he wears or carries, except his racquet in his hand or hands.

Note that this loss of point occurs regardless of whether the play is inside or outside the bounds of his court when the ball touches him. A player is considered to be "wearing or carrying" anything that he was wearing or carrying at the beginning of the point during which the touch occurred.

(h) He throws his racquet at and hits the ball.

Example: Player has let racquet go out of his hand clearly before racquet hits ball, but the ball rebounds from his racquet into proper court. This is not a good return, player loses point.

Case 1. In delivering a first service that falls outside the proper court, the server's racquet slips out of his hand and flies into the net. Does he lose the point?

Decision. If his racquet touches the net while the ball is in play, the server loses the point. (Rule 20)

Case 2. In serving, the racquet flies from the server's hand and touches the net before the ball has touched the ground. Is this a fault, or does the player lose the point?

Decision. The server loses the point because his racquet touched the net while the ball was in play. (Rule 20)

Case 3. A and B are playing against C and D. A is serving to D, C touches the net before the ball touches the ground. A fault is then called because the service falls outside the service court. Do C and D lose the point?

Decision. The call "fault" is an erroneous one. C and D have already lost the point before "fault" could be called, because C touched the net while the ball was in play. (Rule 20e)

Case 4. May a player jump over the net into his opponent's court while the ball is in play and not suffer penalty?

Decision. No, he loses the point. (Rule 20e)

Case 5. A cuts the ball just over the net, and it returns to A's side. B, unable to reach the ball, throws his racquet and hits the ball. Both racquet and ball fall over the net on A's court. A returns the ball outside of B's court. Does B win or lose the point?

Decision. B loses the point. (Rule 20e and h)

Case 6. A player standing outside the service court is struck by the service ball before it has touched the ground. Does he win or lose the point?

Decision. The player struck loses the point. (Rule 20g, except as provided under Rule 14a)

Explanation: The exception referred to is that of a served ball that has touched the net en route into the receiver's court; in that circumstance it is a let service, not loss of point. Such a let does not annul a previous (first service) fault; therefore if it occurs on second service, the server has one serve coming.

Case 7. A player standing outside the court volleys the ball or catches it in his hand and claims the point because the ball was certainly going out of court.

Decision. In no circumstance can he claim the point;

(1) If he catches the ball he loses the pointer under Rule 20g.

(2) If he volleys it and makes a bad return he loses the point under Rule 20c.

(3) If he volleys it and makes a good return, the rally continues.

RULE 21
(Formerly Rule 19)

Player Hinders Opponent

If a player commits any act either deliberate or involuntary which, in the opinion of the umpire, hinders his opponent in making a stroke, the umpire shall in the first case award the point to the opponent, and in the second case order the point to be replayed.

Case 1. Is a player liable to a penalty if in making a stroke he touches his opponent?

Decision. Not unless the umpire deems it necessary to take action under Rule 21.

Case 2. When a ball bounds back over the net, the player concerned may reach over the net in order to play the ball. What is the ruling if the player is hindered from doing this by his opponent?

Decision. In accordance with Rule 21, the umpire may either award the point to the player hindered, or order the point to be replayed. (See also Rule 25.)

USTA Interpretation: Upon appeal by a competitor that an opponent's action in discarding a "second ball" after a rally has started constitutes a distraction (hindrance), the umpire, if he deems the claim void, shall require the opponent to make some other and satisfactory disposition of the ball. Failure to comply with this instruction may result in loss of point(s) or disqualification.

RULE 22

Ball Falling on Line—Good

A ball falling on a line is regarded as falling in the court bounded by that line.

Comment: In matches played without officials, it is customary for each player to make the calls on all balls hit to his side of the net, and if a player cannot call a ball out with surety he should regard it as good.

RULE 23

Ball Touching Permanent Fixture

If the ball in play touch a permanent fixture (other than the net, posts, cord or metal cable, strap, or band) after it has hit the ground, the player who struck it wins the point; if before it hits the ground his opponent wins the point:

Case 1. A return hits the umpire or his chair or stand. The player claims that the ball was going into court. Decision. He loses the point.

RULE 24

Good Return

It is a good return

(a) If the ball touch the net, post (singles stick, if they are in use), cord or metal cable, strap, or band, provided that it passes over any of them and hits the ground within the court.

(b) If the ball, served or returned, hit the ground within the proper court and rebound or be blown back over the net, and the player whose turn is to strike reach over the net and play the ball, provided that neither he nor any part of his clothes or racquet touch the net, post (singles stick), cord or metal cable, strap or band or the ground within his opponent's Court, and that the stroke be otherwise good; or

(c) If the ball be returned outside the post or singles stick, either above or below the level of the top of the net, even though it touch the post or singles stick, provided that it hits the ground within the proper Court; or

(d) If a player's racquet pass over the net after he has returned the ball, provided the ball pass the net before being played and be properly returned; or

(e) If a player succeeds in returning the ball, served or in play, which strikes a ball lying in the Court.

Note: If, for the sake of convenience, a doubles court be equipped with singles posts for the purpose of a singles game, then the doubles posts and those portions of the net, cord or metal cable and band outside such singles posts shall be regarded as "permanent fixtures other than net, post, strap or band," and therefore not posts or parts of the net of that singles game.

A return that passes under the net cord between the singles and adjacent doubles post without touching either net cord, net or doubles post and falls within the area of play, is a good return. (But in doubles this would be a "through"—loss of point.)

Case 1. A ball going out of court hits a net post and falls within the lines of the opponent's court. Is the stroke good?

Decision. If a service; no, under Rule 10c. If other than a service; yes, under Rule 24a.

Case 2. Is it a good return if a player returns the ball holding his racquet in both hands?

Decision. Yes.

Case 3. The service, or ball in play, strikes a ball lying in the court. Is the point won or lost thereby? (A ball that is touching a boundary line is considered to be "lying in the court.")

Decision. No. Play must continue. If it is not clear to the umpire that the right ball is returned a let should be called.

Case 4. May a player use more than one racquet at any time during play?

Decision. No. The whole implication of the rules is singular.

Case 5. Must a player's request for the removal of a ball or balls lying in the opponent's court be honored?

Decision. Yes, but not while the ball is in play.

RULE 25

Interference

In case a player is hindered in making a stroke by anything not within his control except a permanent fixture of the court, or except as provided for in Rule 21, the point shall be replayed.

Case 1. A spectator gets into the way of a player, who fails to return the ball. May the player then claim a let?

Decision. Yes, if in the umpire's opinion he was obstructed by circumstances beyond his control, but not if due to permanent fixtures of the court or the arrangements of the ground.

Case 2. A player is interfered with as in Case 1, and the umpire calls a let. The server had previously served a fault. Has he the right to two services?

Decision. Yes; as the ball was in play, the point, not merely the stroke, must be replayed as the rule provides.

Case 3. May a player claim a let under Rule 25 because he thought his opponent was being hindered, and consequently did not expect the ball to be returned?

Decision. No.

Case 4. Is a stroke good when a ball in play hits another ball in the air?

Decision. A let should be called unless the other ball is in the air by the act of one of the players, in which case the umpire will decide under Rule 21.

Case 5. If an umpire or other judge erroneously calls "fault" or "out" and then corrects himself, which of the calls shall prevail?

Decision. A let must be called, unless, in the opinion of the umpire, neither player is hindered in his game, in which case the corrected call shall prevail.

Case 6. If the first ball served—a fault—rebounds, interfering with the receiver at the time of the second service, may the receiver claim a let?

Decision. Yes. But if he had an opportunity to remove the ball from the court and negligently failed to do so, he may not claim a let.

Case 7. Is it a good stroke if the ball touches a stationary or moving object on the court?

Decision. It is a good stroke unless the stationary object came into the court after the ball was put into play in which case a let must be called. If the ball in play strikes an object moving along or above the surface of the court a let must be called.

Case 8. What is the ruling if the first service is a fault, the second service correct, and it becomes necessary to call a let under the provisions of Rule 25 or if the umpire is unable to decide the point?

Decision. The fault shall be annulled and the whole point replayed.

Comment: See Rule 13 and Explanation thereto.

RULE 26

The Game

If a player wins his first point, the score is called "15" for that player; on winning his second point, the score is called "30" for that player; on winning his third point, the score is called "40" for that player, and the fourth point won by a player is scored "game" for that player except as below:

If both players have won three points, the score is called "deuce"; and the next point won by a player is called "advantage for that player." If the same player wins the next point, he wins the game; if the other player wins the next point the score is again called "deuce"; and so on until a player wins the two points immediately following the score at deuce, when the game is scored for that player.

Comment: In matches played without an umpire the server should announce, in a voice audible to his opponent and spectators, the set score at the beginning of each game, and (audible at least to his opponent) point scores as the game goes on. Misunderstandings will be averted if this practice is followed.

RULE 27

The Set

A player (or players) who first wins six games wins a set; except that he must win by a margin of two games over his opponent and where necessary a set shall be extended until this margin be achieved. Note: See tiebreaker.

RULE 28

Maximum Number of Sets

The maximum number of sets in a match shall be five, or, where women take part, three.

RULE 29

Rules Apply to Both Sexes

Except where otherwise stated, every reference in these rules to the masculine includes the feminine gender.

RULE 30

Decisions of Umpire and Referee

In matches where a chair umpire is appointed his decision shall be final; but where a referee is appointed an appeal shall lie to him from the decision of a chair umpire on a question of law, and in all such cases the decision of the referee shall be final.

In matches where assistants to the chair umpire are appointed (line umpires, net umpire, footfault judge) their decisions shall be final on questions of fact, except that if, in the opinion of the chair umpire, a clear mistake has been made, he shall have the right to change the decision of an assistant or order a let to be played.

When such an assistant is unable to give a decision, he shall indicate this immediately to the chair umpire who shall give a decision. When the chair is unable to give a decision on a question of fact he shall order a let to be played.

In Davis Cup or other team matches where a referee is on court, any decision can be changed by the referee, who may also authorize the chair umpire to order a let to be played.

The referee, in his discretion, may at any time postpone a match on account of darkness or the condition of the ground or the weather. In any case of postponement the previous score and previous occupancy of courts shall hold good, unless the referee and the players unanimously agree otherwise.

RULE 31

Play shall be continuous from the first service till the match be concluded, except that

(a) After the third set, or when women take part the second set, either player is entitled to a rest, which shall not exceed ten minutes, or in countries situated between lat. 15° N and lat. 15°45′S, and except further that when necessitated by circumstances not within the control of the players the chair umpire may suspend play for such a period as he may consider necessary.

If play be suspended and be not resumed until a later day the rest may be taken only after the third set (or when women take part the second set) of play on such later day, completion of an unfinished set being counted as one set.

If play be suspended and not resumed until ten minutes have elapsed in the same day, the rest may be taken only after three consecutive sets have been played without interruption (or when women take part two sets), completion of an unfinished set being counted as one set.

Any nation is at liberty to modify this provision or omit it from its regulations governing tournaments, matches or competitions held in its own country, other than the International Tennis Championships (Davis Cup and Federation Cup).

(b) Play shall never be suspended, delayed, or interfered with for the purpose of enabling a player to recover his strength or his breath.

(c) A maximum of thirty seconds shall elapse from the end of one point to the time the ball is served for the next point, except that when changing ends a maximum of one minute thirty seconds shall elapse from the last point of one game to the time when the ball is served for the first point of the next game.

> Note: The USTA interpretation of the reference to thirty seconds in the above paragraph (new as of mid-1978) is that it is not intended to make it possible for a player who wants to slow the between-points pace of a match exaggeratedly, as a gamesmanship or tactical maneuver, to persistently use almost all of the thirty seconds maximum without liability to being found in violation of the "play shall be continuous" principle; and that a chair umpire who makes such a finding should be empowered to require the player to play at a reasonable tempo under the prevailing temperature conditions.

These provisions shall be strictly construed. The chair umpire shall be the sole judge of any suspension, delay, or interference and after giving due warning he may disqualify the offender.

> ITF Note: A tournament committee has discretion to decide the time allowed for a warm-up period prior to a match. It is recommended that this not exceed five minutes.

USTA Rules Regarding Rest Periods in Age-Limited Categories:

Regular Men's and Women's, and Men's 21 and Women's 21. Paragraph (a) of Rule 31 applies, except that a tournament using tiebreakers may eliminate rest periods provided advance notice is given.

Boys' 18. All matches in this division shall be best of three sets with *no rest period,* except that in interscholastic, state, sectional, and national championships the *final round* may be best-of-five. If such a final requires more than three sets to decide it, a rest of ten minutes after the third set is mandatory. *Special Note:* In severe temperature-humidity conditions a referee may rule that a ten-minute rest may be taken in a Boys' 18 best-of-three. However, to be valid this must be done before the match is started, and as a matter of the referee's independent judgment.

Boys' 16, 14, and 12, and Girls' 18, 16, 14, and 12. All matches in these categories shall be best of three sets. A ten-minute rest before the third set is *mandatory* in Girls' 12, 14, and 16, and in Boys' 12 and 14. The rest period is *optional* in Girls' 18 and Boys' 16. (Optional means at the option of any competitor.)

All Senior divisions (35's, 40's, 45's, 50's, and up), and Father-and-Son. Under conventional scoring, all are matches best-of-three, with rest period optional.

When "No-Ad" scoring is used in a tournament. A tournament committee may stipulate that there will be no rest periods, even in some age divisions where rest periods would be optional under conventional scoring. These divisions are regular Men's (best-of-five) and Women's, Men's 21 (best-of-five) and Women's 21, Men's 35, Seniors (men 45 and over), and Father-and-Son.

N.b. Two conditions of this stipulation are: (1) Advance notice must be given on entry blanks for the event, and (2) the referee is empowered to reinstate the normal rest periods for matches played under unusually severe temperature-humidity conditions; to be valid, such reinstatement must be announced before a given match or series of matches is started, and be a matter of the referee's independent judgment.

Comment: When a player competes in an event designated as for players of a bracket whose rules as to intermissions and length of match are geared to a different physical status, the player cannot ask for allowances based on his or her age, or her sex. For example, a female competing in an intercollegiate (men's) varsity team match would not be entitled to claim a rest period in a best-of-three-sets match unless that were the condition under which the team competition was normally held.

Case 1. A player's clothing, footwear, or equipment becomes out of adjustment in such a way that it is impossible or undesirable for him to play on. May play be suspended while the maladjustment is rectified?

Decision. If this occurs in circumstances not within the control of the player, of which circumstances the umpire is the sole judge, a suspension may be allowed.

Case 2. If, owing to an accident, a player is unable to continue immediately, is there any limit to the time during which play may be suspended?

Decision. No allowance may be made for natural loss of physical condition. Consideration may be given by the umpire for accidental loss of physical ability or condition.

Comment: Case 2 refers to an important distinction that should be made between a disability caused by an accident during the match, and disability attributable to fatigue, illness or exertion (examples: cramps, muscle pull, vertigo, strained back). Accidental loss embodies actual injury from such mishaps as collision with net post or net, a cut from a fall, contact with chair or backstop, or being hit with a ball, or other object.

Even in case of accident, no more than three minutes should be spent in diagnosis/prognosis, and if bandaging or medication is going to require more than that, the decision as to whether any additional time is to be allowed should be reached by the referee after considering the recommendation of the chair umpire; and, of course, taking into account the need for being fair to the noninjured player. In no case should the injured player be permitted to leave the court area, nor should more than approximately fifteen minutes elapse before either play is resumed or a default declared.

(In Grand Prix matches the chair umpire "may allow a one-time, three-minute rest for an accidental injury," but "play must resume in three minutes.")

Case 3. During a doubles game, may one of the partners leave the court while the remaining partner keeps the ball in play?

Decision. Yes, so long as the umpire is satisfied that play is continuous within the meaning of the rules, and that there is no conflict with Rules 36 and 37. (See Case 1 of Rule 36.)

Note: When a match is resumed following an interruption necessitated by weather conditions, it is allowable for the players to engage in a "re-warm-up" period. It may be of the same duration as the warm-up allowed at the start of the match; may be done using the balls that were in play at the time of the interruption, and the time for the next ball change shall not be affected by this.

RULE 32

Coaching

During a match a player may not receive any coaching or advice, except that when a player changes ends he may receive instruction from a captain who is sitting on the court in a team competition.

Note: Since the ITF did not stipulate any specific penalty for violations of this rule it appears that a chair umpire could do little more than admonish the person doing the forbidden coaching and direct him to cease and desist forthwith. The person's failure to follow this directive could be dealt with under paragraph 9a of the USTA Tournament Regulations, which says that "violation of this rule [32] may render the player or his adviser liable to disciplinary action, which may include disqualification of the player or removal of the adviser from the court area."

RULE 33

Ball-Change Error

In cases where balls are changed after an agreed number of games, if the balls are not changed in the correct sequence the mistake shall be corrected when the player, or pair in the case of doubles, who should have served with the new balls is next due to serve.

THE DOUBLES GAME

RULE 34

The above rules shall apply to the doubles game except as below.

RULE 35

Dimensions of Court

For the doubles game the court shall be 36 feet (10.97 m) in width, i.e. 4½ feet (1.37 m) wider on each side than the court for the singles game, and those portions of the singles sidelines that lie beween the two service lines shall be called the service sidelines. In other respects, the court shall be similar to that described in Rule 1, but the portions of the singles sidelines between the baseline and the service line on each side of the net may be omitted if desired.

Case 1. In doubles the server claims the right to stand at the corner of the court as marked by the doubles sideline. Is the foregoing correct or is it necessary that the server stand within the limits of the center mark and the singles sideline?
Decision. The server has the right to stand anywhere between the center mark and the doubles sideline.

RULE 36

Order of Service

The order of serving shall be decided at the beginning of each set as follows:

The pair who have to serve in the first game of each set shall decide which partner shall do so and the opposing pair shall decide similarly for the second game. The partner of the player who served in the first game shall serve in the third; the partner of the player who served in the second game shall serve in the fourth, and so on in the same order in all subsequent games of a set.

Explanation: It is not required that the order of service, as between partners, carry over from one set to the next. Each team is allowed to decide which partner shall serve first for it, in each set. This same option applies with respect to the order of receiving service.
Case 1. In doubles, one player does not appear in time to play, and his partner claims to be allowed to play single-handed against the opposing players. May he do so?
Decision. No.

RULE 37

Order of Receiving

The order of receiving the service shall be decided at the beginning of each set as follows:

The pair who have to receive the service in the first game shall decide which partner shall receive the first service, and that partner shall continue to receive the first service in every odd game, throughout that set. The opposing pair shall likewise decide which partner shall receive the first service in the second game and that partner shall continue to receive the first service in every even game throughout that set. Partners shall receive the serve alternately throughout each game.

Explanation: The receiving formation of a doubles team may not be changed during a set; only at the start of a new set. Partners must receive throughout each set on the same sides of the court which they originally select when the set began. The first server is not required to receive in the right court; he may select either side, but must hold this to the end of the set.
Case 1. Is it allowable in doubles for the server's partner to stand in a position that obstructs the view of the receiver.
Decision. Yes. The server's partner may take any position on his side of the net in or out of the court that he wishes. (The same is true of the receiver's partner.)

RULE 38

Service out of Turn

If a partner serve out of his turn, the partner who ought to have served shall serve as soon as the mistake is discovered, but all points scored, and any faults served before such discovery shall be reckoned. If a game has been completed before such discovery, the order of service remains as altered.

RULE 39

Error in Order of Receiving

If during a game the order of receiving the service is changed by the receivers, it shall remain as altered until the end of the game in which the mistake is discovered, but the partners shall resume their original order of receiving in the next game of that set in which they are receivers of the service.

RULE 40

Ball Touching Server's Partner Is Fault

The service is a fault as provided for by Rule 10, or if the ball served touch the server's partner or anything he wears or carries; but if the ball served touch the partner of the receiver or anything which he wears or carries, not being a let under Rule 14a, before it hits the ground, the server wins the point.

RULE 41

Ball Struck Alternately

The ball shall be struck alternately by one or other player of the opposing pairs, and if a player touches the ball in play with his racquet in contravention of this rule, his opponents win the point.

> Explanation: This means that, in the course of making one return, only one member of a doubles team may hit the ball. If both of them hit the ball, either simultaneously or consecutively, it is an illegal return. The partners themselves do not have to "alternate" in making returns. (Mere clashing of racquets does not make a return illegal, if it is clear that only one racquet touched the ball.)
>
> Should any point arise upon which you find it difficult to give a decision or on which you are in doubt as to the proper ruling, immediately write, giving full details, to John Stahr, USTA Rules Interpretation Committee, 65 Briarcliff Road, Larchmont, New York 10538, and full instructions and explanations will be sent you.

The 7-of-12 TIEBREAKER

Normally in this country this tiebreaker—or any tiebreaker—goes into effect when the set score reaches 6 all, but at the option of the tournament committee it may take effect at 8 all in one or more complete rounds. Also, the ITF description indicates that the tiebreaker normally would *not* be used in the third or fifth set of a best-of-three or best-of-five match, but any nation has the option of stipulating, in a given tournament, that the tiebreaker will be in effect even in those identifiable final sets of matches.

Here is the procedure:

Singles. A serves first point from right court); B serves points 2 and 3 (left and right); A serves points 4 and 5 (left and right); B serves point 6 (left) and after they change ends, point 7 (right); A serves points 8 and 9 (left and right); B serves points 10 and 11 (left and right), and A serves point 12 (left). If points reach 6 all, players change ends and continue as before. A serves point 13 (right); B serves points 14 and 15 (left and right); and so on until one player establishes a margin of two points. Players change ends for one game to start the next set, with Player B to serve first.

Doubles follows the same pattern, with partners preserving the sequence of their serving turns.

(Assuming A and B versus C and D) Player A serves first point (right); C serves points 2 and 3 (left and right); B serves points 4 and 5 (left and right); D serves point 6 (left) and after teams change ends, point 7 (right). A serves points 8 and 9 (left and right); C serves points 10 and 11 (left and right), and B serves point 12 (left). If points reach 6 all, teams change ends and continue as before: B serves point 13 (right); D serves points 14 and 15 (left and right); until one team establishes a margin of two points. Teams change ends for one game to start the next set with Team C and D to serve first.

If a ball change is due on the tiebreaker game, it will be made. A tiebreaker game counts as one game in reckoning time between ball changes.

THE 5-of-9 TIEBREAKER

Singles. If it is Player A's turn to serve the thirteenth game (at 6 all) he shall serve points 1 and 2, right court and left court; Player B then serves points 3 and 4 (right and left). Players then change ends, and A serves points 5 and 6; B serves points 7 and 8. If the score reaches 4 all, Player B serves point 9 from the right or left court at the election of the receiver.

The set shall be recorded as 7 games to 6. The tiebreaker counts as one game in reckoning ball changes.

Player B shall serve first in the set following the playing of the tiebreaker (thus assuring that he will be first server if this set also goes into a tiebreak). The player shall "stay for one" after a tiebreaker.

(Umpires should note that, if a ball change were called for *on* the tiebreaker game, the change should be deferred until the second game of the following set, to preserve the alternation of the right to serve first with new balls.)

Doubles. In doubles the same format as in singles applies, provided that each player serve from the same end of the court in the tie-break game that he has served from during that particular set. (Note that this operates to alter the *sequence* of serving by the partners on the *second*-serving team.)

N.b. There is no "second spin" of racquets in either the 7-of-12 or the 5-of-9 tiebreaker, no matter how many sets, leading up to the final set have been decided by tiebreakers.

VASSS "No-Ad" Scoring

The "No-Ad" procedure is simply and precisely what the name implies:

A player need win only four points to win a game. That is, if the score goes to 3 points all (or deuce) the next point decides the game—it's game point for both players. The receiver has the right to choose to which court the service is to be delivered on the seventh point.

If a No-Ad set reaches 6 games all, a tiebreaker shall be used which normally would be the 5-of-9.

> Note: The score-calling may be either in the conventional terms or in simple numbers, i.e., "zero, one, two, three, game."

Cautionary Note:

Any ITF-sponsored tournament should get special authorization from ITF before using No-Ad.

REGULATIONS FOR MAKING TESTS SPECIFIED

in Rule 3

1. Unless otherwise specified all tests shall be made at a temperature of approximately 68°F (20°C) and a relative humidity of approximately 60 percent. All balls should be removed from their container and kept at the recognized temperature and humidity for twenty-four hours prior to testing, and shall be at that temperature and humidity when the test is commenced.

2. Unless otherwise specified the limits are for a test conducted in an atmospheric pressure resulting in a barometric reading of approximately 30 inches (76 cm).

3. Other standards may be fixed for localities where the average temperature, humidity, or average barometric pressure at which the game is being played differ, materially from 68°F (20°C), 60 percent and 30 inches (76 cm) respectively.

Applications for such adjusted standards may be made by any National Association to the International Lawn Tennis Federation and if approved shall be adopted for such localities.

4. In all tests for diameter a ring gauge shall be used consisting of a metal plate, preferably noncorrosive of a uniform thickness of one-eighth of an inch (.32 cm) in which there are two circular openings 2.575 inches (6.54 cm) and 2.700 inches (6.86 cm) in diameter respectively. The inner surface of the gauge shall have a convex profile with a radius of one-sixteenth of an inch (.16 cm). The ball shall not drop through the smaller opening by its own weight and shall drop through the larger opening by its own weight.

5. In all tests for deformation conducted under Rule 3, the machine designed by Percy Herbert Stevens and patented in Great Britain under Patent No. 230250, together with the subsequent additions and improvements thereto, including the modifications required to take return deformations shall be employed or such other machine which is approved by a national association and gives equivalent readings to the Stevens machine.

6. Procedure for carrying out tests:

(a) *Precompression.* Before any ball is tested, it shall be steadily compressed by approximately one inch (2.54 cm), on each of three diameters at right angles to one another in succession; this process to be carried out three times (nine compressions in all). All tests to be completed within two hours of precompression.

(b) *Bound test* (as in Rule 3). Measurements are

to be taken from the concrete base to the bottom of the ball.

(c) *Size test* (as in paragraph 4 above).

(d) *Weight test* (as in Rule 3).

(e) *Deformation test.* The ball is placed in position on the modified Stevens machine so that neither platen of the machine is in contact with the cover seam. The contact weight is applied, the pointer and the mark brought level, and the dials set to zero. The test weight equivalent to 18 pounds (8.165 kg) is placed on the beam and pressure applied by turning the wheel at a uniform speed so that five seconds elapse from the instant the beam leaves its seat until the pointer is brought level with the mark. When turning ceases, the reading is recorded (forward deformation). The wheel is turned again until figure ten is reached on the wheel scale (one inch (2.54 cm) deformation). The wheel is then rotated in the opposite direction at a uniform speed (thus releasing pressure) until the beam pointer again coincides with the mark. After waiting ten seconds the pointer is adjusted to the mark if necessary. The reading is then recorded (return deformation). This procedure is repeated on each ball across the two diameters at right angles to the initial position and to each other.

SQUASH Source: *The Rules of Squash*, United States Squash Racquets Association, 1977.

SINGLES PLAYING RULES

RULE 1

Server

At the start of a match the choice to serve or receive shall be decided by the spin of a racquet. The server retains the serve until he loses a point, in which event he loses the serve.

RULE 2

Service

(a) The server, until the ball has left the racquet from the service, must stand with at least one foot on the floor within and not touching the line surrounding the service box and serve the ball onto the front wall above the service line and below the 16-foot line before it touches any other part of the court, so that on its rebound (return) it first strikes the floor within, but not touching, the lines of the opposite service court, either before or after touching any other wall or walls within the court. A ball so served is a good service, otherwise it is a fault.

(b) If the first service is a fault, the server shall serve again from the same side. If the server makes two consecutive faults, he loses the point. A service called a fault may not be played, but the receiver may volley any service which has struck the front wall in accordance with this rule.

(c) At the beginning of each game, and each time there is a new server, the ball shall be served by the winner of the previous point from whichever service box the server elects and thereafter alternately until the service is lost or until the end of the game. If the server serves from the wrong box there shall be no penalty and the service shall count as if served from the correct box, provided, however, that if the receiver does not attempt to return the service, he may demand that it be served from the other box, or if, before the receiver attempts to return the service, the referee calls a let (see Rule 9), the service shall be made from the other box.

(d) A ball is in play from the moment at which it is delivered in service until (1) the point is decided, (2) a fault, as defined in 2a is made, or (3) a let or let point occurs. (See Rules 9 and 10.)

RULE 3

Return of Service and Subsequent Play

(a) A return is deemed to be made at the instant the ball touches the racquet of the player making the return. To make a good return of a service or of a subsequent return, the ball must be struck on the volley or before it has touched the floor twice, and reach the front wall on the fly above the telltale and below the 16-foot line, and it may touch any wall or walls within the court before or after reaching the front wall. On any return the ball may be struck only once. It may not be "carried" or "double-hit."

(b) If the receiver fails to make a good return of a good service, the server wins the point. If the receiver makes a good return of service, the players shall alternate making returns until one player fails to make a good return. The player failing to make a good return loses the point.

(c) Until the ball has been touched or has hit the floor twice, it may be struck at any number of times.

(d) If at any time after a service the ball hits outside the playing surfaces of the court (the ceiling and/or lights, or on or above a line marking the perimeters of the playing surfaces of the court), the player so hitting the ball loses the point, unless a let or a let point occurs. (See Rules 9 and 10.)

RULE 4

Score

Each point won by a player shall add one to his score.

RULE 5

Game

The player who first scores 15 points wins the game excepting that:

(a) At "13 all" the player who has first reached the score of thirteen must elect one of the following before the next serve:

(1) Set to 5 points—making the game 18 points.

(2) Set to 3 points—making the game 16 points.

(3) No set in which event the game remains 15 points.

(b) At "14 all," provided the score has not been "13 all," the player who has first reached the score of 14 must elect one of the following before the next serve:

(1) Set to 3 points—making the game 17 points.

(2) No set, in which event the game remains 15 points.

RULE 6

Match

The player who first wins three games wins the match, except that a player may be awarded the match at any time upon the retirement, default or disqualification of an opponent.

RULE 7

Right to Play Ball

Immediately after striking the ball a player must get out of an opponent's way and must

(a) Give an opponent a fair view of the ball, provided, however, interference purely with an opponent's vision in following the flight of the ball is not a let. (See Rule 9.)

(b) Give an opponent a fair opportunity to get to and/or strike at the ball in and from any position on the court elected by the opponent.

(c) Allow an opponent to play the ball to any part of the front wall or to either side wall near the front wall.

RULE 8

Ball in Play Touching Player

(a) If a ball in play, after hitting the front wall, but before being returned again, shall touch either player, or anything he wears or carries (other than the racquet of the player who makes the return) the player so touched loses the point, except as provided in Rule 9a or 9b.

(b) If a ball in play touches the player who last returned it or anything he wears or carries before it hits the front wall, the player so touched loses the point.

(c) If a ball in play, after being struck by a player on a return, hits the player's opponent or anything the opponent wears or carries before reaching the front wall:

(1) The player who made the return shall lose the point if the return would not have been good.

(2) The player who made the return shall win the point if the ball, except for such interference, would have hit the front wall fairly; provided, however, the point shall be a let (see Rule 9) if

(i) The ball would have touched some other wall before so hitting the player's opponent or anything he wears or carries.

(ii) The ball has hit some other wall before hitting the player's opponent or anything he wears or carries.

(iii) The player who made the return shall have turned following the ball around prior to playing the ball.

(d) If a player strikes at and misses the ball, he may make further attempts to return it. If, after being missed, the ball touches his opponent or anything he wears or carries:

(1) If the player might otherwise have made a good return, the point shall be a let.

(2) If the player could not have made a good return, he shall lose the point.

If any further attempt is successful but the ball, before reaching the front wall, touches his opponent or anything he wears or carries and Rule 8c(2) applies, the point shall be a let.

(e) When there is no referee, if the player who made the return does not concede that the return would not have been good, or, alternatively, the player's opponent does not concede that the ball has hit him (or anything he wears or carries) and would have gone directly to the front wall without first touching any other wall, the point shall be a let.

(f) When there is no referee, if the players are unable to agree whether 8d(1) or 8d(2) applies, the point shall be a let.

RULE 9

Let

A let is the playing over of a point.

On the replay of the point the server (1) is entitled to two serves even if a fault was called on the original point, (2) must serve from the correct box even if he served from the wrong box on the original point, and (3) provided he is a new server, may serve from a service box other than the one selected on the original point.

In addition to the lets described in Rules 2c and 8c(3), the following are lets if the player whose turn it is to strike the ball could otherwise have made a good return:

(a) When such player's opponent violates Rule 7.

(b) When owing to the position of such player, his opponent is unable to avoid being touched by the ball.

(c) When such player refrains from striking at the ball because of a reasonable fear of injuring his opponent.

(d) When such player before or during the act of striking or striking at the ball is touched by his opponent, his racquet or anything he wears or carries.

(e) When on the first bounce from the floor the ball hits on or above the 6½-foot line on the back wall *and*

(f) When a ball in play breaks. If a player thinks the ball has broken while play is in progress, he must nevertheless complete the point and then immediately request a let, giving the ball to the referee for inspection. The referee shall allow a let only upon such immediate request if the ball in fact proves to be broken. (See Rule 13c.)

A player may request a let or a let point. (See Rule 10.) A request by a player for a let shall automatically include a request for a let point. Upon such request, the referee shall allow a let, let point, or no let.

No let shall be allowed on any stroke a player makes unless he requests such before or during the act of striking or striking at the ball.

The referee may not call or allow a let as defined in this Rule 9 unless such let is requested by a player; provided, however, the referee may call a let at any time (1) when there is interference with play caused by any factor beyond the control of the players, or (2) when he fears that a player is about to suffer severe physical injury.

RULE 10

Let Point

A let point is the awarding of a point to a player when an opponent unnecessarily violates Rule 7b or 7c.

An unnecessary violation occurs (1) when the player fails to make the necessary effort within the scope of his normal ability to avoid the violation, thereby depriving his opponent of a clear opportunity to attempt a winning shot, or (2) when the player has repeatedly failed to make the necessary effort within the scope of his normal ability to avoid such violations.

The referee may not award a let point as defined in this Rule 10 unless such let point or a let (see Rule 9) is requested by a player.

When there is no referee, if a player does not concede that he has unnecessarily violated Rule 7b or 7c, the point shall be a let.

RULE 11

Continuity of Play

Play shall be continuous from the first service of each game until the game is concluded. Play shall never be suspended solely to allow a player to recover his strength or wind. The provisions of this Rule 11 shall be strictly construed. The referee shall be the sole judge of intentional delay, and, after giving due warning, he must default the offender. Between each game play may be suspended by either player for a period not to exceed two minutes.

Between the third and fourth games play may be suspended by either player for a period not to exceed five minutes. Except during the five-minute period at the end of the third game, no player may leave the court without permission of the referee. Except as otherwise specified in this Rule 11, the referee may suspend play for such reason and for such period of time as he may consider necessary.

If play is suspended by the referee because of injury to one of the players, such player must resume play within one hour from the point and game score existing at the time play was suspended or default the match, provided, however, if a player suffers cramps or pulled muscles, play may be suspended by the referee once during a match for such player for a period not to exceed five minutes after which time such player must resume play or default the match.

In the event the referee suspends play other than for injury to a player, play shall be resumed when the referee determines the cause of such suspension of play has been eliminated, provided, however, if such cause of delay cannot be rectified within one hour, the match shall be postponed to such time as the tournament committee determines. Any such suspended match shall be resumed from the point and game score existing at the time the match was stopped unless the referee and both players unanimously agree to play the entire match or any part of it over.

RULE 12

Attire and Equipment

(a) The color of a player's shirt or trousers may be either white or a solid pastel. The referee's decision as to a player's attire shall be final.

(b) A standard singles ball as specified in the Court, Racquet, and Ball Specifications of this association shall be used.

(c) A racquet as specified in the Court, Racquet, and Ball specifications of this association shall be used.

RULE 13

Condition of Ball

(a) No ball, before or during a match, may be artificially treated, that is, heated or chilled.

(b) At any time, when not in the actual play of a point, another ball may be substituted by the normal consent of the players or by decision of the referee.

(c) A ball shall be determined broken when it has a crack that extends through both its inner and outer surfaces. The ball may be squeezed only enough to determine the extent of the crack. A broken ball shall be replaced and the preceding point shall be a let. (See Rule 9f.)

(d) A cracked (but not broken) ball may be replaced by mutual consent of the players or by decision of the referee, and the preceding point shall stand.

RULE 14

Court

(a) The singles court shall be as specified in the Court, Racquet, and Ball Specifications of this association.

(b) No equipment of any sort shall be permitted to remain in the court during a match other than the ball used in play, the racquets being used by the players, and the clothes worn by them. All other equipment, such as extra balls, extra racquets, sweaters when not being worn, towels, bathrobes, etc., must be left outside the court. A player who requires a towel or cloth to wipe himself or anything he wears or carries should keep same in his pocket or securely fastened to his belt or waist.

RULE 15

Referee

(a) A referee shall control the game. This control shall be exercised from time the players enter the court. The referee may limit the time of the warm-up period to five minutes, or shall terminate a longer warm-up period so that the match commences at the scheduled time.

(b) The referee's decision on all questions of play shall be final except as provided in Rule 15c.

(c) Two judges may be appointed to act on any appeal by a player to a decision of the referee. When such judge are acting in a match, a player may appeal any decision of the referee to the judges, except a decision under Rules 11, 12a, 13, 15a and 15f. If one judge agrees with the referee, the referee's decision stands; if both judges disagree with the referee, the judge's decision is final. The judges shall make no ruling unless an appeal has been made. The decision of the judges shall be announced promptly by the referee.

(d) A player may not request the removal or replacement of the referee or a judge during a match.

(e) A player shall not state his reason for his request under Rule 9 for a let or let point or for his appeal from any decision of the referee provided, however, that the referee may request the player to state his reasons.

(f) A referee serving without judges, after giving due warning of the penalty of this Rule 15f, in his discretion may disqualify a player for speech or conduct unbecoming to the game of squash racquets, provided that a player may be disqualified without warning if, in the opinion of such referee, he has deliberately caused physical injury to his opponent.

When two judges are acting in a match, the referee in his discretion, upon the agreement of both judges, may disqualify a player with or without prior warning for speech or conduct unbecoming to the game of squash racquets.

RACQUETBALL Source: *Official Racquetball Rules,* United States Racquetball Association, 1978.

PART I. THE GAME

RULE 1.1

Types of Games

Racquetball may be played by two or four players. When played by two it is called "singles"; and when played by four, "doubles."

RULE 1.2

Description

Racquetball is a competitive game in which a racquet is used to serve and return a ball.

RULE 1.3

Objective

The objective is to win each rally by serving or returning the ball so the opponent is unable to keep the ball in play. A rally is won when a side is unable to return the ball before it touches the floor twice.

RULE 1.4

Points and Outs

Points are scored only by the serving side when it serves an ace or wins a rally. When the serving side loses a rally; it loses the serve. Losing the serve is called a "sideout" or "handout."

RULE 1.5

Game

A game is won by the side first scoring 21 points.

RULE 1.6

Match

A match is won by the side first winning two games.

RULE 1.7

Tiebreaker

In the event each side wins a game, the third game will be won by the side first scoring 11 points. This 11 point third game is called "tiebreaker."[1]

[1] The tiebreaker in International Racquetball Association matches is 15 points.

PART II. COURT AND EQUIPMENT

RULE 2.1

Court

The specifications for a standard four-wall racquetball court are:

(a) *Dimensions.* The dimensions shall be 20 feet wide, 20 feet high, and 40 feet long with each back wall at least 12 feet high.

(b) *Lines and zones.* Racquetball courts shall be divided and marked on the floors with 1½-inch-wide red or white lines as follows:

(1) *Short line.* The short line divides the court in half, parallel to the front and back walls. The back edge of the short line shall be equal distance between the front and back walls, 20 feet from both.

(2) *Service line.* The service line is parallel with the short line with the front edge of the service line 5 feet in front of the back edge of the short line.

(3) *Service zone.* The service zone is the space between the outer edges of the short line.

(4) *Service box lines.* The service box lines are located at each end of the service zone and designated by lines 18 inches from and parallel with each side wall.

(5) *Service boxes.* The service boxes are the spaces between the side walls and the service box lines.

(6) *Receiving lines.* Five feet back of the short

line, vertical lines shall be marked on each side wall extending 3 inches from the floor. The back edges of the receiving lines shall be 5 feet from the back edge of the short line.

RULE 2.2

Ball Specifications

The specification for the standard racquetball are:
(a) *Size*. The ball shall be 2¼ inches in diameter.
(b) *Weight*. The ball shall weigh approximately 1.4 ounces.
(c) *Bounce*. The ball shall bounce 68 to 72 inches from a 100-inch drop at a temperature of 76° F.
(d) *Official ball*. The official ball of the USRA is the black Seamco 558; the official ball of the NRC is the green Seamco 559—or any other racquetball deemed official by the USRA or NRC from time to time.

RULE 2.3

Ball Selection

A ball shall be selected by the game referee for use in each match in all tournaments. During a game the referee may, at his discretion or at the request of both players or teams, select another ball. Balls that are not round or which bounce erratically shall not be used.

(a) In tournament play, the referees all choose at least two balls for use, so that in the event of breakage, the second ball can be put into play immediately.

RULE 2.4

Racquet

The official racquet will have a maximum head length of 11 inches and a width of 9 inches. These measurements are computed from the outer edge of the racquet head rims. The handle may not exceed 7 inches in length. Total length and width of the racquet may not exceed a total of 27 inches.

(a) The racquet must include a thong which must be securely wrapped on the player's wrist.

(b) The racquet frame may be made of any material, as long as it conforms to the above specifications.

(c) The strings of the racquet may be gut, monofilament, nylon, or metal.

RULE 2.5

Uniform

All parts of the uniform, consisting of shirt, shorts and socks, shall be clean. Color is optional provided, in the judgment of the referee, it does not affect the opposing player's view of the ball. Warm-up pants and shirts, if worn in actual match play, shall also be white or of acceptable colors, but may be of any color if not used in match play. Only club insignia, name of club, name of racquetball organization, name of tournament, or name of sponsor may be on the uniform. Players may not play without shirts.[2]

[2]Eye protection is required in all IRA-sanctioned junior events and for any participant under eighteen years of age in any IRA tournament.

PART III. OFFICIATING

RULE 3.1

Tournaments

All tournaments shall be managed by a committee or chairman, who shall designate the officials.

RULE 3.2

Officials

The officials shall include (a) a referee for all matches, (b) a referee and two linesmen for all quarterfinal, semifinal, championship, and third-place matches, and (c) additional officials, assistants, scorekeepers, or recordkeepers may be designated as desired.

RULE 3.3

Qualifications

All officials shall be experienced or trained, and shall be thoroughly familiar with these rules and with the local playing conditions.

RULE 3.4

Briefing

Before each match the officials and players shall be briefed on rules and on local court hinders or other regulations.

RULE 3.5

Referees

(a) *Prematch duties.* Before each match commences, it shall be the duty of the referee to

(1) Check on adequacy of preparation of the court with respect to cleanliness, lighting, and temperature.

(2) Check on availability and suitability of all materials necessary for the match such as balls, towels, scorecards, and pencils.

(3) Check readiness and qualifications of assisting officials.

(4) Explain court regulations to players and inspect the compliance of racquets with rules upon request.

(5) Remind players to have an adequate supply of extra racquets and uniforms.

(6) Introduce players, toss coin, and signal start of first game.

(b) *Decisions.* During games the referee shall decide all questions that may arise in accordance with these rules. In national events (i.e., pro tour, regionals, national championships, national juniors, or any other event deemed "national" by the USRA or NRC, a protest shall be decided by the national director, or in his absence the national commissioner, or in his absence the national coordinator, or any other person delegated by the national director. On all questions involving judgment and on all questions not covered by these rules, the decision of the referee is final.

(c) *Protests.* Any decision not involving the judgment of the referee may on protest by decided by the chairman, if present, or his delegated representative.

(d) *Forfeitures.* A match may be forfeited by the referee when

(1) Any player refuses to abide by the referee's decision, or engages in unsportsmanlike conduct.

(2) After warning, any player leaves the court without permission of the referee during a game.

(3) Any player for a singles match, or any team for a doubles match fails to report to play. Normally, ten minutes from the scheduled game time will be allowed before forfeiture. The tournament chairman may permit a longer delay if circumstances warrant such a decision.

(4) If any player for a singles, or any team for a doubles fail to appear to play any matches or playoffs, they shall forfeit their ratings for future tournaments and forfeit any trophies, medals, awards, or prize money.

(e) *Referee's technical.* The referee is empowered, after giving due warning, to deduct one point from a contestant's or his team's total score when in the referee's sole judgment, the contestant during the course of the match is being overtly and deliberately abusive beyond a point of reason. The warning referred to will be called a "technical warning" and the actual invoking of this penalty is called a "referee's technical." If after the technical is called against the abusing contestant and the play is not immediately continued within the allotted time provided for under the existing rules, the referee is empowered to forfeit the match in favor of the abusing contestant's opponent or opponents as the case may be. The referee's technical can be invoked by the referee as many times during the course of a match as he deems necessary.

(f) *Profanity.* No warning need be given by the referee, and an immediate referee's technical may be invoked by the referee if a player utters profane language in any way.

RULE 3.6

Scorers

The scorer may keep a record of the progress of the game in the manner prescribed by the committee or chairman. As a minimum the progress record shall include the order of serves, time-outs, and points. The referee may at his discretion also serve as scorer.

RULE 3.7

Recordkeepers

In addition to the scorer, the committee may designate additional persons to keep more detailed records for statistical purposes of the progress of the game.

RULE 3.8

Linesmen

Two linesmen will be designated by the tournament chairman or referee and shall, at the referee's signal, either agree or disagree with the referee's ruling.

The official signal by a linesman to show agreement with the referee is "thumbs up." The official signal to show disagreement is "thumbs down." The official signal for no opinion is an "open palm down."

If both linesmen disagree with the referee, the referee must reverse his ruling. If one linesman agrees and one linesman disagrees or has no opinion, the referee's call shall stand. If one linesman disagrees and one linesman has no opinion, the rally shall be replayed.

RULE 3.9

Appeals

In any match using linesmen, a player or team may appeal certain calls by the referee. These calls are (1) kill shots (whether good or bad), (2) fault serves, and (3) double-bounce pickups. At no time may a player or team appeal hinder, avoidable hinder, or technical foul calls.

The appeal must be directed to the referee, who will then request opinions from the linesmen. Any appeal made directly to a linesman by a player or team will be considered null and void, and forfeit any appeal rights for that player or for that particular rally.

(a) *Kill-shot appeals*. If the referee makes a call of "good" on a kill-shot attempt that ends a particular rally, the loser of the rally may appeal the call, if he feels the shot was not good. If the appeal is successful and the referee's original call reversed, the player who originally lost the rally is declared winner of the rally and is entitled to every benefit under the rules, i.e., point and/or service.

If the referee makes a call of "bad" or "skip" on a kill-shot attempt, he has ended the rally. The player against whom the call went has the right to appeal the call, if he feels the shot was good. If the appeal is successful and the referee's original call reversed, the player who originally lost the rally is declared winner of the rally and is entitled to every benefit under the rules as winner of a rally.

(b) *Fault-serve appeals*. If the referee makes a call of "fault" on a serve that the server felt was good, the server may appeal the call. If his appeal is successful, the server is then entitled to two additional serves.

If the served ball was considered by the referee to be an ace and in his opinion there was absolutely no way for the receiver to return the serve, then a point shall be awarded to the server.

If the referee makes a "no call" on a particular serve (therefore making it a legal serve) but either player feels the serve was short, either player may appeal the call at the end of the rally. If the loser of the rally appeals and wins his appeal, then the situation reverts back to the point of service with the call becoming fault. If it was a first service, one more

serve attempt is allowed. If the server already had one fault, the second fault would cause a side out.

(c) *Double-bounce pickup appeals*. If the referee makes a call of "two bounces," thereby stopping play, the player against whom the call was made has the right of appeal, if he feels he retrieved the ball legally. If the appeal is upheld, the rally is replayed.

If the referee makes no call on a particular play during the course of a rally in which one player feels his opponent retrieved a ball on two or more bounces, the player feeling this way has the right of appeal. However, since the ball is in play, the player wishing to appeal must clearly motion the referee and linesmen by raising his non-racquet hand, thereby alerting them to the exact play which is being appealed. At the same time, the player appealing must continue to retrieve and play the rally.

If the appealing player should win the rally, no appeal is necessary. If he loses the rally, and his appeal is upheld, the call is reversed and the "good" retrieve by his opponent becomes a "double-bounce pickup," making the appealing player the winner of the rally and entitled to all benefits thereof.

RULE 3.10

If at any time during the course of a match the referee is of the opinion that a player or team is deliberately abusing the right of appeal, by either repetitious appeals of obvious rulings, or as a means of unsportsmanlike conduct, the referee shall enforce the technical foul rule.

PART IV. PLAY REGULATIONS

RULE 4.1

Serve—Generally

(a) *Order*. The player or side winning the toss becomes the first server and starts the first game. The loser of the toss will serve first in the second game. The player or team scoring more points in games one and two combined shall serve first in the tiebreaker. In the event that both players or teams score an equal number of points in the first two games, another coin toss shall be held prior to the tiebreaker with the winner of the toss serving first.

(b) *Start*. Games are started from any place

within the service zone. No part of either foot may extend beyond either line of the service zone. Stepping on the line (but not beyond it) is permitted. Server must remain in the service zone until the served ball passes the short line. Violations are called "footfaults."

(c) *Manner.* A serve is commenced by bouncing the ball to the floor in the service zone, and on the first bounce the ball is struck by the server's racquet so that it hits the front wall and on the rebound hits the floor back of the short line, either with or without touching one of the side walls.

(d) *Readiness.* Serves shall not be made until the receiving side is ready, or the referee has called play ball.

(c) *Deliberate delays.* Deliberate delays on the part of the server or receiver exceeding ten seconds shall result in an out or point against the offender.

(1) This "ten-second rule" is applicable to both server and receiver, each of whom is allowed up to ten seconds to serve or be ready to receive. It is the server's responsibility to look and be certain the receiver is ready. If the receiver is not ready, he must signal so by raising his racquet above his head. Such raising of the racquet is the only legal signal that the receiver may make to alert the referee and server that he is not ready.

(2) If the server serves a ball while the receiver is signaling "not ready," the serve shall go over with no penalty.

(3) If the server looks at the receiver and the receiver is not signaling "not readiness," the server may then serve. If the receiver attempts to signal "not ready," after this point such signal shall not be acknowledged and the serve becomes legal.

(f) *Time-outs.* At no time shall a call of "time-out" by a player be acknowledged by the referee if the "time-out" call does not precede the serve; i.e., the so-called 'Chabot time-out," is not legal. The beginning of the serve, as indicated in Rule 4.1(c), is with the bounce of the ball.

RULE 4.2

Serve—In Doubles

(a) *Server.* At the beginning of each game in doubles, each side shall inform the referee of the order of service which order shall be followed throughout the game. Only the first server serves the first time up and continues to serve first throughout the game. When the first server is out—the side is out. Thereafter both players on each side shall serve until a handout occurs. It is not necessary for the server to alternate serves to their opponents.

(b) *Partner's position.* On each serve, the server's partner shall stand erect with his back to the side wall and with both feet on the floor within the service box until the served ball passes the short line. Violations are called "foot faults" subject to penalties thereof.

RULE 4.3

Defective Serves

Defective serves are of three types resulting in penalties as follows:

(a) *Dead-ball serve.* A dead-ball serve results in no penalty and the server is given another serve without canceling a prior illegal serve.

(b) *Fault serve.* Two fault serves result in a handout.

(c) *Out serves.* An out serve results in a handout.

RULE 4.4

Dead-Ball Serves

Dead-ball serves do not cancel any previous illegal serve. They occur when an otherwise legal serve:

(a) *Hits partner.* Hits the server's partner on the fly on the rebound from the front wall while the server's partner is in the service box. Any serve that touches the floor before hitting the partner in the box is a short.

(b) *Screen balls.* Passes so close to[3] the server or the server's partner as to obstruct the view of the returning side. Any serve passing behind the server's partner and the side wall is an automatic screen.

[3] IRA: within 18 inches of

(c) *Court hinders.* Hits any part of the court that under local rules is a dead ball.

RULE 4.5

Fault Serves

The following serves are faults and any two in succession results in a handout:

(a) *Footfaults.* A footfault results

(1) When the server leaves the service zone before the served ball passes the short line.

(2) When the server's partner leaves the service box before the served ball passes the short line.

(b) *Short service.* A short service is any served ball that first hits the front wall and on the rebound hits the floor in front of the back edge of the short line either with or without touching one side wall.

(c) *Three-wall serve.* A three-wall serve is any ball served that first hits the front wall and on the rebound hits two side walls on the fly.

(d) *Ceiling serve.* A ceiling serve is any served ball that touches the ceiling after hitting the front wall either with or without touching one side wall.

(e) *Long serve.* A long serve is any served ball that first hits the front wall and rebounds to the back wall before touching the floor.

(f) *Out-of-court serve.* Any ball going out of the court on the serve.

RULE 4.6

Out Serves

Any one of the following serves results in a handout:

(a) A serve in which the ball is struck after being bounced outside the service zone.

(b) *Missed ball.* Any attempt to strike the ball on the first bounce that results either in a total miss or in touching any part of the server's body other than his racquet.

(c) *Nonfront serve.* Any served ball that strikes the server's partner, or the ceiling, floor or side wall, before striking the front wall.

(d) *Touched serve.* Any served ball that on the rebound from the front wall touches the server or touches the server's partner while any part of his body is out of the service box or the server's partner intentionally catches the served ball on the fly.

(e) *Out-of-order serve.* In doubles, when either partner serves out of order.

(f) *Crotch serve.* If the served ball hits the crotch in the front wall it is considered the same as hitting the floor and is an out. A crotch serve into the back wall (or side wall on three-wall serves) is good and in play.

RULE 4.7

Return of Serve

(a) The receiver or receivers may not infringe on the "five foot zone" until the server strikes the ball. The receiver may then return the serve after the ball passes the short line, as long as no part of the receiver's body or racquet breaks the plane of the service zone. He may not return the serve on the fly in front of the five foot line.

(b) *Defective serve.* To eliminate any misunderstanding, the receiving side should not catch or touch a defectively served ball until called by the referee or it has touched the floor the second time.

(c) *Fly return.* In making a fly return, the receiver must end up with both feet back of the five foot line. A violation by a receiver results in a point for the server.

(d) *Legal return.* After the ball is legally served, one of the players on the receiving side must strike the ball with his racquet either on the fly or after the first bounce and before the ball touches the floor the second time to return the ball to the front wall either directly or after touching one or both side walls, the back wall or the ceiling, or any combination of those surfaces. A returned ball may not touch the floor before touching the front wall. (1) It is legal to return the ball by striking the ball into the back wall first, then hitting the front wall on the fly or after hitting the side wall or ceiling. (2) If the ball should strike the front wall, then back wall and then front wall again without striking the floor, the player whose turn it is to strike the ball, may do so by letting the ball bounce after hitting the front wall a second time. (3) If the ball strikes the front wall, then back wall, and then front wall again after striking the floor, the player whose turn it is to strike the ball must do so by striking it before it hits the floor a second time.

(e) *Failure to return.* The failure to return a serve results in a point for the server.

RULE 4.8

Changes of Serve

(a) *Handout.* A server is entitled to continue serving until:

(1) *Out serve.* He makes an out serve under Rule 4.6.

(2) *Fault serves.* He makes two fault serves in succession under Rule 4.5.

(3) *Hits partner.* He hits his partner with an attempted return.

(4) *Return failure.* He or his partner fails to keep the ball in play by returning it as required by Rule 4.7d.

(5) *Avoidable hinder.* He or his partner commits an avoidable hinder under Rule 4.11.

(b) *Sideout.*

(1) *In singles.* In singles, retiring the server retires the side.

(2) *In doubles.* In doubles, the side is retired when both partners have been put out, except on the first serve as provided in Rule 4.2a.

(c) *Effect.* When the server or the side loses the serve, the server or serving side shall become the receiver; and the receiver or receiving side, the server; and so alternately in all subsequent services of the game.

RULE 4.9

Rallies

Each legal return after the serve is called a rally. Play during rallies shall be according to the following rules:

(a) *One or both hands.* Only the head of the racquet may be used at any time to return the ball. The ball must be hit with the racquet in one or both hands. Switching hands to hit a ball is an out. The use of any portion of the body is an out.

(b) *One touch.* In attempting returns, the ball may be touched only once by one player on the returning side. In doubles both partners may swing at, but only one may hit the ball. Each violation of (a) or (b) results in a handout or point.

(c) *Return attempts.*

(1) *In singles.* In singles if a player swings at but misses the ball in play, the player may repeat his attempts to return the ball until it touches the floor the second time.

(2) *In doubles.* In doubles if one player swings at but misses the ball, both he and his partner may make further attempts to return the ball until it touches the floor the second time. Both partners on a side are entitled to an attempt to return the ball.

(3) *Hinders.* In singles or doubles, if a player swings at but misses the ball in play and in his or his partner's attempt again to play the ball there is an unintentional interference by an opponent it shall be a hinder. (See Rule 4.10.)

(d) *Touching Ball.* Except as provided in Rule 4.10a(2), any touching of a ball before it touches the floor the second time by a player other than the one making a return is a point or out against the offending player.

(e) *Out-of-court ball.*

(1) *After return.* Any ball returned to the front wall which on the rebound or on the first bounce goes into the gallery or through any opening in a side wall shall be declared dead and the serve replayed.

(2) *No return.* Any ball not returned to the front wall, but which caroms off a player's racquet into the gallery or into any opening in a side wall either with or without touching the ceiling, side or back wall, shall be an out or point against the player or players failing to make the return.

(f) *Dry ball.* During the game and particularly on service every effort should be made to keep the ball dry. Deliberate wetting shall result in an out.

(g) *Broken ball.* If there is any suspicion that the ball has broken during the serve, or during a rally, play shall continue until the end of the rally. The referee or any player may request the ball be examined. If the referee decides the ball is broken or otherwise defective, a new ball shall be put into play and the rally replayed.

(h) *Ball inspection.* The ball may be inspected by the referee between rallies at any time during a match.

(i) *Play stoppage.* (1) If a player loses a shoe or other equipment, or foreign objects enter the court, or any other outside interference occurs, the referee shall stop the play. (2) Players wearing protective eye glasses have the responsibility of having such eyeglasses securely fastened. In the event that such protective eye glasses should become unfastened and enter the court, the play shall be stopped as long as such eyeglasses were fastened initially. In the event such eyeglasses are not securely fastened, no stoppage of play shall result and the player wearing such glasses plays at his own risk. (3) If a player loses control of his racquet, time should be called after the point has been decided, providing the racquet does not strike an opponent or interfere with ensuing play.

RULE 4.10

Dead-Ball Hinders

Hinders are of two types—"dead ball" and "avoidable." Dead-ball hinders as described in this rule result in the rally being replayed. Avoidable hinders are described in Rule 4.11.

(a) *Situations.* When called by the referee, the following are dead-ball hinders:

(1) *Court hinders.* Hits any part of the court which under local rules is a dead ball.

(2) *Hitting opponent.* Any returned ball that touches an opponent on the fly before it returns to the front wall.

(3) *Body contact.* Any body contact with an opponent that interferes with seeing or returning the ball.

(4) *Screen ball.* Any ball rebounding from the front wall close to[4] the body of a player on the side which just returned the ball to interfere with or prevent the returning side from seeing the ball. See Rule 4.4(b).

[4] IRA: within 18 inches of

(5) *Straddle ball.* A ball passing between the legs of a player on the side which just returned the ball, if there is no fair chance to see or return the ball.

(6) *Backswing hinder.* If there is body contact on the back swing, the player must call it immediately. This is the only hinder call a player can make.

(7) *Other interference.* Any other unintentional interference that prevents an opponent from having a fair chance to see or return the ball.

(b) *Effect.* A call by the referee of a hinder stops the play and voids any situation following such as the ball hitting a player. No player is authorized to call a hinder, except on the backswing and such a call must be made immediately, as provided in Rule 4.10a(6).

(c) *Avoidance.* While making an attempt to return the ball, a player is entitled to a fair chance to see and return the ball. It is the duty of the side that has just served or returned the ball to move so that the receiving side may go straight to the ball and not be required to go around an opponent. The referee should be liberal in calling hinders to discourage any practice of playing the ball where an adversary cannot see it until too late. It is no excuse that the ball is "killed," unless in the opinion of the referee the ball couldn't be returned. Hinders should be called without a claim by a player, especially in close plays and on game points.

(d) *In doubles.* In doubles, both players on a side are entitled to a fair and unobstructed chance at the ball and either one is entitled to a hinder even though naturally it would be his partner's ball and even though his partner may have attempted to play the ball or that he may already have missed it. It is not a hinder when one player hinders his partner.

RULE 4.11

Avoidable Hinders

An avoidable hinder results in an "out" or a point depending upon whether the offender was serving or receiving.

(a) *Failure to move.* Does not move sufficiently to allow opponent his shot.

(b) *Blocking.* Moves into a position effecting a block, on the opponent about to return the ball, or, in doubles, one partner moves in front of an opponent as his partner is returning the ball.

(c) *Moving into ball.* Moves in the way and is struck by the ball just played by his opponent.

(d) *Pushing.* Deliberately pushing or shoving an opponent during a rally.

RULE 4.12

Rest Periods

(a) *Delays.* Deliberate delay exceeding ten seconds by server, or receiver shall result in an out or point against the offender. (See Rule 4.1(e).)

(b) *During game.* During a game each player in singles, or each side in doubles, either while serving or receiving may request a time-out for a towel, wiping glasses, change, or adjustment. Each time-out shall not exceed thirty seconds. No more than three time-outs in a game shall be granted each singles players or each team in doubles. Two time-outs shall be allotted each player in singles or each team in doubles in the tiebreaker.

(c) *Injury.* No time shall be charged to a player who is injured during play. An injured player shall not be allowed more than a total of fifteen minutes of rest. If the injured player is not able to resume play after total rests of fifteen minutes, the match shall be awarded to the opponent or opponents. On any further injury to same player, the tournament director, if present, or committee after considering any available medical opinion shall determine whether the injured player will be allowed to continue.

(d) *Between games.* A five-minute rest period is allowed between the first and second games and a five-minute rest period between the second and third games.[5] Players may leave the court between games, but must be on the court and ready to play at the expiration of the rest period.

[5] In IRA tournaments, a two-minute rest period is allowed between the first and second games and a ten-minute rest period between the second and third games.

(e) *Postponed Games.* Any games postponed by referee due to weather elements shall be resumed with the same score as when postponed.

APPENDIX

PART V TOURNAMENTS

RULE 5.1

Draws

The seeding method of drawing shall be the standard method approved by the USRA and NRC. All draws in professional brackets shall be the responsibility of the national director of the NRC.

RULE 5.2

Scheduling

(a) *Preliminary matches.* If one or more contestants are entered in both singles and doubles they may be required to play both singles and doubles on the same day or night with little rest between matches. This is a risk assumed on entering both singles and doubles. If possible the schedule should provide at least a one-hour rest period between all matches.

(b) *Final matches.* Where one or more players have reached the finals in both singles and doubles, it is recommended that the doubles match be played on the day preceding the singles. This would assume more rest between the final matches. If both final matches must be played on the same day or night, the following procedure should be followed:

(1) The singles match be played first.

(2) A rest period of not less than *one hour* be allowed between the finals in singles and doubles.

RULE 5.3

Notice of Matches

After the first round of matches, it is the responsibility of each player to check the posted schedules to determine the time and place of each subsequent match. If any change is made in the schedule after posting, it shall be the duty of the committee or chairman to notify the players of the change.

RULE 5.4

Third Place

In championship tournaments, national, state, district, etc. (if there is a playoff for third place), the loser in the semifinals must play for third place or lose his ranking for next year unless he is unable to compete because of injury or illness. (See Rule 3.5d (4).)

RULE 5.5

USRA Regional Tournaments

Each year the United States and Canada are divided into regions for the purpose of sectional competition preceding the national championships. The exact boundaries of each region are dependent on the location of the regional tournaments. The locations are announced in *National Racquetball* magazine.

(a) Only players residing in the area defined can participate in a local tournament.

(b) Winners of open singles and ladies open singles in regional tournaments will receive round-trip air-coach tickets to the USRA national tourney. Remuneration will be made after arrival at the nationals.

(c) A USRA officer will be in attendance at each regional tournament and will coordinate with the host chairman.

(1) *Awards.* No individual award in USRA-sanctioned tournaments should exceed value of more than $25.

(2) *Tournament management.* In all USRA-sanctioned tournaments the tournament chairman and/or the national USRA official in attendance may decide on a change of courts after the completion of any tournament game if such a change will accommodate better spectator conditions.

(3) *Tournament conduct.* In all USRA-sanctioned tournaments the referee is empowered to default a match if an individual player or team conducts itself to the detriment of the tournament and the game.

(4) *Professional definition.* Any player who has accepted $1,000 or more in prizes and/or prize money in the most recent twelve calendar months is considered a professional racquetball player and ineligible for participation in any USRA-sanctioned tournament bracket.

(5) *Pick-a-partner.* The essence of the "player's fraternity" has been to allow player to come to tournaments and select a doubles partner, if necessary, regardless what organization or city he might represent.

(6) *Age brackets.* The following age brackets, determined by the age of the player on the first day of the tournament, are:

Open: Any age can compete.

Juniors: 17 and under.

Seniors: 35 and over.

Masters: 45 and over.

Golden Masters: 55 and over.

In doubles both players must be within the specified age bracket.

ONE- AND THREE-WALL RACQUETBALL

Source: *Official Rules of Racquetball,* International Racquetball Association, 1979

Basically, racquetball rules for one-wall three-wall, and four-wall are the same, with the following exceptions:

ONE WALL

Court size. Wall shall be 20 feet in width and 16 feet high, floor 20 feet in width and 34 feet from the wall to the back edge of the long line. There should be a minimum of 3 feet beyond the long line and 6 feet outside each side line and behind the long line to permit movement area for the players.

Short line. Back edge 16 feet from the wall.

Service markers. Lines at least 6 inches long parallel to and midway between the long and short lines, extending in from the side lines. The imaginary extension and joining of these lines indicates the service line. Lines are 1½ inches in width.

Service zone. Floor area inside and including the short, side, and service lines.

Receiving zone. Floor area in back of short line bounded by and including the long and side lines.

THREE-WALL

Serve. A serve that goes beyond the side walls on the fly in player or side out. A serve that goes beyond the long line on a fly but within the side walls is the same as a "short."

Court size. Short side wall—20 feet in width, 20 feet in height and 40 feet in length. Side wall shall extend back on either side from the front wall parallel 20 feet along the side wall markers. Side wall may extend from 20 feet at the front wall and taper down to 12 feet at the end of the side wall. All other markings are the same as for four wall racquetball.

Court size. Long side wall 20 feet in width and 20 feet in height and 40 feet in length. Side wall shall extend back on either side 40 feet. The side wall may but is not restricted to tapering from 20 feet of height at the front wall down to 12 feet at the 40-foot marker. All lines are the same as four-wall racquetball.

PADDLE TENNIS Source: *The Game of Paddle Tennis,* United States Paddle Tennis Association, 1978

RULE 1

Dimensions of Court

Fifty feet long by 20 feet wide. Same court for singles and doubles; there are no doubles alleys.

There are four service courts 22 feet long by 10 feet wide.[1]

[1] On the West Coast, courts have a restraint line 12 feet from the net, parallel to the baseline on each side of the net.

There shall be space behind each baseline of not less than 15 feet, and at the sides of not less than 10 feet wherever possible.

RULE 2

Height of Net

Thirty-one inches at net posts with cable pulled taut; not more than 1 inch allowable sag at center if there is no steel cable. Net posts shall be 18 inches from sidelines.

RULE 3

Official Ball

A deadened tennis ball. A "deadened" tennis ball is a pressurized ball approved by the USTA which has its internal pressure reduced by being punctured so that when dropped from a height of 6 feet to the court surface the bounce will be not less than 31 inches (the height of net) nor more than 33 inches. In other words, the punctured ball shall rebound 6 to 8 inches lower than a regular tennis ball. Puncturing with a safety pin or hypodermic needle is a simple method of achieving the required bounce.

RULE 4

The Paddle

The paddle shall be not more than 17½ inches long and 8½ inches wide, and may be perforated or solid. No spongy or other extraneous material may be applied to paddle face; and no strung racquet shall be used in any sanctioned tournament.

RULE 5

Service

Only one underhand serve is allowed. If serve is a fault, the server loses that point. Before commencing to serve, the server shall stand with both feet at rest behind the baseline and within the imaginary extensions of the center and side lines. The server shall then project the ball by hand into the air and strike it with the paddle at a point not higher than 31 inches above the court surface at the instant of impact; or, the server may bounce or drop the ball to the court surface behind the baseline and strike it with the paddle upon its rebound at a point not higher than 31 inches above the court surface. Delivery shall be deemed complete at the instant of impact of paddle and ball.

The server may choose either method of serving, that is, bouncing the ball or projecting it into the air before striking it with the paddle. However, whichever alternative he chooses, he must continue to serve in that manner for the entire set. In other words, he cannot switch from a bounce serve to the projecting serve at will; although he may change his manner of serving at the commencement of a new set.

The server shall throughout the delivery of the service not take two full steps (nor more) in the natural progression of making the serve. The server may take a step with either foot, with the other foot making the follow-through step. If either foot touches or swings over any area other than that behind the baseline before contact between ball and paddle it is a footfault.

Service shall begin in the right-hand court at the start of every game. The ball served shall pass over the net and hit the ground within the 22-foot-by-10-foot service court which is diagonally opposite, or upon any line bounding such court, and progress from there to the left-hand court, alternating at each point until game is completed. If the ball is served from the wrong court, and is not detected, all points will stand as played, but the correct station shall be assumed as soon as the mistake is discovered.

One ball only shall be used during a set. Server may not substitute another ball during an unfinished set without consent of opponent or tournament official; nor may server hold another ball when serving.[2]

[2] On the West Coast, in doubles, the restraint rule applies:

> Both feet of all players must be *clearly behind* the "restraint" line until clearly after the receiver's paddle strikes the ball. A player may lean into the "bucket" area as long as his feet are behind the restraint line. Foot progress into the bucket area simultaneous, or nearly so, with the paddle versus ball impact constitutes a violation, and the point shall be awarded the other side.
>
> If there is a reasonable doubt as to the violation, the umpire may call a "let" and the point shall be replayed. Restraint ends for the receiving team the moment the receiver crosses the restraint line prior to contact being made by receiver in order to *return a short serve*.
>
> The receiver's paddle must contact the service in order for play to continue. Receiver may not swing at a served ball, miss the ball, and charge the server with violation of the restraint rule.
>
> —SOURCE: *Official Rules of Play,* American Paddle Tennis League

RULE 6

"One Bounce" Rule (Applies to Singles Only)

Each player must allow the ball to bounce once on his side before being permitted to volley; in other words, the server must return the return of service as a ground stroke.

RULE 7

Good Return

It is a good return.

(a) If the ball touches the net, posts, cord or metal cable, strap, or band, provided that it passes over any of them and hits the ground within the court.

(b) If the ball, served or returned, hits the ground within the proper court and rebounds or is blown back over the net, and the player whose turn it is to strike reaches over the net and plays the ball, provided that neither he nor any part of his clothes or paddle touch the net, posts, cord or metal cable, strap or band, or the ground within his opponent's court, and that the stroke be otherwise good.

(c) If the ball be returned outside the post, either above or below the level of the top of the net, even though it touch the post, provided that it hits the ground within the proper court.

(d) If a player's paddle follow through over the net after he has properly returned the ball, provided the ball was hit on the striker's side of net.

RULE 8

Professionals

There shall be no distinction between professionals in any sport and amateurs. All players are eligible for USPTA tournament play.

Except as noted above, the rules of play and scoring of the United States Tennis Association shall govern.

(See p. 222) The 12-point tiebreaker is played when games reach 6 all.

Source: *Official Rules of Platform Tennis,* American Platform Tennis Association, 1978

RULE 1

Dimensions and Terminology

The court is a rectangle 44 feet long and 20 feet wide, laid out on a surface with a playing area 60 feet by 30 feet which is enclosed by a screen 12 feet high. The screen is held taut by a superstructure around the perimeter of the deck. Screens are made of 1-inch hexagonal galvanized wire mesh.

The court is divided across the middle by a net the ends of which are attached to posts. The posts are 37 inches high and 18 inches outside the court (acceptable tolerance ± 6 inches). The height of the net at the posts is 37 inches and at center is 34 inches. The net is held down taut and adjusted for height by a vertical center strap 2 inches wide.

The lines at the ends of the court, parallel to the net, are called "baselines." The lines at the sides of the court, perpendicular to the net, are called "sidelines." Two feet inside the sidelines and running parallel to them for the length of the court are the "alley lines." Twelve feet from the net on either side and running parallel to it from alley line to alley line are the "service lines." The segments of the alley lines between the service lines and the net are called the "service sidelines." The area between the net and the service lines is divided in half by a line perpendicular to them. This line is called the "center service line." Each baseline is bisected by an imaginary extension of the center service line called the "center mark." The center mark appears as a line 4 inches long extending into the court at right angles to, and touching the baselines.

The area between the baseline and the service line is called the "backcourt." The area between the service line and the net is called the "forecourt," which in turn is divided into two "service courts," left and right. The area between the side line and the alley line is called the "alley."

All lines are customarily 2 inches wide and all measurements are made to the outside of the lines from the net or the center of the center service line. This line is in both service courts and is itself centered on the imaginary center line of the court. All lines are within the court.

There is a space of 8 feet between each baseline and the back screen, and a space of 5 feet between each side line and the side screen. These spaces are part of the playing area, but they are not part of the court.

On either side of the court, or on both sides, an access door is cut into the superstructure. The door is located near the center of the court.

RULE 2

Court Fixtures

Court fixtures are the net, the posts, the cord (or metal cable) that holds up the net, the band across the top of the net, the center strap, the screens, the snow boards, the superstructure, the doors, the lighting poles and lights, any crossbeams or corner supports within the enclosure, and, when they are present, the umpire and his chair.

RULE 3

The Ball and the Paddle

The ball is a rubber ball with either orange or yellow flocking, conforming to APTA specifications for diameter, weight, bounce and other standards as set forth in Table A.

The paddle is 17 inches in overall length with a playing area 10⅜ inches long and a handle 6⅝ inches long. The paddle is perforated with a number of ⅜-inch holes. The surface of the paddle must be flat and the finish smooth. APTA paddle standards are set forth in Table B.

RULE 4

Use of Ball and Paddle

Only one ball shall be used continuously during each set unless otherwise specified by the tournament committee. Server may not substitute another ball during an unfinished set without the permission of tournament officials, nor may server hold two balls while serving.

A player may not carry a second paddle during play, although it is permissible to use both hands on the paddle and to switch the paddle from hand to hand in the course of play.

RULE 5

Singles Game

A singles game has been approved, on a one-year trial basis, which utilizes the standard singles court, all four wires, and a single serve.

RULE 6

Choice of Sides and Service

The choice of sides and the right to serve first or to receive first is decided by toss, which is generally accomplished by spinning the paddle.

The team that does not toss has the right to call the toss. The team winning the toss has the following options:

(a) The right to serve first, in which case the other team has the right to choose from which end of the court to receive.

(b) The right to receive first, in which case the other team has the right to choose from which end of the court to serve.

(c) The right to choose the end, in which case the other team has the right to elect to serve first or to receive first.

(d) The right to require the other team to make the first choice.

RULE 7

Server and Receiver

After the toss has been concluded, the teams take their places on opposite sides of the net. The member of the serving team who elects to serve first becomes the server. The member of the receiving team who elects to play the right court becomes the first receiver.

The server must deliver service from a position behind the baseline and between the center mark and the sideline, diagonally cross-court from the receiver.

The receiver may stand wherever he pleases on his own side of the net, on or off the court. Likewise the server's partner and the receiver's partner may take any position they choose on their own sides of the net, on or off the court.

The server alternates serving, first from behind his own right court into the receiver's right service court, then from behind his own left court into the receiver's left service court, and so on. Members of the receiving team alternate receiving service.

If the server serves from behind the wrong court and his mistake is not discovered until the point has been completed, the point stands as played, but thereafter the server must serve from the correct court according to the score. If the server serves from behind the wrong court and the mistake is detected by the receiving team after the service has been delivered and that team does not attempt to return the service, the server loses the point.

The ball served must pass over the net cleanly and hit the deck within the proper service court before the receiver may return it. The receiver may not volley the serve, i.e., strike the ball before it has bounced. If he does so, the receiver loses the point outright.

RULE 8

Delivery of the Service

The service is delivered as follows: the server takes an initial position behind the baseline and between an imaginary extension of the center mark and the sideline, as described in Rule 7. The server then projects the ball by hand into the air in any direction, and before it hits the ground strikes the ball with his paddle. At the moment of impact the service delivery is completed.

Note: The serve may be delivered overhand, underhand, or sidearm as the server chooses. There is no obligation on server's part to inform receiver as to his intention, and server may vary his type of delivery.

RULE 9

Only One Service

Only one service is allowed. If the service is a fault, the server loses the point. If the service is a let, the server serves the point again.

RULE 10

Fault or Out

The serve is a fault if

(a) The server does not take a legal position as described in Rules 7 and 8.

(b) The server commits a footfault. (See Rule 11.)

(c) The server misses the ball completely in attempting to strike it.

(d) The ball does not land in the proper service court.

(e) The ball served hits the server's partner.

(f) The ball touches a court fixture other than the net, band, or center strap before it hits the deck. If it touches any of the above fixtures and then lands within the proper service court, it is a let. (See Rule 13.)

> Comment: It is customary for the receiving team, especially receiver's partner, to determine whether the serve is a fault by reason of (a) the ball's having landed outside the proper service court or (b) the server's having violated the footfault rule. The first such call of a footfault on each server in a match not being officiated shall be a let. After his "grace fault" it is loss of point.
>
> Under tournament conditions, if there are linesmen, they assume the responsibility for calling all footfaults. At any time in any round of a tournament match any player is entitled to request a footfault judge and/or linesmen.

A ball in play (other than a serve) is out if it does not land within the court on the proper side of the net after either crossing the net or touching the net, post, cord, band, or center strap.

> Note: Since all parts of the lines bounding the court are deemed to be within the court, a ball that touches any part of a line is good.
>
> The usual procedure is for the receiving team to make line calls on its own side of the net in matches in which there are no linesmen. Any doubts should be resolved in favor of the opponents.

RULE 11

Footfault

The server shall, throughout delivery of the service, up to the moment of impact of paddle and ball:

(a) Not change his position by walking or running.

(b) Not touch, with either foot, any area other than that behind the baseline within the imaginary extension of the center mark and the sideline.

> Note: The server shall not by the following movements of his feet be deemed to "change his position by walking or running":

(1) Slight movements of the feet which do not materially affect the location originally taken by him;

(2) An unrestricted movement of one foot, so long as the other foot maintains continuously its original contact with the deck;

(3) Leaving the deck with both feet.

RULE 12

Receiving Team Must Be Ready

The server must not deliver his serve until the receiving team is ready. If the receiver makes any attempt to return the ball, he is deemed to be ready. Also, if the receiver attempts to return the ball, it is deemed that his partner also is ready.

If the receiver says that he is not ready as a serve is being delivered, the serve shall be played again, provided the receiver does not attempt to return the ball. In such case, the receiver may not claim a fault should the serve land outside the service court.

RULE 13

A Let

In all cases where a let is called, the point is to be replayed.

The service is a let if

(a) It touches the net cord, center strap or band and then lands in the proper service court.

(b) After touching the net, band or center strap it touches either member of the receiving team or anything they are wearing or carrying before hitting the deck, regardless of where they might be standing, on or off the court.

(c) It is delivered when the receiving team is not ready. (See Rule 12.)

A ball in play is a let if

(d) It hits an overhanging obstruction such as a tree limb or a crossbeam.

(e) The ball becomes broken in the course of a point.

(f) Play is interrupted by an accidental occurrence such as a ball from another court bouncing into the court.

> Note: In any situation during the play of a point when a let may be called, if the player who could call the let does not do so immediately and permits play to

continue, that decision is binding on his team. It is not reasonable to opt not to call a let, strike the ball for loss of point, and then ask for a let to be called.

RULE 14

Serve Touching Receiving Team

If the serve touches the receiver or the receiver's partner or anything they are wearing or carrying before the ball has hit the deck, the server wins the point outright, provided the serve is not a let as described in Rule 13b. This ruling applies whether the member of the receiving team is hit while he is standing on or off the court.

RULE 15

When Receiver Becomes Server

At the end of the first game of a set, the receiving team becomes the serving team. The partners decide between them who will serve first in each set. The order of service remains in force for that entire set.

RULE 16

Serving or Receiving out of Turn

If a player serves out of turn the player who should be serving must take over the serving from the point that the mistake is discovered. All points stand as played.

If an entire game is served by the wrong player the game score stands as played, but the order of service remains as altered, so that in no case may one player on a team serve three games in a row.

If the receiving team receives from the wrong sides of their court (as established in their first receiving game of the set), they must play that entire game from the "wrong courts" but must revert to the original sides of their court the next game they are receivers.

RULE 17

Ball Remains in Play

Once a ball is put into play by service, it remains in play until the point is decided, unless a fault or a let is called.

> Explanation: A player may not catch a ball that appears to be going out of bounds and claim the point.

The ball is in play until it actually hits the screen on the fly, or bounces on the deck. A player catching or stopping a ball and calling "out" before the ball is legally out loses the point for his team.

RULE 18

Loss of Point

A team loses the point if

(a) The ball bounces a second time on its side of the net, provided the first bounce was within the court:

> Discussion: Sometimes it is difficult to determine whether a player attempting to retrieve a ball, especially a drop shot, that has bounced once and is about to bounce again, actually strikes the ball before it bounces the second time. Propriety dictates that the player attempting to hit the ball is honor bound to call "not up" if he feels the ball did in fact bounce twice. A player who has any doubt in this situation will ask the nearest opponent, after the point has been decided, "Was I up?" If the opponent says no, the point should be conceded.

(b) A player returns the ball in such a way that it hits
   (1) The deck on the other side of the net outside the side lines or baseline.
   (2) Any object, other than an opposing player, on the other side of the net outside the sidelines or baseline.
   (3) The net, post, cord, band, or center strap and does not then land within the court on the other side of the net.

(c) A player volleys the ball and fails to make a good return, even when standing outside the court:

> Explanation: A player standing outside the court volleys at his own risk. It is not proper to volley the ball and simultaneously call it "out" for if the ball is volleyed it is in play.

(d) A player touches or strikes the ball more than once in making a stroke (commonly called a "double hit," or "carry").

(e) A player volleys the ball before it has crossed over to his side of the net, i.e., reaches over the net to strike the ball, making contact on the opponents' side of the net. (See Rule 20b.)

(f) A player is touched by a ball in play, unless it is a let service. (See Rule 13b.)

> Note: It does not matter whether the player is inside or outside the court, whether he is hit squarely or his clothing merely grazed, or whether the contact is accidental or purposeful. If a ball touches anything other than a player's paddle it is loss of point.

(g) A player throws his paddle at the ball in play and hits it.

(h) A player bounces the ball over the screen and out of the enclosure or into a lighting fixture, whether or not the ball rebounds back into the court.

(i) A player or anything he wears or carries, touches the net, post, cord, band, or center strap, or the court surface on the opponents' side of the net, within the boundary lines, while the ball is in play.

> Note: If the point has already been concluded, it is not a violation to touch any of these fixtures. Also, if in rushing to retrieve a drop shot, a player's momentum carries him past the net post onto the opponents' side of the net, this is not loss of point unless the player actually steps inside the opponents' court or interferes with one of the opponents. Mere physical contact with an opponent is not loss of point unless such contact hinders the opponent.
>
> When a player is standing at the net and the opponent hits the ball into the net in such a way that it pushes the net against his paddle or his person, the net player loses the point. It does not matter that the ball was not going over the net. The net player loses the point because he made contact with the net while the ball was still in play.

RULE 19

Ball Touching Court Fixtures

If the ball in play touches a court fixture (as defined in Rule 2) after it has hit the deck within the boundaries of the court, the ball remains in play and may be returned, so long as it has not hit the deck a second time on the same side of the net.

> Exceptions: If the ball hits a lighting fixture, the point is concluded—loss of point for striker. If the ball hits a crossbeam, it is a let.

In matches in which an umpire and an umpire's chair are inside the enclosure, a ball striking either the umpire or his chair prior to landing in the opponents' court is loss of point for the striker.

RULE 20

Good Return

It is a good return if

(a) The ball touches the net, posts, cord, band, or center strap and then hits the deck within the proper court.

(b) The ball, served or returned, hits the deck within the proper court and rebounds or is blown back over the net, and the player whose turn it is to strike reaches over the net and plays the ball, provided that neither he nor any part of his clothing or equipment touches the net, posts, cord, band, or center strap or the deck within his opponents' court, and that the stroke is otherwise good. (See also Rule 21, ''Interference.'')

(c) The ball is returned outside the post, either above or below the level of the top of the net, whether or not it touches the post, provided that it then hits the deck within the proper court.

> Note: It is not a good return if the ball is hit through the open space between the net and the post.

(d) A player's paddle passes over the net after he has returned the ball, provided that the ball had crossed to his side of the net before being struck by him, and that the stroke is otherwise good.

RULE 21

Interference

In case a player is hindered in making a stroke by anything not within his control, the point is replayed.

> Clarification: If a tree branch or a ball from another court should interfere with play, a let should be called immediately. However, if a player bumps into his own partner or is interfered with by a court fixture, that is not grounds for a let.
>
> In the situation covered by Rule 20b, if the player who is attempting to strike the ball is willfully hindered by his opponent, the player is entitled to the point by reason of interference, whether such interference is verbal or physical. However, if it is agreed that such interference was unintentional, a let should be called.

RULE 22

Scoring

(a) *The game*

The first point is called ''15,'' although it is also commonly called ''5.''

The second point is called ''30.''

The third point is called ''40.''

The fourth point is ''game.''

When both teams score 15, or both score 30, the score is called ''15 all'' or ''30 all.''

When both teams score 40, the score is called ''deuce.''

The next point after deuce is called ''advantage'' for the team winning it, thus ''advantage server'' (or more usually "ad in"), if the serving team wins, and "advantage receiver" (or "ad out"), if the receiving team wins.

If the team with the advantage wins the next point, it wins the game. If the other team wins that point, the score reverts to deuce. This continues indefinitely until one or the other team wins two points in a row from deuce, which wins the game. Zero or no points is called "love." A game that is won "at love" means that the losing team scored no points.

(b) *The set*

The team that first wins six games wins the set. However, the winning team must have a margin of two games, and a set played under the traditional rules continues until one team has such a two-game margin, e.g., 8–6 or 11–9.

A set that is won "at love" means that the losing team scored no games.

Should the players or the tournament committee decide to play a tiebreaker, a special procedure is followed when the game score is 6 all. (See p. 247.) The APTA recommends the use of the 12-point tiebreaker, especially when time is a problem. Tournament committees should announce in the tournament rules whether the tiebreaker is to be played.

(c) *The match*

Customarily a match is best of three sets but a tournament committee has the right to require best of five in the late rounds or the finals of a men's tournament.

> Comment: In matches played without an umpire the server should announce the point scores as the game goes on, and the game score at the end of his service game. Misunderstandings will be averted if this practice is followed.

RECOMMENDED NUMBER OF SETS TO BE PLAYED IN DIFFERENT EVENTS

Junior Girls—Ages 18 and 15
    2 out of 3 all through the tournament
Junior Boys—Age 15
    2 out of 3 all through the tournament
Junior Boys—Age 18
    2 out of 3 to the finals
    3 out of 5 finals
Men's—Ranking Tournaments
    2 out of 3 to the finals
    3 out of 5 finals

Men's—National
    2 out of 3 to quarters,
    then 3 out of 5
Men's—45
    2 out of 3 to finals
    finals—3 out of 5
Men's—Seniors
    2 out of 3 all the way
Men's—Veterans
    2 out of 3 all the way
Ladies'
    2 out of 3 all the way
Mixed
    2 out of 3 all the way

RULE 23

When Teams Change Sides

Teams change sides at the end of the first, third, fifth, and every subsequent odd-numbered game of each set.

When a set ends on an odd total of games, e.g., 6–3, the teams "change for one"—that is, they change sides for one game, and then change sides again after the first game of the next set. When the set ends on an even total of games, e.g., 6–4, the teams "stay for one" and then change sides after the first game of the next set.

RULE 24

Continuous Play

Play shall be continuous from the first serve of the first game until the conclusion of the match, except:

(a) Rest periods are permitted by tournament officials.

(b) When changing sides on the odd games, a maximum of one minute is allowed for players to towel off, change equipment, rest, etc.

(c) Play shall never be suspended, delayed, or interfered with for the purpose of enabling a player to recover his strength or to receive instruction or advice. The umpire shall be the sole judge of such suspension, delay, or interference, and after giving due warning he may disqualify the offender. No allowance may be made for natural loss of physical condition such as cramps, faintness, or loss of wind. Consideration may be given by the umpire for accidental loss of physical ability or condition.

> Note 1: In the event of an accident, a fall, collision with a net post, a sprained ankle, and the like, up to a ten-minute suspension in play may be authorized. A

default will be mandatory if play is not resumed immediately after the suspension.

Note 2: If a player's clothing, footwear, or equipment becomes out of adjustment in such a way that it is impossible or undesirable for him to play on, the provisions in Note 1 shall apply.

Clarification: The intent of the Continuous Play Rule is to prevent unauthorized rest periods for players who are tired and to discourage stalling tactics for whatever purpose. In the event of an accident, the umpire or tournament chairman shall consider a temporary suspension of play.

If a match is adjourned for a legitimate reason, e.g., a sudden rainstorm, when the match is resumed (a) the teams are entitled to a full warm-up and (b) the match must begin precisely where it left off, with the same game and point score, same server, same sides of the court, and same order of service.

RULE 25

Only One Hit

In the course of making a return, only one player may hit the ball. If both players, either simultaneously or consecutively, hit the ball, it is an illegal return and loss of point. Mere clashing of paddles does not constitute an illegal return, provided that only one player strikes the ball.

RULE 26

Balls Off Screens

If a ball in play or on the serve hits the deck in the proper court and then touches any part of the back or side screens, or both screens, or the horizontal top rails, or the snow boards, it may be played, so long as it does not bounce on the deck a second time on the same side of the net before being hit by the player.

Note: A ball taken off the screen must be returned directly over the net into the opponents' court. It may not be caromed back indirectly by being hit from paddle to screen and thence into the opponents' court.

THE APTA—APPROVED 12-POINT TIEBREAKER FOR PLATFORM TENNIS

Revised 12-point Tiebreaker

At six games all the players continue to serve in order and from the same side as before. *The server of the first point of the tiebreaker will serve only one*

point and that to the ad court. Each player will then, in normal service rotation, serve twice; first to the deuce court then to the ad court. The single point served by the initial server of the tiebreaker results in an immediate change of sides and teams will continue to change sides in the normal pattern as if the server had served an entire game. First team to win 7 points wins set, although if it be 6 points all, the team must win by 2 points in a row. The set shall be scored at 7–6. The team receiving service for the first point of the tiebreaker shall begin serving the next set from the opposite side from which it received the first point. The teams shall change sides after the first game.

Example
North

A	B
C	D

South

A started serving the set from N side.
It's 6 games all and it's A's turn to serve again.
A serves once (ad court) from N side.
Change sides
C serves twice from N side.*
(deuce court first; ad court second)
B serves twice from S side.
(deuce court first; ad court second)
Change sides
D serves twice from S side.
(deuce court first; ad court second)
A serves twice from N side.
(deuce court first; ad court second)
Change sides and repeat this order until one team reaches 7 points or wins by 2 points after each team reaches 6 points.
Team C-D starts serving next set from N side
Teams change sides after one game.

*Assuming that C has been following A in service order.

THE DETERMINING SET OF THE FINAL ROUND OF EACH TOURNAMENT MUST BE PLAYED OUT WITHOUT A TIEBREAKER (THIRD SET OF TWO-OUT-OF-THREE SET MATCH, AND FIFTH SET OF THREE-OUT-OF-FIVE SET MATCH).

If a ball change is called for on a tiebreaker game, the change should be deferred until the second game of the following set, to preserve the alternation of the right to serve first with the new ball.

TABLE A
BALL PERFORMANCE STANDARDS AND ACCEPTABLE TOLERANCES

The APTA has established the following Performance Standards and Acceptable Tolerances for ball.

The APTA reserves the right to withhold or terminate approval if the association feels the standards have not been met by a manufacturer, and to approve balls for sanctioned play as it sees fit.

I. *Bounce Test for Rebound*

Balls conditioned at 70°F for twenty-four hours, then dropped from 90 inches to a concrete slab, and the rebound measured. Bounce to be measured from bottom of ball.

	Acceptable Tolerance
Rebound	43″–48″

II. Weight Test

	Acceptable Tolerance
	70 g–75 g

III. Diameter Test

Measure diameter along two perpendicular axes of the ball. Both readings must be within tolerance.

	Standard	Acceptable Tolerance
Diameter	2½″	2½″ ± $\frac{1}{32}$″

TABLE B
PLATFORM TENNIS PADDLE STANDARDS AND ACCEPTABLE TOLERANCES

	Standard	Tolerance
Total Length	17″ maximum	none
Thickness (including rim)	$\frac{3}{8}$″ ± $\frac{1}{16}$″	
Handle Length	6⅝″ maximum	none
Width of Head (at widest point)	8¼″ maximum	
Play Length (handle to outside edge of rim)	10⅜″ maximum	
Bolts and Nuts	Flat and flush (Preferably concealed by grip)	none
Holes—Number	87 maximum	
Holes—Diameter	⅜″	none
Edges—Shape	Squared or rounded	none
Surface Finish	Smooth	none
Surface	Flat	none

FOUR-WALL PADDLEBALL

Source: *Official Paddleball Rules,* National Paddleball Association.

RULE 1

The game

(a) *Players.* Paddleball may be played by two players (singles), three players (cutthroat), or four players (doubles).

(b) *Description.* The game is played with a wooden paddle and a paddleball in a four-wall, one-wall, or three-wall court.

(c) *Game score.* A game is won by the side first scoring 21 points. Points are scored only by the serving side when it serves an ace or wins a volley.

(d) *Match score.* A match consists of the best two out of three games.

RULE 2

Court

The standard four-wall court is 40 feet long, 20 feet wide with front and side walls 20 feet high, a back wall at least 12 feet high, and a ceiling. A line midway between and parallel with the front and back walls divides the court in the center and is called the "short line." A line 5 feet in front of the short line and parallel to it is called the "service line." The space between and including these two lines is called the "service zone." A line 18 inches from and parallel with the side wall at each end of the service zone is called the "service box." All lines are 1½ inches wide and are red or black.

RULE 3

Equipment

(a) *Paddle.* The official paddle is wooden and is approximately 8 inches wide; 16 inches long, weighing approximately 16 ounces, with a leather thong attached to the end of the handle, which must be worn around the wrist during play. Racquets with strings are not permitted. (An "official" paddle is manufactured by Marcraft Recreation Corp., 20 Chestnut Street, Garfield, N.J. 07026.)

(b) *Ball.* The official paddleball is the Pennsy Official National Paddleball made by General Tire–Pennsylvania Athletic Products, Akron, Ohio. When dropped from a height of 6 feet, it should rebound approximately 3½ feet. Balls shall be approved for play by the referee prior to the start of the match.

(c) *Uniform.* For tournament play players are required to wear white shirts, white socks, white shorts, and white shoes. A team name or club insignia may be worn on the shirt. A glove may be worn on the hand holding the paddle. Knee and elbow pads of a soft material may be worn. Warm-up suits, if worn in a match, must also be white.

RULE 4

Serving Regulations

(a) *Serve.* The serve shall be determined by a toss of a coin. In informal play contestants can rebound the ball from the front wall with the player landing closest to the short line winning the serve. The server of the first game also serves first in the third game, if any. Prior to each serve the server calls the score, giving the server's score first.

(b) *Position of server.* The server may serve from anywhere in the service zone with no part of either foot extending *beyond* either line of the service zone. The server must start and remain in the service zone until the served ball has passed the short line. Stepping on the line is allowed.

(c) *Violation.* A violation of the serve is called a foot fault and is an illegal serve. Two illegal serves in succession result in a serve-out.

(d) *Method of serving.* The ball must be dropped to the floor within the service zone and struck with the paddle on the first bounce, hitting the front wall first and rebounding back of the short line, either with or without touching one side wall. The server shall not serve until his opponent is ready.

(e) *Service in doubles.* In doubles the side starting each game is allowed only one serve-out. Thereafter, in that game, both players on each side are permitted to serve until a serve-out occurs. The service order established at the beginning of each game must be followed throughout that game. Servers do not have to alternate serves to their opponents. Serving out of order or the same player serving both serves is a serve-out.

(f) *Partner's position.* During the serve the server's partner is required to stand within the service box with his back against the wall and both feet on the floor until the ball passes the short line. Failure to take this position during a serve is a footfault. If, while in legal position, a player is hit by a served ball on the fly it is a dead ball giving the server another serve. If hit by the serve when out of the box it is a serve-out. A ball passing behind a player legally in the box is a hinder. A dead ball serve does not eliminate a previous fault on that particular service.

(g) *Illegal serves.* Any two illegal serves in succession put the server out. An illegal serve cannot be played. The following are illegal serves:

(1) *Short serve.* A served ball which hits the floor before crossing the short line.

(2) *Long serve.* A served ball rebounding from the front wall to the back wall before hitting the floor.

(3) *Ceiling serve.* A served ball rebounding from the front wall and hitting the ceiling before hitting the floor.

(4) *Two-side serve.* A served ball rebounding from the front wall and hitting two or more walls before hitting the floor.

(5) *Out-of-court serve.* A served ball going out of the court.

(6) *Footfault.* The server stepping out of or leaving the service zone before the ball passes the short line or server's partner in doubles, not staying in service box as required.

(h) *Serve-out serves.* The following "out serves" result in a serve-out:

(1) Bouncing the ball more than twice before striking it when in the act of serving.

(2) Bouncing the ball and having it hit the side wall.

(3) Dropping the ball and hitting it in the air (accidentally dropping the ball does not put the server out).

(4) Striking at and missing the dropped serve.

(5) Touching the server's body or clothing with the ball in the act of serving.

(6) Any serve which simultaneously strikes the front wall and the floor, ceiling, or side wall.

RULE 5

Playing Regulations

(a) *Return of service.*

(1) The receiver(s) must remain at least five feet back of the short line until the ball is struck by the server.

(2) A legally served ball must be returned on the fly or after the first bounce to the front wall either directly or after touching the side wall(s), ceiling, or back wall. A return touching the front wall and floor simultaneously is not a good return.

(3) In returning a service on the fly, no part of the receiver's body may cross the short line before making the return.

(4) Failure to legally return the service results in a point for the server.

(b) *Playing the ball.* A legal return of service or of an opponent's shot is called a volley. The following rules must be observed. Failure to do so results in a serve-out or point.

(1) The ball must be hit with the paddle in one or both hands. The safety thong must be around the wrist at all times.

(2) Hitting the ball with the arm, hand, or any part of the body is prohibited.

(3) In attempting a return the ball may be touched only once. If a player swings at the ball but misses it, he or his partner in doubles may make a further attempt to return it until it touches the floor a second time.

(4) In doubles both partners may swing at and simultaneously strike a ball.

(5) Any ball struck at in play which goes out of court or which is returned to the front wall and then on the rebound or on the first bounce goes out of court is a serve-out or point.

(c) *Unintentional hinders* (point replayed). It is a hinder if a player unintentionally interferes with an opponent preventing him from having a fair opportunity to hit the ball. Each player must get out of his opponent's way immediately after he has struck the ball and

(1) Must give his opponent a fair opportunity to get to and/or strike at the ball. If a player in attempting to get into position goes in the wrong direction and his opponent stands still this does *not* constitute a hinder.

(2) Must give his opponent a fair view of the ball provided, however, interference with his opponent's vision in following the flight of the ball is *not* a hinder.

(3) Must allow his opponent an opportunity to play the ball from any part of the court.

(4) Must allow his opponent to play the ball to any part of the front wall and to either side wall or the back wall in three and four-wall courts.

(5) Unnecessary interference with an opponent or unnecessary crowding, even though the opposing player is not actually prevented from reaching or striking the ball, is a hinder.

(d) *Other unintentional hinders.*

(1) A returned ball striking an opponent on the fly on its return to the front wall.

(2) Hitting any part of the court that under local rules is a dead ball.

(3) A ball rebounding from the front wall on the serve so close to the body of the server that the opponent is interfered with or prevented from seeing the ball. (Called a shadow ball.)

(4) A ball going between the legs of a player on the side which just returned the ball so that the opponent does not have a fair chance to see or return the ball. (Called a straddle ball.)

(5) Body contact with an opponent which interferes with his seeing or returning the ball.

(6) Any other unintentional interference that prevents an opponent from seeing or returning the ball.

(7) It is not a hinder when a player hinders his partner.

(8) A player is not entitled to a hinder unless the interference occurred before or simultaneously with his paddle's contact with the ball.

(e) *Intentional hinder* (serve-out or point).

(1) A player failing to move sufficiently to allow his opponent a fair shot.

(2) Intentionally pushing an opponent during play.

(3) Blocking the movement of an opponent by moving into his path.

(f) *Wet Ball.* On the service and during play the ball and the paddle must be dry.

(g) *Replay of point.* Any foreign object entering the court or any other outside interference causes play to stop and the point is replayed.

(h) *Broken ball.* If a ball breaks during play the point is replayed.

(i) *Rest periods between games.* A two-minute rest period is allowed between games one and two. Players are not permitted to leave the court. A ten-minute rest period is allowed between the second and third game during which time players are allowed to leave the court.

(j) *Continuity of play.* Play shall be continuous from the first serve of each game until the game is concluded except that during a game each player in singles, or each side in doubles, either during serving or receiving, may request a time-out not to exceed thirty seconds. No more than two time-outs per game shall be allowed each player or each team in doubles. Deliberate delay shall result in a point or side-out against the offender.

(k) *Safety.* The safety thong must be around the wrist at all times. The paddle may *not* be switched from one hand to the other. Both hands on the paddle together may be used in striking the ball.

(l) *Injuries.* Play may be suspended for up to fifteen minutes for an injury. If the injured player is unable to continue, the match is forfeited. If the match is resumed and must then be stopped again for the same player, the match is forfeited.

(m) Prior to each serve the server should call the score, giving the server's score first.

RULE 6

Officiating

All tournament matches should be conducted with a referee and scorer whose duties are as follows:

REFEREE

(a) Brief all players and officials on the rules and local playing regulations.

(b) Check the playing area for suitability for play.

(c) Check the playing equipment and uniform of players and approve of same.

(d) Check availability of other necessary equipment such as extra balls, towels, scorecards, pencils.

(e) Introduce players, toss coin for choice of serving or receiving.

(f) Take position in center and above the back wall of the back court and signal start of game.

(g) During game decide on all questions that arise in accordance with the rules. He is responsible for the entire conduct of the game including

    (1) Legality of the serve and its return.

    (2) Calling of unintentional hinders, intentional hinders and faults.

    (3) Preventing any unnecessary delay during match.

    (4) Announcing when a point is made or server is out.

    (5) Deciding on all questions in accordance with the rules and all questions not covered by the rules.

    (6) Forfeiting or postponing a match at his discretion.

(h) Matches may be forfeited when

    (1) A player refuses to abide by the referee's decision.

    (2) A player fails to appear for a scheduled contest within fifteen minutes.

    (3) A player is unable to continue play for physical reasons.

(i) The decision of the referee is final.

(j) Approve the final score after announcing the name of the winner of the match and the scores of all games played.

SCORER

(a) Assist referee in prematch responsibilities.

(b) Obtain necessary equipment for scoring match including scorecard, pencils, extra balls, towels, etc.

(c) Assist the referee in any and all capacities at the referee's discretion.

(d) Keep a record of the progress of the game as prescribed by the tournament committee.

(e) Keep players and spectators informed on the progress of the game by announcing score after each exchange. The scorecard should then be given to the referee for his approval.

Note: Referee may assume the responsibility for announcing running game score.

ONE-WALL PADDLEBALL

Source: *Paddleball Players Association Official Rules One Wall Paddleball,*
Howard Solomon and Joel Skolnick, 1976

RULE 1

The Game

(a) *Players.* The game may be played by two or four persons.

(b) *Game.* A game shall be won by the side first scoring 21 points. All games must be won by a 2-point margin (i.e., 22–20, 23–21).

(c) *Match.* A match shall be won by a side winning the majority of the games.

(d) *Scoring.* Only the team serving may score points. When the receiving team makes an out the serving team is awarded 1 point.

RULE 2

Court and Equipment

(a) *Court.* The court shall be the fair playing surface of the wall and floor.

(b) *Wall.* The wall shall be 20 feet in width from the outside edge of one sideline to the outside edge of the other sideline, and 16 feet high including any top line.

(c) *Floor.* The floor shall be 20 feet in width between the outside edges of the sidelines which shall be perpendicular to the wall lines. It shall be 34 feet from the wall to the back edge of the long line. The side lines should be extended at least 3 feet farther from the wall than the long line. There should be a minimum of 10 feet of floor outside each side line and in back of the long line to allow sufficient movement area for the players.

(d) *Short line.* There shall be a short line running parallel with the wall between the side lines with its back edge 16 feet from the wall.

(e) *Service markers.* There shall be service markers (lines) at least 6 inches long, parallel to, and midway between, the long and short lines, extending inward from the sidelines. The imaginary further extension and joining of these markers indicate the service line.

(f) *Lines.* All lines shall be 1½ inches in width.

(g) *The service area* is the floor bounded by
(1) The short line
(2) The area up to and including the sidelines and the service line.

(h) *Receiving area.* The receiving area is the floor area in back of the short line, bounded by and including the long and sidelines.

(i) *The ball.* The ball shall be rubber with a 1⅞-inch diameter with a 1/32-inch variance. The weight shall be 2/10 to 3/10 ounces with a 2/10 variance. The rebound shall be 44 inches to 52 inches from a 70-inch drop at 68°F.

(j) *The paddle.* The paddle can be no longer than 18 inches and no wider than 9 inches. The paddle can not have any stringing such as that of a tennis racquet. Any paddle having a metal or exposed wood edge must be covered with enough tape to fully cover the edge of the paddle. The surface of the paddle may also be taped with an adhesive type material but no rough textured surface can be created. A paddle found unfit for play by a referee will not be permitted for use in any tournament.

(k) *Attire.* All players are requested to wear proper attire preferably light or white in color. The referee will rule on any controversial attire.

(l) *New ball.* All games will start with a new ball. The referee will replace any ball that becomes substandard in performance during the game.

RULE 3

Officials

(a) *Officials.* For all championship matches there shall be a referee, 4 linespersons, and a scorer.

(b) *Referee.* The referee shall
(1) Have an exact knowledge of the playing rules, tournament regulations, and their proper enforcement and be responsible for the proper conduct of the game.

(2) Decide on all questions in accordance with the rules.

(3) Decide on all questions and interpretations not covered in these rules.

(4) Check the playing area for suitability of play and establishing any local ground rules relative to any deficiencies in the playing area.

(5) Check the player's attire and equipment.

(6) Administer penalties in accordance with the rules.

(7) Administer forfeitures when (i) a player engages in unsportsmanlike conduct; (ii) a player leaves the court without the referee's permission; (iii) a team fails to report to play—normally fifteen minutes are allowed.

(8) Introduce players and toss coin for choice of serving or receiving.

(c) *Linesperson.* There shall be a linesperson for each of the sidelines, short line, and long line. The linesperson shall

(1) Stand facing the line he/she is to call.

(2) Call "out" the balls which strike the wall or floor off the court.

(3) Call faults on their respective lines.

(4) Call decisions as quickly as is consistent with accuracy.

(5) Be confident, however, feel free to yield on an appeal request. (See Rule 13.)

(d) *Scorer.* The scorer shall keep an accurate record of the score, and shall keep the contestants informed as to the progress of the game. He shall announce the score after allowing the players time to return to their position on the court.

RULE 4

Safety

(a) *Introduction.* The game of single-wall paddleball is such that there must be great concern for the safety of all participants. It is therefore imperative to exercise an extreme degree of caution at all times. Because of the potential for dangerous situations, this committee includes an entire section of safety rules and regulations, thereby demonstrating the importance we place on playing and conducting a safe paddleball game. It is the intent of this safety section to discourage or eliminate any reckless or wild player from participating in this sport. Safety is a primary concern in this sport and will be considered as such in any judgments that may arise.

(b) *Stopping play.* The referee will stop the game with the call of "hold" or "stop" whenever he believes there is danger of a player being struck.

(c) *Room to swing.* When opponents are close together, the player or team that has just struck the ball, must whenever possible yield sufficient room to allow the striker to swing at the ball. Violation will result in an out or point against the offender.[1]

[1] This rule is not included in the American Paddleball Association's version.

(d) *Striker's obligation.* If, in the judgment of the referee, a striker has a reasonable view of his opponent, and the opponent does not move into the area of the striker's swing, it shall be the striker's obligation at all such times to avoid hitting his opponent with the paddle. Failure to do so will result in one or more of the penalties listed in Rule 11 at the referee's discretion.

(e) *Safety block.* A striker must call "block" whenever he believes there is danger of hitting his opponent in the course of a normal swing. Upon the "block" call the striker must refrain from hitting the ball. Any player swinging in a situation where there is an obvious potential for injury will be penalized at the discretion of the referee in accordance with the penalties listed in Rule 11. The player calling "block" must be in position to have returned the ball. The referee will then rule on the block call. If the referee confirms the call the point will be replayed. If the referee denies the call the player or side who made the call will lose a point or service.

(f) *Backswing contact.* If an opponent unintentionally causes contact with a player's backswing a block will be called.

(g) *Moving into swing.* Penalties, as listed in Rule 11, will be administered to any player forcing contact by moving into the swinging area of the striker.

(h) *Follow-through contact.* If a player contacts an opponent in the course of a normal follow-through, one or more of the following may occur at the referee's discretion:

(1) Play will continue and no call made because neither player reacted significantly to the contact.

(2) The play will stand.

(3) The play will be stopped.

(4) Penalties will be invoked due to violation.

RULE 5

Service

(a) *First service.*

(1) To decide which player shall serve first in singles, a coin is tossed and called. The winner of the toss may elect to serve or receive.

(2) To decide which team shall serve first in doubles, a coin is tossed and called. The winners have the choice of the following: (i) To serve first and be retired after making only one out. (ii) To receive first with the conditions stated in (i) applying to the opposing team.

If the teams are playing a match, the choice of serving or receiving first shall alternate from team to team with each new game.

(b) *Service order.* (1) After the team that serves first is retired, the partners of each team will serve in successive order (one after the other).

(2) In doubles, either player on a team may serve first.

(c) *Sideout.* In doubles, the first server on a team will serve until his team makes one out. The second server will then serve until his team makes a second out. That side will then be retired and the opposing team will serve. In singles, each server will be retired after making one out.

(d) *Serving position.* The server must stand and remain within the service area at all times when in the act of serving (from his starting position to his concluding move). Violation will be a fault except as in Rule 5(d) (1)

(1) The serving team can not step backward, beyond the service markers until the return of service. To do so will result in a loss of service to the server.

(2) The server's paddle may extend beyond the short line or sidelines.

(3) The server's paddle may not extend beyond the "imaginary" service line. Violation of this is a fault.

(e) *Legal service.* In serving the ball, the ball is required to hit the wall first and then rebound into the receiving area. Failure to do so will be an out except as in Rule 6(d) and 6(e).

(f) *Service bounces.* (1) The server will be permitted practice bounces before serving. Normally no more than three bounces are allowed. Violation of this can result in a fault call at the referee's discretion.

(2) In serving, the ball shall be bounced in the service area. Violation is a fault.

(3) When serving, after the ball is bounced it must be struck on the first rebound. Striking the ball on subsequent bounces will be a violation resulting in a fault.

(g) *Service miss.* If the server strikes at the ball and misses it he will be out. The server may swing any number of times before the second bounce.

(h) *Partner's position.* In doubles, the server's partner must stand off the court, between the extensions of the short line and service line, while his teammate is serving. Violation will be a fault.

(i) *Partner's service entry.* In doubles, the server's partner must not enter the court until the served ball passes him. Violation will be a fault.

(j) *No service restriction.* In doubles, a served ball may pass on either side of the server's body. For singles service refer to Rule 14.

(k) *Behind partner's back.* A served ball may pass between the server's partner and short line.

RULE 6

Faults

(a) *Two consecutive faults.* Two consecutive faults will be an out. (See Rule 14(d).)

(b) *Fault elimination.* A fault will remain with a server until a point or an out is achieved. Blocks do not cancel faults.

The following will cause the penalty of fault against the server.

(c) *Footfault.* Stepping out of the service area before completing the serve is a fault. Refer to Rule 5(d).

(d) *Short fault.* Serving the ball in the court not past the short line. Refer to Rule 5(e).

(e) *Long fault.* Serving the ball between and including the side lines past the long line. Refer to Rule 5(e).

(f) *Service bounces.* (1) Striking the ball on any but the first rebound from the ground while serving is a fault. Refer to Rule 5(f)(3).

(2) Bouncing the ball out of the service area when serving is a fault.

(g) *Server's paddle.* If the server's paddle extends over the service line it is a fault. Refer to Rule 5(d)(3).

(h) *Between the legs.* A served ball passing between the legs of the server or his partner will be a fault.

(i) *Partner's position.* The server's partner not standing off the court between the extensions of the service line and the short line while his partner is serving is a fault. Refer to Rule 5(h).

(j) *Partner's service entry.* If the server's partner enters the court before the served ball has passed him it will be a fault. Refer to Rule 5(i).

RULE 7

Receiving Service

(a) *Receiver's position.* The receiving team can stand anywhere behind the service line and its extensions.

(b) *Returning service.* The player who is going to return a served ball must strike at the ball and complete his follow-through before crossing the service line with his body or his paddle. Violation will be an out.

(c) *Returning longs.* The receiving team must allow all long faults which they do not wish to play to bounce. Any contact made with a ball on a fly will be considered an attempt to play the ball.

(d) *Missed fly return.* A served fly ball, struck at and entirely missed by the receiver, which strikes long, is a long fault.

RULE 8

General

(a) *Legally played ball.* A fairly played ball will be one that is struck in proper turn on a fly or on one bounce and hits the fair playing surface of the wall and floor respectively. Violation will be an out.

(b) *Rally order.* Opposing teams must alternately strike the ball. Any team hitting the ball consecutively will be out.

(c) *Out overrides block.* A team which is struck with its own ball will be out even though a block has been called.

(d) *Double swing.* A team may swing and miss any number of times at a ball until it has bounced twice.

(e) *Hand and paddle.* The paddle hand, from the wrist down, will be considered part of the paddle.

(f) *Switching.* Players are allowed to switch the paddle from hand to hand.

(g) *Loss of paddle.* (1) Should a player lose his paddle he is out.

(2) Should a paddle be accidentally dislodged from a player's hand by an opponent, the play will stop and the rally replayed.

(h) *Late appeal.* Once a ball is served no appeal can be entered in reference to any prior play.

(i) *Substitutions.* Substitution of partners is not permitted once a tournament has started.

(j) *Conversation between players.* Conversation between players on the court shall be kept at a minimum. Excessive conversation will be penalized.

(k) *Time-outs.* A team is entitled to three one-minute time-outs in any one game. Ten-second time-outs may be requested for wiping hands glasses, or tying laces. Flagrant abuse of requesting such time-outs will result in a penalty. Time-outs may be taken consecutively.

(l) *Rest periods.* Periods between games and matches will be decided before the start of the tournament by the tournament directors.

(m) *Interruption in play.* Should play be interrupted for reasons outside the game (i.e., stray ball, etc.) the rally will stop and any fault shall remain.

(n) *Passing your opponents.* (1) If a ball rebounds off the wall and passes both opponents, who clearly have no chance for a play, and then hits the striking team *without bouncing,* the referee shall rule whether or not the ball would have landed fair or out. If the ball is judged to have obviously landed fair, the point will be awarded to the striking team. Otherwise the striking team will be out.

(2) Similarly, if the ball passes both opponents, bounces fair, and then hits either one of the striking team, the point will go to the striking team.

(o) *Ball hitting opponent.* If a team strikes a ball and that ball on the way to the wall, hits an opponent without bouncing, and the referee judges that the ball would have been fair on the wall and floor, a block will be granted. If the referee judges otherwise the striking team is out.

(p) *Intentional loss of ball.* Any player intentionally hitting or throwing the ball out of the playing area may be penalized including forfeiture of game at the discretion of the referee.

(q) *Continuity of play.* The server shall have ten seconds after the scorer announces the score to put the ball into play. Failure to do so may result in delay of game penalty. The receiving team must also be ready to play in the same ten seconds

(r) *Severest penalty rules.* If a fault on a serve is followed by an out call, the out prevails. If a block call is followed by an out call, the out will prevail. Refer to Rule 8(c).

RULE 9

Blocks

(a) *Unintentional block.* The nature of the unintentional block is such that it requires the following explanation. For the purpose of this explanation we shall evaluate the block situation in light of the relative advantages and disadvantages caused by the movements of the team that has just struck the ball.

(1) When the teammate that has just struck the ball moves in a manner that creates an advantage for his team by causing interference with the opponent's ability to move or chance to play the ball, the opponent should request a block from the referee by saying the word "block" out loud and continuing to play the ball. The referee will confirm the opponent's block request by calling "stop" or deny the opponent's request by remaining silent and making no call.

(2) If the player who has just finished striking the ball moves in a manner that places his/her team at a disadvantage (even though technically a block has occurred) the opponent may refrain from calling block and thereby attempt to capitalize on the improper movements of the player moving in such a manner.

(3) It must be understood that it shall be the decision of the opponent whether or not to call the unintentional block. The referee will make no such call unless it is requested as in (1) The referee, however, will call all other blocks.

(b) *Safety block.* Refer to Rule 4(d).

(c) *Granting a block.* At all times a player must be in position to strike the ball to call a block.

(d) *Between the legs.* A ball passing between the legs of an opponent will be a block only when the striker has a reasonable chance for a play and calls "block" in the manner prescribed in Rule 9(a) (1).

(e) *Backward movement.* The opposing team must give full freedom to a player moving in a backward direction in pursuit of the ball. Intentional violation will be an out. Accidental violation will be a block.

(f) *Taking position.* (1) In doubles, a player will be called out if he moves alongside or in front of an opponent while his partner is striking the ball. (See Fig. 10.)

(2) In singles, a player will be called out if he moves alongside or in front of an opponent who is about to strike the ball.

(g) *Vision block.* No block shall be granted by the referee when a player's body blocks the opponent's view of the ball. However, should a player's movement block an opponent's vision to the ball, block can be granted.

(h) *Blocking the ball.* A player will be called out if he intentionally uses his body or his paddle to prevent a ball from reaching the wall.

(i) *Blocking pursuit of ball.* If a player deliberately moves to block an opponent's pursuit of the ball, the player is out.

(j) *Moving into swing.* Refer to Rule 4(g).

(k) *Cutting down wall.* Any intentional movement that cuts down an opponent's opportunity to play the ball to the wall will be called out. (See Fig. 12.)

(l) *Pushing off.* A player will be called out if he intentionally or unintentionally pushes or pushes off an opponent.

(m) *Accidental bumping.* If a player after striking the ball accidently bumps an opponent and in so doing prevents him from playing the next shot, a block will be called. However, if the ball is out the player is out.

(n) A player will be called out if he is about to strike the ball and moves in a sudden backward direction so that

(1) He forces his opponent to move out of the play.

(2) He creates a potential hazard with the backswing of his racket

(3) He forces unavoidable contact to occur with the opponent behind him.

RULE 10

Outs or Points

(a) *Outside ball.* Any ball in play, after the service striking outside the sidelines or past the long line, is an out or point.

(b) *Not hitting wall.* Any ball hitting the floor before the wall will be out.

(c) *Improper return.* If a player fails to legally and properly return opponent's play, it shall be an out or point.

(d) *Hitting twice.* Refer to Rule 8(b).

(e) *Loss of paddle.* Refer to Rule 8(g).

(f) *Serving out of turn.* Refer to Rule 5(b).

(g) *Illegal service.* Refer to Rule 5(e).

(h) *Service miss.* Refer to Rule 5(g).

(i) *Two consecutive faults.* Refer to Rule 6(a).

(j) *Illegal receiving.* A receiver crossing the service line with his body or paddle before completing his follow through will be out. Refer to Rule 7(b).

(k) *Delay of game.* Refer to Rule 8(g).

(l) *Excessive conversation.* Refer to Rule 8(j).

(m) *Taking position illegally.* Refer to Rule 9(f).

(n) *Intentional block.* Refer to Rule 9(i).

(o) *Intentional backward blocking.* Refer to Rule 9(e).

(p) *Pushing off.* Refer to Rule 9(l).

(q) *Cutting down wall.* Refer to Rule 9(k).

RULE 11

Penalties

(a) Removal from tournament.

(b) Removal from game.

(c) Loss of service or point accompanied by a warning.

Appeal Play

If in the course of a game a player disagrees with

the call of an official, he may approach the head referee and request an appeal play. Should the head referee feel there is merit for the request, he will then ask the official who made the disputed call if he/she will yield the call. If the official says no the head referee will inform the player that the appeal has been disallowed. Play will continue with no further discussion or comment. If the official yields his/her call the head referee will consult with any or all officials to reach a decision on the play.

All officials are encouraged to yield to an appeal request whenever any doubt exists in their minds as to the accuracy of a call made or if the play went unobserved by the linesperson involved.

Players shall not discuss calls with linespersons at any time. Any player doing so will be penalized at the discretion of the referee.

RULE 13

Injuries

(a) If a player becomes injured or unable to continue to play due to conditions other than an injury caused by an opponent, he shall be allowed an injury time-out not to exceed five minutes. If after five minutes play has not resumed, that player or side shall default the game. If this occurs during a match, the player or side will default if they fail to report to play the next game by the normal line period allowed between games in a match.

(b) In singles play, if a player is injured by an opponent and that opponent has been disqualified, the injured player will be awarded the win. However, if he is unable to play any of his subsequent matches he will default.

(c) In singles play, if a player is injured by an opponent and the referee declares no violation or disqualification, and the injured player after five minutes can not resume play, he shall default. If this occurs during a match, the player will default if he fails to report to play the next game by the normal time period allowed between games in a match.

(d) In doubles play, if a player is injured by an opponent and the opponents have been disqualified, the injured player's team will be awarded the win. If the injured player is unable to play his subsequent games his partner may if he so desires, continue by himself until the injured player can resume.

(e) In doubles play, if a player is injured by an opponent and the referee declares no violation or disqualification and the injured player after five minutes can not resume play, his partner may continue by himself until the injured player can resume.

RULE 14

Singles Service

(a) Defining major service area, minor service area, and automatic fault area.

The position of the server's feet from the start to the conclusion of his/her serve shall divide the court into three areas: the major service area, the minor service area, and the automatic fault area.

Automatic fault area. The automatic fault area will be determined by drawing two imaginary lines perpendicular to the wall and parallel to the side lines which pass through the extreme right and left foot positions of the server. If the server moves from his starting position to another point where the serve is completed, the entire area from start to finish will be an automatic fault area.

Major service area. The major service area of the court will be the larger of the two areas to either the left or right of the automatic fault area.

Minor service area. The minor service area of the court will be the smaller of the two areas to either the left or right of the automatic fault area.

If in the opinion of the referee the server during his serve (from start to finish) creates two relatively equal areas on either side of the automatic fault area, both areas will be considered minor service areas.

(b) The server has the option to serve to either the major or minor service area.

(c) The server must designate to his opponent and the referee when serving to the minor service area. This will be done by pointing to the minor service area. Violation will be a fault.

(d) *Singles service variation.* At the discretion of the tournament committee, singles competition may be conducted where a player will be retired when he makes one fault.

The APA recently introduced a new rule that puts a limit on the number of appeals allowed per game:

15 *Limit on appeals.* (The tournament director may or may not invoke the following rule for any or all games in a tournament, at his discretion.)

Play must be continuous at all times and in accordance with the rules. Any pause in play to question or dispute a call by a linesperson or the referee shall be deemed an appeal whether or not the appeal is made only to the referee as the rule stipulates. In a 15-point game each side is limited to two appeals and in a game of 21 or more points each side is limited to three appeals. Once a side has exhausted their appeals they may not halt play to question, dispute, or appeal any further calls in that game. Failure to abide by this rule will result in a penalty as outlined in Rule 11.

Source: *Official Rules and Regulations of Paddleball, American Paddleball Association, 1979*